Advancing Critical Reading, Writing, And Study Skills

8th Edition

Lawrence Scheg

Modesto Junior College/Chapman University

This book belongs to :

Name: Maranatha Bo-Llay
Street: 2327 Robertson Bd.
City: Modesto   State: CA
Phone: (209) 450-6183

The information above is optional

Sierra Publishing
South Lake Tahoe, California

i

ISBN: 0-9742756-8-9, 978-09742756--8-0

Published by
Sierra Publishing
1034 Emerald Bay Road #125
South Lake Tahoe, CA 96150-6200

Contact for Domestic and International Orders:
Send E-mail to: mailsierrapublishing@yahoo.com
or visit www.SierraPublishing.com

Printed in the United States of America

Acknowledgements

Michael Brown, an essay "Love Canal and the Poisoning of America," Copyright © 1979 by Michael Brown. Reprinted by permission of the author.

Rachel Carson, "Elixirs of Death" *From Silent Spring by Rachel Carson. Copyright © 1962 The Houghton Mifflin Company. Reprinted with permission from Houghton Mifflin.*

Martin Luther King Jr., "I Have a Dream," Copyright © 1963 by Martin Luther King, Jr., copyright renewed © 1991 by Coretta Scott King. "Letter From Birmingham Jail," copyright © 1963, 1964 by Martin Luther King Jr., copyright © renewed 1991, 1992 by Coretta Scott King. Both selections reprinted with the permission of the Heirs to the Estate of Martin Luther King Jr., c/o Joan Daves Agency as the proprietor's agent.

Lawrence Scheg, "Landmines," Copyright © 2003 by Lawrence Scheg, Reprinted by permission of the author

Table of Contents:

Section 1:

A. Skills Needed to Advance Your Reading Proficiency

B. How to Get the Most Benefit from the Thematic Reading Selections:

Section 2:

A Thematic Approach to Advancing Reading Skills:

Theme 1: Health and the Environment

Theme 2: Government and Politics:

Theme 3: Civil Rights:

Theme 4: Philosophies That Shape Our World:

Appendix

Skills Needed to Advance Your Reading Proficiency

Skills to Build On

The Foundation

Most of us are aware of the fact that a building needs a good solid foundation before any other construction can begin. Likewise a good reader needs a solid foundation of essential reading skills before that reader can advance to a higher level of reading proficiency. The essential skills are the ability to locate the main idea and thesis, the ability to identify supporting evidence or details, the ability to understand the reason behind the writer writing that reading selection, the ability to separate facts from opinions, the ability to identify the structure or patterns used in the writing, and the ability to draw correct conclusions based on the evidence given and your own background knowledge and experience.

Only when these skills are mastered is the reader ready to advance to a deeper level of reading analysis. This deeper level will build on the foundation mentioned above while adding a probing analysis, commentary, and discussion of some of the most influential writings to date.

The readings in the thematic section of this text will challenge your reading and thinking skills. You will struggle with some readings. Your emotions will run from sorrow to joy, from anger to praise, from a feeling of identifying with another's helplessness to one of sharing in their overcoming incredible odds, and much more.

The thematic readings are designed for a reader who wishes to advance to a mature level of reading and understanding that few in our modern world ever achieve. This, however, is the lever of achievement that has made ordinary men and women into the most influential members of our world. The successful completion of this text, with its reading selections, is the completion of a journey such as Plato writes about in *"The Allegory of the Cave"* - where the individual is transformed from only seeing the shadows of this world to understanding the reality behind those shadows.

Many of the reading selections will need to be analyzed using certain more advanced skills than those mentioned above. Because many writers use certain techniques in their writings, it would be of great benefit for you to know what those techniques are, how to identify them, and how to assess their relevance to the various reading selections. The most common techniques used are those that relate to Argumentation and Propaganda.

Introduction to the Techniques Used For Argumentation

Argumentation (or debate) is an integral part of nearly every person's life, and we need to be aware of the techniques that relate to this arena of thought and action. When we debate or argue, we shouldn't get into a heated, out of control, exchange – for that will usually lead to defeat for all concerned. Rather, we should listen to the opponent's point and support, and in turn our opponent should listen to our point and support. This is similar to lawyers in a courtroom, or a diplomat on assignment in a foreign country.

There are techniques, and if we are aware of them, we may use them to our advantage - or at least we will be able to recognize them when they are being used by others.

As you progress through this section, the various techniques, and their applications, will be discussed. These techniques may be applied to verbal exchanges as well as exchanges between a writer and a reader.

Debate/Argumentation Basics

The basic element when working with these techniques is to first identify the **point being made**, then look at the **support** being given.

The **point** should be clear and well stated. The **support** should be relevant, and adequate. By being **relevant** is meant that it truly relates to the point being presented, and being **adequate** means there is enough evidence to convince a person that the point is well supported.

Basically the person is making a point and providing support as a means of lending validity to that point. As a reader, it is our responsibility to make certain that the writer has accomplished that task.

Relevant Support

As stated above, the support must be relevant – it must relate to the topic. You must decide if each point really does relate to the topic, or if the writer has somehow strayed from the main point under discussion. If they have strayed, we need to note that weakness in their argument.

Adequate Support

How much support is adequate? Are three items of support enough? Are thirty pieces of support enough? Actually the answer is left to the reader. You must decide when there is adequate support – much like a judge or jury must decide during a trial which side is most convincing. You may be right, but, if you are not adequate in your support, you may lose your argument.

The Importance of Point and Support in Everyday Life

Many times we will read controversial material and that is where these techniques need to be applied most of all. You must evaluate the evidence being presented in the form of supporting details, and you must weigh all of the support (evidence) given from all sides if you are to make wise, informed decisions.

Remember this, most people write from a personal point of view, or conviction. Writers are able to present many items in support of an argument, but other writers may be able to present many other conflicting items in support of their argument also. As analytical readers, we need to explore all sides of an issue, not just the side that agrees with our way of thinking, if we are to make intelligent decisions affecting all aspects of our lives. Reading is not just a tool, it is a skill, and it can affect every part of our existence.

Outlining Point and Support Arguments

A very good way to evaluate arguments is to create point and support outlines. First, you should create a T chart. Then, you should label the T chart with the topic being argued placed at the top. Now, state the point being argued followed by the support being presented by each side. (If more than two sides are presenting evidence, then modify the chart to include more sides by adding to the columns.

Once you have created this T chart outline of each point of view, you will be better able to see the relevance and adequacy of the various points and support presented by each side.

An example of a T comparison/contrast chart:

Topic Being Argued

Point being made by Presenter A	Point being made by Presenter B
Support given by Presenter A B	Support given by Presenter
I.	I.
A.	A.
1.	1.
2.	2.
B.	3.
1.	B.
2.	C.
3.	1.
C.	2.
D.	3.
1.	D.
2.	E.
E.	1.
1.	2.
2.	3.
3.	4.
a.	a.
b.	b.
c.	c.

By creating point and support outlines, we will have a clearer view of the support presented by each side. Your outline should also include minor and refining supporting details as well when they exist.

Writing and Argumentation

Writers should strive to be objective in their presentation of material. The reality of many writers is that they often contain biases. You must never lose sight of the fact that all writers are people, not machines. Some persons are better able to remain objective and unbiased, but many others are not able to do so.

Writers generally support their arguments, and information in general, with the types of support that we would expect – surveys, experiments, studies, various opinions, examples, eyewitness reports, and other forms of evidence. Depending on many factors, those items may be more or less valid. Here again, the analytical reader must evaluate all of the support given.

Surveys, for example, may be more or less valid depending on who was surveyed, when they were surveyed, where they were surveyed, and who they were surveyed by.

Studies may be valid, or they may be flawed, by special interest money, the bias of those doing the study, and the size of the study.

Eyewitness reports may be valid, or they may be flawed, because eyewitnesses rarely agree upon the events that they witness.

Opinions are the weakest support of all since people are generally able to come up with a multitude of opinions on just about any topic or event. We need to investigate further to see if the opinions given have any validity. It's nice to have an opinion but what is that opinion based upon? What supports that opinion for stating something?

Examples are perhaps the strongest form of support. Even here much manipulation may occur. An opposing side may come up with their own conflicting examples in an attempt to show a weakness in their opponent's example. The writer's job is to have such strong examples that they cannot be refuted or disproved because it is very difficult to refute good solid examples. The reader must be able to judge the various examples given and decide which are valid and strong.

The End Result

Ultimately, we must question everyone, every idea, and every point, presented to us. We cannot go through life successfully if we fail to question and analyze the many viewpoints that exist in the world. People who fail in that regard often end up being gullible (accepting almost anything), or close-minded (closed to any point of view but their own). Neither lopsided approach will produce a competent reader or a competent citizen.

Fallacies in Argumentation:

A fallacy in reasoning indicates weaknesses, or errors, existing in the support given for the point being argued. An easy way to remember what fallacy means is that it contains the word fall. The argument is able to fall because of weak support. Some Common Fallacies Are:

Changing the Subject

People who are losing an argument will often try to change the subject. Others may change the subject inadvertently (by accident). In either case, we need to spot this error and bring them back to the original point in conversation, or make an annotation when reading.

Hasty Generalization

Sometimes a person may come to a conclusion too quickly, and that is called a Hasty Generalization. Hasty means they've arrived at their conclusion too quickly. Generalization means too broad or wide in scope. This person has arrived at a conclusion without serious study of most of the available information.

Circular Reasoning

In Circular Reasoning, the person reasons in circles, perhaps repeating the point in many different ways, but never giving additional support for the point. Nothing new is being added to the discussion. You want to say to this person, "Tell me something new, something that hasn't already been said."

Personal Attack

In Personal Attack, the person attacks the opponent on a personal level. They may bring up unrelated issues to try to sidetrack the real point under discussion, or they may state, or imply, that the opponent holds some unpopular view. This, they hope, will divert attention from the real issues and away from the weaknesses of their own argument.

Straw Man

Like the straw man in the Wizard of Oz, a Straw Man is a weak character who can easily be defeated. If an opponent is putting forth a good argument, the adversary may try to create an image of that person which is false. They will try to convince the audience that this person is the false image they've created. Then, they will battle that false image instead.

They may also imply that this person holds an unpopular view, or favors an unpopular cause, when that is not the truth.

False Cause

In a False Cause fallacy, the assumption is that because one event follows another, the first event must have caused the second event to happen. Other causes may have contributed to the final result (the effect). The reader, or listener, must look for other possible causes, and not too readily accept any cause/effect relationship as being valid until that has been done.

A T chart would help you to evaluate a cause/effect relationship. Simply put the cause(s) to the left side of the chart and the effect(s) to the right side. Now you will be able to more clearly see the cause /effect relationship.

False Comparison

A false comparison assumes that two things are more alike than they really are. A person must study all of the similarities, and all of the differences, before judging whether the things being compared are really similar enough to warrant the comparison.

Either-Or

In this situation, only two sides to a point are presented when more sides actually exist. Offering only two choices limits the discussion and thinking. We need to look at the sides presented, and then decide if any other sides may exist that would be relevant to the point being discussed.

Two Wrongs make a Right

An author using this argument may argue that because some other individual, or group, has engaged in unethical behavior, that, now his/her group has a similar right to engage in unethical behavior. The author may try to downplay, ignore, or dispute past laws, traditions, and practices based on this argument.

(That which is ethical or unethical is a hotly debated issue. Society is moving away from the traditions of the past ages, and we need to ask ourselves if those past traditions (laws & behaviors) have benefited humans and should be kept, or are they unnecessary and should be eradicated or modified. We first have to make the judgment as to whether laws, practices, and past rules are good ethical standards, or not, before we let an author reject them as unworthy and justify unethical actions based on the unethical actions of others. This is a difficult area for people to from a consensus because beliefs vary so greatly from one culture, religion, philosophy, and country to another.)

Propaganda Techniques

Writers often use Propaganda techniques in their writings. The word propaganda generally has a strong negative connotation associated with it. These techniques, however, may be used in deceiving people for unethical reasons or they may be used for legitimate and good purposes too. A discussion of the most common techniques follows:

Euphemisms

A Euphemism is a pleasant sounding word, or phrase, used in place of one that might be considered harsh or too precise. It may be the innocent use of a word to replace one that would not be as agreeable to the listener's ears. For example the use of "rest room" instead of toilet, the use of "passed away" instead of died, or the use of "intoxicated" for drunk, etc.

A second use of Euphemisms involves the deliberate technique of speaking in a way that will not be understood by most people. The words, or phrases, have meanings that only a few select persons know the real meanings to. One example might be: Joe is going on a long vacation. The actual meaning might be that Joe is going to die. Another example might be: Sam is going deep sea diving. The actual meaning is that he is being fed to the sharks.

Testimonial

A testimonial is the use of a famous person who will give verbal, or written, support for a person, idea, place, nation, product, political agenda, religious promotion, etc. The idea is that this famous person will influence others to follow without giving the agenda in question too much thought. This person may believe in what they are supporting, but often they are not experts in that area. We must also remember that these people are usually paid for their endorsement and that may be their only interest in promoting it.

A good example of testimonial being used is the many actors who promote the various telephone calling plans that we see on television. They rarely have full knowledge of those plans, and if they did, they probably would not want to do the advertisements.

A testimonial by a famous person does not always indicate deception. Some testimonials may be legitimate and sincere. The reader, or listener, has to be the judge.

Transfer

The Transfer technique involves the attempt to associate someone, or something, with a symbol or image that people already admire and love. It can be used in a positive manner, or for deception.

The United States post office displays the American Eagle on many of their trucks because most people admire the American Eagle, and that transfers to a greater love and respect for the post office.

Pictures of Princess Diana, even though she is now deceased, are still used to promote the banning of landmines.

Martin Luther King Jr. used the backdrop of the Lincoln Memorial to present his "I Have A Dream" speech. It was an effective backdrop, transferring good feelings for Lincoln, and his signing of the Emancipation Proclamation, to the call for Civil Rights in 1960's America.

Also, transfer may be used to lure us in, or soften our reaction to something. Products are often advertised to us with appealing backgrounds that tend to make us less aware of the product being promoted, and very comfortable with the scenery. Medicines, household cleaners, automobiles, and many other products are often promoted in this way.

Sex appeal and good looks are also used to as ways to transfer good feelings to a product, cause, candidate, etc. Certainly, most of us would be less inclined to buy some products, such as beer, if they showed drunken and overweight, persons instead.

Appeal to Authority

Often those in positions of authority are used to support an argument. They know that most people rarely question those presented as authorities. This may have merit if the person(s) are really authorities, but all too often the so called authorities disagree among themselves, so, in a case like that, no real definitive authority really exists.

Authorities are often in disagreement over issues like: acid rain, whether global warming is real, abortion, evolution, politics, health issues, and so forth. Therefore, a skilled reader wants to look at all sides of an issue and to study many "authorities" / "experts" before coming to a conclusion.

A good example of this point would be that the authorities/experts said eggs raised cholesterol, and years later other authorities said eggs actually lowered cholesterol levels. Which expert do you believe? We must research important information ourselves, and the Internet is a good place *to start*.

Bandwagon

This technique involves getting a person to follow, or accept something, because so many others do. It derives its name from earlier times, before radio and television, when a band would accompany a wagon into town. The band would be heard throughout the town or countryside and draw attention to the wagon loaded with goods to sell, or perhaps an agenda to promote.

People would see nearly everyone else running toward the center of excitement so often they would join in the rush. Today we might label this technique as Political Correctness. As others rush to support a cause, or vote in a certain way, people tend to join in – not wanting to be left out. It's suggested that everyone else is doing it, so why don't you?

Plain Folks

This technique is used to try to convince us that they are plain ordinary citizens like us. The truth may be that they are not like us at all, and they may even feel superior to the rest of us. This technique masks their true economic, political, and societal status.

Don't lose sight of the fact that many people who appear to be like the rest of us, despite their prestige, money, power, or status, may actually be genuinely humble persons. Again, we have to evaluate the sincerity, or lack of it, in these situations.

Name Calling

This is one technique that most of us are familiar with. It involves the use of negative, or emotionally-loaded, language in describing a person, situation, place, country, product and so forth.

The person using this tactic hopes to throw the listener off balance by creating a bad image of the opponent. This usually results in the reader, or listener, not wanting to read, or hear, anything that the opponent has to say. It can ultimately shut down an open minded evaluation of the point being discussed. This is especially evident in political campaigns, but may also be encountered in any area of life's interactions.

Glittering Generalities

The key to this approach is in understanding the two words that make up this term. It glitters like gold, but it is fools gold. Also, it is very broad and hard to pin down. The ideas being presented sound great but they don't amount to much – if anything at all. It's all fluff and show with no real substance. When you strip away the nice sounding words, there is little, if anything, of substance left.

Card Stacking

When researchers investigate something, they usually create 4x6 cards containing the various pros and cons of the information collected. Card stacking involves ignoring the negatives and only presenting the positives.

It can also refer to any situation in which the negatives are ignored, downplayed, or concealed when presenting evidence. This technique is most often used by people trying to hide something from us, which if we knew existed, would turn us away from whatever it is that they are promoting. In legal terms it is referred to as "concealing evidence."

Gradualism

A writer may use this technique so that the reader does not become alarmed by the material being presented. The writer presents new information in very small increments so that the new information is almost imperceptible by the reader. Historically, rulers have used this technique to produce changes in society, or in their kingdom, that may take decades, or even centuries, for the slow desired change to come to full effect.

A good way to understand this technique is by the example of the frog and the kettle of water. If you toss a frog into a kettle of hot water, it will react immediately and try to jump out. However, if you put a frog in a kettle of cold water, and slowly heat the water, it will probably not resist, and will cook to death. Likewise, some deceptive writers know that radical ideas presented too quickly may cause the audience to react strongly against their ideas so they present the new information in a very gradual manner called gradualism.

Recognizing Connotative and Denotative Language

An extremely important skill to develop is the ability to know the difference between connotative and denotative language. Authors often use words that stir our emotions and affect our thinking. The use of these connotative words may be positive - as is the case in the beautiful connotative language that permeates the works of Martin Luther King Jr. Or the words may be used to stir up negative emotions - as is the case in the Communist Manifesto. An inability to recognize these words and their messages will hamper good comprehension of anything that you read which contains such connotative words.

Following is a brief study of the difference between denotative and connotative language.

Denotative Language

•Denotative language consists of words that have little or no power to sway our emotions. Words like table, chair, tree, etc are all examples of denotative language.
•It is language that is highly objective, or impersonal.
•Authors rely on denotative language when they don't want to reveal their own feelings or don't wish to affect the feelings of their audience.
•Statements relying primarily on denotative language are likely to be factual.

Connotative Language

•Consists of words that evoke positive or negative associations called "connotations."
•Connotative language sways our emotions and encourages us to feel or think in a certain way.
•Connotative language reveals the author's point of view.
•Statements that include words with strong connotations are more than likely statement of opinion.

The Importance of Context

•Change the context, or setting of a word, and it is possible to make it more connotative than denotative.

✳ Additional Techniques. Test Tuesday

- Lies - Some author knowinly will lie
- Bias/Prejudice - Ex: Global Warming
- Statistic - used to twist the truth, and to lie with number.
- Class Werfare - The social standings of people is used to create divisions among the population. The classes are usually: the elite/privileged/rich, the middle class and upper middle class, the poor/underprivilegde.
- Race - (accusation of race) used to drive a wedge between people
- Religion - (anti-religious prejudice) " "
- Political Corretness - Pressure often put on people to conform to ideas that may may not have valitity.

✳ - Demonization - Creating a very evil or sinister view of a person or group that is not true.
- Double talk/speak - Using coded words that only a few selet individuals will know the true meaning of. The words will often apera innocent
- Spin - Turining argument away from the truth, or reality to make the opposit look.
- Anonymous Sources - Using sources that are not identified and cannot be questioned to deceive the readers
- Social change Agenda - An agenda to change the way society thinks and function. This is a manipulation that often convince readers to accept ideas that was not acceptel.
- Two wrongs make a Righ - the author puts forth an argument that because someone esle violated the law.
- scapegoat - puts blame to anothe person

How to Get the Most Benefit from the Thematic Reading Selections

Reading and Highlighting

A few individuals have photographic memories, but most people do not. I once asked a class to raise their hand if they possessed a photographic memory, and after a long pause, one individual's hand went up and he said, "I have a photographic memory, but I'm usually out of film."

It was funny and also revealing as to how most people deal with their inability to remember what they read. Very few people have photographic memories (probably less than 1%) but most students feel inadequate, unintelligent, develop poor self-esteem, and a host of other problems because they assume most other people easily remember what they read when the actual truth is that it takes certain skills to remember what you've read, heard, or even seen.

One of the best ways to become focused and to aid in you memory of things read is to highlight the reading selection. Highlighting is a skill that one must learn and practice. To highlight correctly, a person must be able to identify the main point (or main idea) presented in each paragraph by the writer. Then, the reader must be able to identify the information that supports that main idea. Also, in connection with those skills is the ability to filter out the information that is not essential to the core understanding of the reading selection. These skills are covered in my text entitled *Improving Essential Reading and Study Skills*. It is extremely important that you have mastered those skills before you start the thematic readings later in this text. If you have not mastered those skills, now would be a good time to go back to that text and review them.

Highlighting correctly can reveal to us the author's main point, support, organization, point of view, purpose, and so forth. It is essential to probing more deeply into the reading selections.

Annotations

Once you have highlighted the text, it is time to return to the text highlights for a second time and time to do some deeper thinking about the ideas uncovered there. When you do that, it is time to annotate your reading selection. To annotate means to create critical commentary or notes relating to the selection read. It is your analysis of the author's ideas. You may agree or disagree. You may question or doubt the writer's thesis. You may formulate ideas of your own or you may even make a note that further research is needed before you draw any conclusions. You may even state bewilderment, anger, or amusement in the face of that person's ideas. How you respond is ultimately left up to you – but respond you must, or you are in danger of being gullible, close minded, or even brainwashed.

Our brains are like computers and they can be easily programmed to think and function in a certain way. However, what separates us from the cold computer is the ability to take input, analyze it, accept it or reject it, and rather than being programmed, we create a view of the world that is uniquely our own.

The reading selections in this text are set in templates that make it easier for you to read and respond. The templates have lined side bars that make it easy to write your commentary next to the ideas that you have highlighted.

Discussion of Reading Selections

Once you have read, highlighted, and annotated your reading selections, it will be time to discuss those selections in order to obtain an even deeper understanding of the works and their influence on our modern society.

By sharing our ideas with others, we will come to a fuller understanding of where our conclusions are solid and where they may have weaknesses. Our fellow students will be bringing their own perceptions to the discussion as well. Since we are not cookie cutter carbon copies or clones, we may have different perceptions, opinions, and conclusions. Sometimes all may be in agreement but still different students, with different perceptions will often add their own unique perspectives to the discussion.

I have found that discussions are best when sharing is done in small groups of three to four individuals. The class may be divided into any number of these small groups as the instructor finds necessary. The instructor then circulates around the room, listening to the various discussions and may at times offer limited input. After the instructor feels that the groups have had had sufficient time to share their ideas, he/she may have the groups report on the major points of discussion or may open the discussion up in a more broad sense to the entire class.

Because the students have had time to discuss and refine their ideas, the discussion should now move into a deeper classroom discussion. From that point, each individual will grow even more in their understanding of the selection since many points of view, interpretations and analysis of the reading will have been put forth by the various members of the class.

Writing and Additional Research

After completing the exercises above, each individual will have written responses to the various readings, discussed the works in small group settings and in the larger classroom setting. The instructor may have suggested or shown movies, videos, or other items of interest to help in the understanding of the selection(s). Now, if time allows, you may be asked to write a more formal paper.

Taking all of the ideas that you have been exposed to, you may now be asked to create a paper that reflects your thoughts, and unique perspective, on the subject matter or theme. It should reflect growth from your initial analysis of the reading(s) to your deeper analysis after much more thought and discussion.

Ultimately, in a writing course, students would be asked to take an idea that was discussed and probe that vein of thought deeper by doing research that involves the use of the Internet, the library, personal interviews, periodical research, film, and any other research that would be appropriate.

A Thematic Approach To Advancing Reading Skills

Theme 1
Health and the Environment

Rachel Carson wrote the book that changed how the world looks at the Environment. Her book <u>Silent Spring</u> (1962) has been translated into nearly every major language on planet earth. It is one of the best examples of truly great research and writing – a model for all research writers. She provides clear and powerful examples as evidence for her often controversial positions.

To understand toxins in the environment today, we need to read and digest Rachel's awesome work.

Sixteen years after her book was published, Michael Brown found that he was writing about the cancerous effects so clearly warned about in her book.

The pollution did not stop with pesticides and industrial waste. Now we must look the very ingredients added to our food. We must ask ourselves whether it is through ignorance or greed that the very food that we eat, the air that we breathe, and the water that we drink is so horribly polluted.

Elixirs of Death
(From Silent Spring 1962)
RACHEL CARSON

(1907-1964)

For the first time in the history of the world, every human being is now subjected to contact with dangerous chemicals, from the moment of conception until death. In the less than two decades of their use, the synthetic pesticides have been so thoroughly distributed throughout the animate and inanimate world that they occur virtually everywhere. They have been recovered from most of the major river systems and even from streams of groundwater flowing unseen through the earth. Residues of these chemicals linger in soil to which they may have been applied a dozen years before. They have entered and lodged in the bodies of fish, birds, reptiles, and domestic and wild animals so universally that scientists carrying on animal experiments find it almost impossible to locate subjects free from such contamination. They have been found in fish in remote mountain lakes, in earthworms burrowing in soil, in the eggs of birds— and in man himself. For these chemicals are now stored in the bodies of the vast majority of human beings, regardless of age. They occur in the mother's milk, and probably in the tissues of the unborn child.

2   All this has come about because of the sudden rise and prodigious growth of an industry for the production of man-made or synthetic chemicals with insecticidal properties. This industry is a child of the Second World War. In the course of developing agents of chemical warfare, some of the chemicals created in the laboratory were found to be lethal to insects. The discovery did not by chance: insects were widely used

to test chemicals as agents of death for man.

3   The result has been a seemingly endless stream of synthetic insecticides. In being man-made-by ingenious laboratory manipulation of the molecules, substituting atoms, altering their arrangement— they differ sharply from the simpler inorganic insecticides of prewar days. These were derived from naturally occurring minerals and plant products— compounds of arsenic, copper, lead, manganese, zinc, and other minerals, pyrethrum from the dried flowers of chrysanthemums, nicotine sulphate from some of the relatives of tobacco, and rotenone from leguminous plants of the East Indies.

Enormous Biological Potency

4   What sets the new synthetic insecticides apart is their enormous biological potency. They have immense power not merely to poison but to enter into the most vital processes of the body and change them in sinister and often deadly ways. Thus, as we shall see, they destroy the very enzymes whose function is to protect the body from harm, they block the oxidation processes from which the body receives its energy, they prevent the normal functioning of various organs, and they may initiate in certain cells the slow and irreversible change that leads to malignancy.

5   Yet new and more deadly chemicals are added to the list each year and new uses are devised so that contact with these materials has become practically worldwide. The production of synthetic pesticides in the United States soared from 124,259,000 pounds in 1947 to 637,666,000 pounds in 1960—more than a fivefold increase. The wholesale value of these products was well over a quarter of a billion dollars. But in the plans and hopes of the industry this enormous production is only a beginning.

6   A Who's Who of pesticides is therefore of concern to us all. If we are going to live so intimately with these chemicals—eating and drinking them, taking them into the very marrow of our bones— we had better know something about their nature and their power.

Arsenic

7   Although the Second World War marked a turning away inorganic chemicals as pesticides into the wonder world of carbon molecule, a few of the old materials persist. Chief among these is arsenic, which is still the basic ingredient in a variety weed and insect killers. Arsenic is a highly toxic mineral occurring widely in association with the ores of various metals, and in very small amounts in volcanoes, in the sea, and in spring water. Its relations to man are varied and historic. Since many of its compounds are tasteless, it has been a favorite agent of homicide from long before the time of the Borgias to the present. Arsenic was the first recognized elementary carcinogen (or cancer-causing substance), identified in chimney soot and linked to cancer nearly two centuries ago by an English physician. Epidemics of chronic arsenical poisoning involving whole populations over long periods are on record. Arsenic-contaminated environments have also caused sickness and death among horses, cows, goats, pigs, deer, fishes, and bees; despite this record arsenical sprays and dusts are widely used. In the arsenic-sprayed cotton country of southern United States beekeeping as an industry has nearly died out. Farmers using arsenic dusts over long periods have been afflicted with chronic arsenic poisoning; livestock have been poisoned by crop sprays or weed killers containing arsenic. Drifting arsenic dusts from blueberry lands have spread over neighboring farms, contaminating streams, fatally poisoning bees and cows, and causing human illness. "It is scarcely possible…to handle arsenicals with more utter disregard of the general health than that which has been practiced in our country in recent years," said Dr. W. C. Hueper of the National Cancer Institute, an authority on environmental cancer. "Anyone who has watched the dusters and sprayers of arsenical insecticides at work must have been impressed by the almost supreme carelessness with which the poisonous substances are dispensed."

Carbon

8   Modern insecticides are still more deadly. The vast majority fall into one of two large groups of chemicals. One, represented by DDT, is known as the "chlorinated hydrocarbons." The other group consists of the organic phosphorus insecticides, and is represented by the reasonably familiar malathion and parathion. All have one thing in common. As mentioned above, they are built on a basis of carbon atoms, which are also the indispensable building blocks of the living world, and thus classed as "organic." To understand them, we must see of what they are made, and how, although linked with the basic chemistry of all life, they lend themselves to the modifications which make them agents of death.

9   The basic element, carbon, is one whose atoms have an almost infinite capacity for uniting with each other in chains and rings and various other configurations, and for becoming linked with atoms of other substances. Indeed, the incredible diversity of living creatures from bacteria to the great blue whale is largely due to this capacity of carbon. The complex protein molecule has the carbon atom as its basis, as have molecules of fat, carbohydrates, enzymes, and vitamins. So, too, have enormous numbers of nonliving things, for carbon is not necessarily a symbol of life.

10   Some organic compounds are simply combinations of carbon and hydrogen. The simplest of these is methane, or marsh gas, formed in nature by the bacterial decomposition of organic matter under water. Mixed with air in proper proportions, methane becomes the dreaded "fire damp" of coal mines. Its structure is beautifully simple, consisting of one carbon atom to which four hydrogen atoms have become attached:

$$C + H + H + H + H = Methane$$

Chemists have discovered that it is possible to detach

one or all of the hydrogen atoms and substitute other elements. For example, by substituting one atom of chlorine for one of hydrogen we produce methyl chloride:

$$C + H + H + H + Cl = \text{Methl Chloride}$$

Take away three hydrogen atoms and substitute chlorine and we have the anesthetic chloroform:

$$C + H + Cl + Cl + Cl = \text{Aneshetic Chloroform}$$

Substitute chlorine atoms for all of the hydrogen atoms and the result is carbon tetrachloride, the familiar cleaning fluid:

$$C + Cl + Cl + Cl + Cl = \text{Carbon TetraChloride}$$

11   In the simplest possible terms, these changes rung upon the basic molecule of methane illustrate what a chlorinated hydrocarbon is. But this illustration gives little hint of the true complexity of the chemical world of the hydrocarbons, or of the manipulations by which the organic chemist creates his infinitely varied materials. For instead of the simple methane molecule with its single carbon atom, he may work with hydrocarbon molecules consisting of many carbon atoms, arranged in rings or chains, with side chains or branches, holding to themselves with chemical bonds not merely simple atoms of hydrogen or chlorine but also a wide variety of chemical groups. By seemingly slight changes the whole character of the substance is changed; for example, not only what is attached but the place of attachment to the carbon atom is highly important. Such ingenious manipulations have

produced a battery of poisons of truly extraordinary power.

DDT

12   DDT (short for dichloro-diphenyl-trichloro-ethane) was first synthesized by a German chemist in 1874, but its properties as an insecticide were not discovered until 1939. Almost immediately DDT was hailed as a means of stamping out insect-borne disease and winning the farmers' war against crop destroyers overnight. The discoverer, Paul Muller of Switzerland, won the Nobel Prize.

13   DDT is now so universally used that in most minds the product takes on the harmless aspect of the familiar. Perhaps the myth of the harmlessness of DDT rests on the fact that one of its first uses was the wartime dusting of many thousands of soldiers, refugees, and prisoners, to combat lice. It is widely believed that since so many people came into extremely intimate contact with DDT and suffered no immediate ill effects the chemical must certainly be innocent of harm. This understandable misconception arises from the fact that--unlike other chlorinated hydrocarbons— DDT *in powder form* is not readily absorbed through the skin. Dissolved in oil, as it usually is, DDT is definitely toxic. If swallowed, it is absorbed slowly through the digestive tract; it may also be absorbed through the lungs. Once it has entered the body it is stored largely in organs rich in fatty substances (because DDT itself is fat-soluble) such as the adrenals, testes, or thyroid. Relatively large amounts are deposited in the liver, kidneys, and the fat of the large, protective mesenteries that enfold the intestines.

14   This storage of DDT begins with the smallest conceivable intake of the chemical (which is present as residues on most foodstuffs) and continues until quite high levels are reached. The fatty storage depots act as biological magnifiers, so that an intake of as little as 1\10 of 1 part per million in the diet results in storage of about 10 to 15 parts per million, an increase of one hundredfold or more. These terms of reference, so

commonplace to the chemist or the pharmacologist, are unfamiliar to most of us. One part in a million sounds like a very small amount— and so it is. But such substances are so potent that a minute quantity can bring about vast changes in the body. In animal experiments, 3 parts per million has been found to inhibit an essential enzyme in heart muscle; only 5 parts per million has brought about necrosis or disintegration of liver cells; only 2.5 parts per million of the closely related chemicals dieldrin and chlordane did the same.

15   This is really not surprising. In the normal chemistry of the human body there is just such a disparity between cause and effect. For example, a quantity of iodine as small as two ten-thousandths of a gram spells the difference between health and disease. Because these small amounts of pesticides are cumulatively stored and only slowly excreted, the threat of chronic poisoning and degenerative changes of the liver and other organs is very real.

16   Scientists do not agree upon how much DDT can be stored in the human body. Dr. Arnold Lehman, who is the chief pharmacologist of the Food and Drug Administration, says there is neither a floor below which DDT is not absorbed nor a ceiling beyond which absorption and storage ceases. On the other hand, Dr. Wayland Hayes of the United States Public Health Service contends that in every individual a point of equilibrium is reached, and that DDT in excess of this amount is excreted. For practical purposes it is not particularly important which of these men is right. Storage in human beings has been well investigated, and we know that the average person is storing potentially harmful amounts. According to various studies, individuals with no known exposure (except the inevitable dietary one) store an average of 5.3 parts per million to 7.4 parts per million; agricultural workers 17.1 parts per million; and workers in insecticide plants as high as 648 parts per million! So the range of proven storage is quite wide and, what is even more to the point, the minimum figures are above the level at which damage to the liver and other organs or tissues may begin.

17   One of the most sinister features of DDT and related chemicals is the way they are passed on from one organism to another through all the links of the food chains. For example, fields of alfalfa are dusted with DDT; meal is later prepared from the alfalfa and fed to hens; the hens lay eggs which contain DDT. Or the hay, containing residues of 7 to 8 parts per million, may be fed to cows. The DDT will turn up in the milk in the amount of about 3 parts per million, but in butter made from this milk the concentration may run to 65 parts per million. Through such a process of transfer, what started out as a very small amount of DDT may end as a heavy concentration. Farmers nowadays find it difficult to obtain uncontaminated fodder for their milk cows, though the Food and Drug Administration forbids the presence of insecticide residues in milk shipped in interstate commerce.

18   The poison may also be passed on from mother to offspring. Insecticide residues have been recovered from human milk in samples tested by Fond and Drug Administration scientists. This means that the breast-fed human infant is receiving small but regular additions to the load of toxic chemicals building up in his body. It is by no means his first exposure, however: there is good reason to believe this begins while he is still in the womb. In experimental animals the chlorinated hydrocarbon insecticides freely cross the barrier of the placenta, the traditional protective shield between the embryo and harmful substances in the mother's body. While the quantities so received by human infants would normally be small, they are not unimportant because children are more susceptible to poisoning than adults. This situation also means that today the average individual almost certainly starts life with the first deposit of the growing load of chemicals his body will be required to carry thenceforth.

19   All these facts— storage at even low levels, subsequent accumulation, and occurrence of liver damage at levels that may easily occur in normal diets, caused Food and Drug Administration scientists to declare as early as 1950 that it is "extremely likely the potential hazard of DDT has been underestimated." There has been no such parallel situation in medical

history. No one yet knows what the ultimate consequences may be.

Chlordane

20   Chlordane, another chlorinated hydrocarbon, has all these unpleasant attributes of DDT plus a few that are peculiarly its own. Its residues are long persistent in soil, on foodstuffs, or on surfaces to which it may be applied. Chlordane makes use of all available portals to enter the body. It may be absorbed through the skin, may be breathed in as a spray or dust, and of course is absorbed from the digestive tract if residues are swallowed. Like all other chlorinated hydrocarbons, its deposits build up in the body in cumulative fashion. A diet containing such a small amount of chlordane as 2.5 parts per million may eventually lead to storage of 75 parts per million of the fat of experimental animals.

21   So experienced a pharmacologist as Dr. Lehman has described chlordane in 1950 as "one of the most toxic of insecticides— anyone handling it could be poisoned." Judging by the carefree liberality with which dusts for lawn treatments by suburbanites are laced with chlordane, this warning has not been taken to heart. The fact that the suburbanite is not instantly stricken has little meaning, for the toxins may sleep long in his body, to become manifest months or years later in an obscure disorder almost impossible to trace to its origins. On the other hand, death may strike quickly. One victim who accidentally spilled a 25 percent industrial solution on the skin developed symptoms of poisoning within forty minutes and died before medical help could be obtained. No reliance can be placed on receiving advance warning which might allow treatment to be had in time.

Heptachlor

22   Heptachlor, one of the constituents of chlordane, is marketed as a separate formulation. It has a particularly high capacity for storage in fat. If the diet contains as little as 1\10 of 1 part per million there will

be measurable amounts of heptachlor in the body. It also has the curious ability to undergo change into a chemically distinct substance known as heptachlor epoxide. It does this in soil and in the tissues of both plants and animals. Tests on birds indicate that the epoxide that results from this change is more toxic than the original chemical, which in turn is four times as toxic as chlordane.

23   As long ago as the mid-1930s a special group of hydrocarbons, the chlorinated naphthalenes, was found to cause hepatitis, and also a rare and almost invariably fatal liver disease in persons subjected to occupational exposure. They have led to illness and death of workers in electrical industries; and more recently, in agriculture, they have been considered a cause of a mysterious and usually fatal disease of cattle. In view of these antecedents, it is not surprising that three of the insecticides that are related to this group are among the most violently poisonous of all the hydrocarbons. These are dieldrin, aldrin, and endrin.

Dieldren

24   Dieldrin, named for a German chemist, Diels, is about 5 times as toxic as DDT when swallowed but 40 times as toxic when absorbed through the skin in solution. It is notorious for striking quickly, and with terrible effect at the nervous system, sending the victims into convulsions. Persons thus poisoned recover so slowly as to indicate chronic effects. As with other chlorinated hydrocarbons, these long-term effects include severe damage to the liver. The long duration of its residues and the effective insecticidal action make dieldrin one of the most used insecticides today, despite the appalling destruction of wildlife that has followed its use. As tested on quail and pheasants, it has proved to be about 40 to 50 times as toxic as DDT.

25   There are vast gaps in our knowledge of how dieldrin is stored or distributed in the body, or excreted, for the chemists' ingenuity in devising insecticides has long ago outrun biological knowledge

36

of the way these poisons affect the living organism. However, there is every indication of long storage in the human body, where deposits may lie dormant like a slumbering volcano, only to flare up in periods of physiological stress when the body draws upon its fat reserves. Much of what we do know has been learned through hard experience in the antimalarial campaigns carried out by the World Health Organization. As soon as dieldrin was substituted for DDT in malaria-control work (because the malaria mosquitoes had become resistant to DDT), cases of poisoning among the spraymen began to occur. The seizures were severe--from half to all (varying in the different programs) of the men affected went into convulsions and several died. Some had convulsions as long as *four months* after the last exposure.

Aldrin

26   Aldrin is a somewhat mysterious substance, for although it exists as a separate entity it bears the relation of alter ego to dieldrin. When carrots are taken from a bed treated with aldrin they are found to contain residues of dieldrin. This change occurs in living tissues and also in soil. Such alchemistic transformations have led to many erroneous reports, for if a chemist, knowing aldrin has been applied, tests for it he will be deceived into thinking all residues have been dissipated. The residues are there, but they are dieldrin and this requires a different test.

27   Like dieldrin, aldrin is extremely toxic. It produces degenerative changes in the liver and kidneys. A quantity the size of an aspirin tablet is enough to kill more than 400 quail. Many cases of human poisonings are on record, most of them in connection with industrial handling.

28   Aldrin, like most of this group of insecticides, projects a menacing shadow into the future, the shadow of sterility. Pheasants fed quantities too small to kill them nevertheless laid few eggs, and the chicks that hatched soon died. The effect is not confined to birds. Rats exposed to aldrin had fewer pregnancies and their young were sickly and short-lived. Puppies

37

born of treated mothers died within three days. By one means or another, the new generations suffer for the poisoning of their parents. No one knows whether the same effect will be seen in human beings, yet this chemical has been sprayed from airplanes over suburban areas and farmlands.

Endrin

29   Endrin is the most toxic of all the chlorinated hydrocarbons. Although chemically rather closely related to dieldrin, a little twist in its molecular structure makes it 5 times as poisonous. It makes the progenitor of all this group of insecticides, DDT, seem by comparison almost harmless. It is 15 times as poisonous as DDT to mammals, 30 times as poisonous to fish, and about 300 times as poisonous to some birds.

30   In the decade of its use, endrin has killed enormous numbers of fish, has fatally poisoned cattle that have wandered into sprayed orchards, has poisoned wells, and has drawn a sharp warning from at least one state health department that its careless use is endangering human lives.

31   In one of the most tragic cases of endrin poisoning there was no apparent carelessness; efforts had been made to take precautions apparently considered adequate. A year-old child had been taken by his American parents to live in Venezuela. There were cockroaches in the house to which they moved, and after a few days a spray containing endrin was used. The baby and the small family dog were taken out of the house before the spraying was done about nine o'clock one morning. After the spraying the floors were washed. The baby and dog were returned to the house in midafternoon. An hour or so later the dog vomited, went into convulsions, and died. At 10 P.M. on the evening of the same day the baby also vomited, went into convulsions, and lost consciousness. After that fateful contact with endrin, this normal, healthy child became little more than a vegetable— unable to see or hear, subject to frequent muscular spasms, apparently completely cut off from contact with his

If this continues we're going to have a huge issue of food and product of the manufactured goods

38

surroundings. Several months of treatment in a New York hospital failed to change his condition or bring hope of change. "It is extremely doubtful," reported the attending physicians, "that any useful degree of recovery will occur."

Alkyl or Organic Phosphates

32   The second major group of insecticides, the alkyl or organic phosphates, are among the most poisonous chemicals in the world. The chief and most obvious hazard attending their use is that of acute poisoning of people applying the sprays or accidentally coming in contact with drifting spray, with vegetation coated by it, or with a discarded container. In Florida, two children found an empty bag and used it to repair a swing. Shortly thereafter both of them died and three of their playmates became ill. The bag had once contained an insecticide called parathion, one of the organic phosphates; tests established death by parathion poisoning. On another occasion two small boys in Wisconsin, cousins, died on the same night. One had been playing in his yard when spray drifted in from an adjoining field where his father was spraying potatoes with parathion; the other had run playfully into the barn after his father and had put his hand on the nozzle of the spray equipment.

33   The origin of these insecticides has a certain ironic significance. Although some of the chemicals themselves—organic esters of phosphoric acid— had been known for many years, their insecticidal properties remained to be discovered by a German chemist, Gerhard Schrader, in the late 1930s. Almost immediately the German government recognized the value of these same chemicals as new and devastating weapons in man's war against his own kind, and the work on them was declared secret. Some became the deadly nerve gases. Others, of closely allied structure, became insecticides.

Destruction of Enzymes

34   The organic phosphorus insecticides act on the living organism in a peculiar way. They have the ability to destroy enzymes— enzymes that perform necessary functions in the body. Their target is the nervous system, whether the victim is an insect or a warm-blooded animal. Under normal conditions, an impulse passes from nerve to nerve with the aid of a "chemical transmitter" called acetylcholine, a substance that performs an essential function and then disappears. Indeed, its existence is so ephemeral that medical researchers are unable, without special procedures, to sample it before the body has destroyed it. This transient nature of the transmitting chemical is necessary to the normal functioning of the body. If the acetylcholine is not destroyed as soon as a nerve impulse has passed, impulses continue to flash across the bridge from nerve to nerve, as the chemical exerts its effects in an ever more intensified manner. The movements of the whole body become uncoordinated: tremors, muscular spasms, convulsions, and death quickly result.

35   This contingency has been provided for by the body. A protective enzyme called cholinesterase is at hand to destroy the transmitting chemical once it is no longer needed. By this means a precise balance is struck and the body never builds up a dangerous amount of acetylcholine. But on contact with the organic phosphorus insecticides, the protective enzyme is destroyed, and as the quantity of the enzyme is reduced that of the transmitting chemical builds up. In this effect, the organic phosphorus compounds resemble the alkaloid poison muscarine, found in a poisonous mushroom, the fly amanita.

36   Repeated exposures may lower the cholinesterase level until an individual reaches the brink of acute poisoning, a brink over which he may be pushed by a very small additional exposure. For this reason it is considered important to make periodic examinations of the blood of spray operators and others regularly exposed.

Parathion

37   Parathion is one of the most widely used of the organic phosphates. It is also one of the most powerful and dangerous. Honeybees become "wildly agitated and bellicose" on contact with it, perform frantic cleaning movements, and are near death within half an hour. A chemist, thinking to learn by the most direct possible means the dose acutely toxic to human beings, swallowed a minute amount, equivalent to about .00424 ounce.

Paralysis followed so instantaneously that he could not reach the antidotes he had prepared at hand, and so he died. Parathion is now said to be a favorite instrument of suicide in Finland. In recent years the State of California has reported an average of more than 200 cases of accidental parathion poisoning annually. In many parts of the world the fatality rate from parathion is startling: 100 fatal cases in India and 67 in Syria in 1958, and an average of 336 deaths per year in Japan.

38   Yet some 7,000,000 pounds of parathion are now applied to fields and orchards of the United States--by hand sprayers, motorized blowers and dusters, and by airplane. The amount used on California farms alone could, according to one medical authority, "provide a lethal dose for 5 to 10 times the whole world's population."

39   One of the few circumstances that save us from extinction by this means is the fact that parathion and other chemicals of this group are decomposed rather rapidly. Their residues on the crops to which they are applied are therefore relatively short-lived compared with the chlorinated hydrocarbons. However, they last long enough to create hazards and produce consequences that range from the merely serious to the fatal. In Riverside, California, eleven out of thirty men picking oranges became violently ill and all but one had to be hospitalized. Their symptoms were typical of parathion poisoning. The grove had been sprayed with parathion some two and a half weeks earlier; the residues that reduced them to retching, half-blind,

41

semiconscious misery were sixteen to nineteen days old. And this is not by any means a record for persistence. Similar mishaps have occurred in groves sprayed a month earlier, and residues have been found in the peel of oranges six months after treatment with standard dosages.

40 The danger to all workers applying the organic phosphorus insecticides in fields, orchards, and vineyards, is so extreme that some states using these chemicals have established laboratories where physicians may obtain aid in diagnosis and treatment. Even the physicians themselves may be in some danger, unless they wear rubber gloves in handling the victims of poisoning. So may a laundress washing the clothing of such victims, which may have absorbed enough parathion to affect her.

Malathion

41 Malathion, another of the organic phosphates, is almost as familiar to the public as DDT, being widely used by gardeners, in household insecticides, in mosquito spraying, and in such blanket attacks on insects as the spraying of nearly a million acres of Florida communities for the Mediterranean fruit fly. It is considered the least toxic of this group of chemicals and many people assume they may use it freely and without fear of harm. Commercial advertising encourages this comfortable attitude.

42 The alleged "safety" of malathion rests on rather precarious ground, although--as often happens— this was not discovered until the chemical had been in use for several years. Malathion is "safe" only because the mammalian liver, an organ with extraordinary protective powers, renders it relatively harmless. The detoxification is accomplished by one of the enzymes of the liver. If however, something destroys this enzyme or interferes with its action, the person exposed to malathion receives the full force of the poison.

43 Unfortunately for all of us, opportunities for this sort of thing to happen are legion. A few years ago a

Similarities

team of Food and Drug Administration scientists discovered that when malathion and certain other organic phosphates are administered simultaneously a massive poisoning results— up to 50 times as severe as would be predicted on the basis of adding together the toxicities of the two. In other words, 1\100 of the lethal dose of each compound may be fatal when the two are combined.

Potentiation

44   This discovery led to the testing of other combinations. It is now known that many pairs of organic phosphate insecticides are highly dangerous, the toxicity being stepped up or "potentiated" through the combined action. Potentiation seems to take place when one compound destroys the liver enzyme responsible for detoxifying the other. The two need not be given simultaneously. The hazard exists not only for the man who may spray this week with one insecticide and next week with another; it exists also for the consumer of sprayed products. The common salad bowl may easily present a combination of organic phosphate insecticides. Residues well within the legally permissible limits may interact.

45   The full scope of the dangerous interaction of chemicals is as yet little known, but disturbing findings now come regularly from scientific laboratories. Among these is the discovery that the toxicity of an organic phosphate can be increased by a second agent that is not necessarily an insecticide. For example, one of the plasticizing agents may act even more strongly than another insecticide to make malathion more dangerous. Again, this is because it inhibits the liver enzyme that normally would "draw the teeth" of the poisonous insecticide.

46   What of other chemicals in the normal human environment? What, in particular, of drugs? A bare beginning has been made on this subject, but already it is known that some organic phosphates (parathion and malathion) increase the toxicity of some drugs used as muscle relaxants, and that several others (again including malathion) markedly increase the sleeping

time of barbiturates.

Systemic Insecticides

47   In Greek mythology the sorceress Medea, enraged at being supplanted by a rival for the affections of her husband Jason, presented the new bride with a robe possessing magic properties. The wearer of the robe immediately suffered a violent death. This death-by-indirection now finds its counterpart in what are known as "systemic insecticides." These are chemicals with extraordinary properties which are used to convert plants or animals into a sort of Medea's robe by making them actually poisonous. This is done with the purpose of killing insects that may come in contact with them, especially by sucking their juices or blood.

48   The world of systemic insecticides is a weird world, surpassing the imaginings of the brothers Grimm— perhaps most closely akin to the cartoon world of Charles Addams. It is a world where the enchanted forest of the fairy tales has become the poisonous forest in which an insect that chews a leaf or sucks the sap of a plant is doomed. It is a world where a flea bites a dog and dies because the dog's blood has been made poisonous, where an insect may die from vapors emanating from a plant it has never touched, where a bee may carry poisonous nectar, back to its hive and presently produce poisonous honey.

49   The entomologists' dream of the built-in insecticide was born when workers in the field of applied entomology realized they could take a hint from nature: they found that wheat growing in soil containing sodium selenate was immune to attack by aphids or spider mites. Selenium, a naturally occurring element found sparingly in rocks and soils of many parts of the world, thus became the first systemic insecticide.

50   What makes an insecticide a systemic is the ability to permeate all the tissues of a plant or animal and make them toxic. This quality is possessed by some chemicals of the chlorinated hydrocarbon group and by others of the organophosphorus group, all

In some ways I find it beneficial that fleas can get killed by sucking on the dogs blood, but it also had bad effects, to the be hives which is a major food income for the humans

synthetically produced, as well as by certain naturally occurring substances. In practice, however, most systemics are drawn from the organophosphorus group because the problem of residues is somewhat less acute.

51   Systemics act in other devious ways. Applied to seeds, either by soaking or in a coating combined with carbon, they extend their effects into the following plant generation and produce seedlings poisonous to aphids and other sucking insects. Vegetables such as peas, beans, and sugar beets are sometimes thus protected. Cotton seeds coated with a systemic insecticide have been in use for some time in California, where twenty-five farm laborers planting cotton in the San Joaquin Valley in 1959 were seized with sudden illness, caused by handling the bags of treated seeds.

52   In England someone wondered what happened when bees made use of nectar from plants treated with systemics This was investigated in areas treated with a chemical called schradan. Although the plants had been sprayed before the flowers were formed, the nectar later produced contained the poison. The result, as might have been predicted, was that the honey made by the bees also was contaminated with schradan.

53   Use of animal systemics has concentrated chiefly on control of the cattle grub, a damaging parasite of livestock. Extreme care must be used in order to create an insecticidal effect in the blood and tissues of the host without setting up a fatal poisoning. The balance is delicate and government veterinarians have found that repeated small doses can gradually deplete an animal's supply of the protective enzyme cholinesterase, so that without warning a minute additional dose will cause poisoning.

54   There are strong indications that fields closer to our daily lives are being opened up. You may now give your dog a pill which, it is claimed, will rid him of fleas by making his blood poisonous to them. The hazards discovered in treating cattle would presumably apply to the dog. As yet no one seems to have proposed a human systemic that would make us lethal to a mosquito. Perhaps this is the next step.

45

Herbicides

55 So far . . . we have been discussing the deadly chemicals that are being used in our war against the insects. What of our simultaneous war against the weeds?

56 The desire for a quick and easy method of killing unwanted plants has given rise to a large and growing array of chemicals that are known as herbicides, or, less formally, as weed killers. The… question that here concerns us is whether the weed killers are poisons and whether their use is contributing to the poisoning of the environment.

57 The legend that the herbicides are toxic only to plants and so pose no threat to animal life has been widely disseminated, but unfortunately it is not true. The plant killers include a large variety of chemicals that act on animal tissue as well as on vegetation. They vary greatly in their action on the organism. Some are general poisons, some are powerful stimulants of metabolism, causing a fatal rise in body temperature, some induce malignant tumors either alone or in partnership with other chemicals, some strike at the genetic material of the race by causing gene mutations. The herbicides, then, like the insecticides, include some very dangerous chemicals, and their careless use in the belief that they are "safe" can have disastrous results.

58 Despite the competition of a constant stream of new chemicals issuing from the laboratories, arsenic compounds are still liberally used, both as insecticides (as mentioned above) and as weed killers, where they usually take the chemical form of sodium arsenite. The history of their use is not reassuring. As roadside sprays, they have cost many a farmer his cow and killed uncounted numbers of wild creatures. As aquatic weed killers in lakes and reservoirs they have made public waters unsuitable for drinking or even for swimming. As a spray applied to potato fields to destroy the vines they have taken a toll of human and nonhuman life.

59   In England this latter practice developed about

1951 as a result of a shortage of sulfuric acid, formerly used to burn off the potato vines. The Ministry of Agriculture considered it necessary to give warning of the hazard of going into the arsenic-sprayed fields, but the warning was not understood by the cattle (nor, we must assume, by the wild animals and birds) and reports of cattle poisoned by the arsenic sprays came with monotonous regularity. When death came also to a farmer's wife through arsenic-contaminated water, one of the major English chemical companies (in 1959) stopped production of arsenical sprays and called in supplies already in the hands of dealers, and shortly thereafter the Ministry of Agriculture announced that because of high risks to people and cattle restrictions on the use of arsenites would be imposed. In 1961, the Australian government announced a similar ban. No such restrictions impede the use of these poisons in the United States, however.

60   Some of the "dinitro" compounds are also used as herbicides. They are rated as among the most dangerous materials of this type in use in the United States. Dinitrophenol is a strong metabolic stimulant. For this reason it was at one time used as a reducing drug, but the margin between the slimming dose and that required to poison or kill was slight—so slight that several patients died and many suffered permanent injury before use of the drug was finally halted.

61   A related chemical, pentachlorophenol, sometimes known as "penta," is used as a weed killer as well as an insecticide, often being sprayed along railroad tracks and in waste areas. Penta is extremely toxic to a wide variety of organisms from bacteria to man. Like the dinitros, it interferes, often fatally, with the body's source of energy, so that the affected organism almost literally burns itself up. Its fearful power is illustrated in a fatal accident recently reported by the California Department of Health. A tank truck driver was preparing a cotton defoliant by mixing diesel oil with pentachlorophenol. As he was drawing the concentrated chemical out of a drum, the spigot accidentally toppled back. He reached in with his bare hand to regain the spigot. Although he washed

immediately, he became acutely ill and died the next day.

62 While the results of weed killers such as sodium arsenite or the phenols are grossly obvious, some other herbicides are more insidious in their effects. For example, the now famous cranberry-weed-killer aminotriazole, or amitrol, is rated as having relatively low toxicity. But in the long run its tendency to cause malignant tumors of the thyroid may be far more significant for wildlife and perhaps also for man.

63 Among the herbicides are some that are classified as "mutagens," or agents capable of modifying the genes, the materials of heredity. We are rightly appalled by the genetic effects of radiation; how then, can we be indifferent to the same effect in chemicals that we disseminate widely in our environment?

The questions that follow may be used for further discussion of the reading selection or as topics for essay writing.

1. Do background research on Rachel Carson. Write a brief essay discussing your findings.

2. In *Elixirs of Death*, Rachel Carson mentions many different classes of chemicals. List four of the major classes of chemicals.

3. Choose one class of chemicals that Rachel Carson wrote about and list the chemicals mentioned within that class. Do a web search to see if those chemicals are still available for purchase today.

3. Visit your local Garden or Nursery supply store on the web and write down some of the pesticides available. Do a second web search and search for possible dangers associated with those chemicals.

4. Research alternative methods of weed and/or pest control. Write a paragraph or more discussing the method that impressed you the most.

5._____
_____
_____
_____
_____

6._____
_____
_____
_____
_____

Applying Reading Skills
(Neatly **PRINT** all answers using ink **not** pencil)

Title of the Reading Selection: _Elixir of Death_

1. What is the author's overall main idea, (central point, or thesis)?
    To be aware of the toxic chemicals that exist in the common a dbily living of the environment

2. There are two kinds of supporting details--major and minor. Major details are the primary points that support the main idea and minor details expand major details. List **three** details and explain how they support the author's primary point?

Details used	Explanation of how they support the thesis
1. Endrin -	Fatality of th baby and dog that caused by the spray of endrin.

Details used	Explanation of how they support the thesis
2. Herbicdles	Plant killeri are detrimental to many animals.

Details used	Explanation of how they support the thesis
3. Systemic Insecticides	- bee hives are poisonous and caused the bees to die off.

3. The five major patterns of organization are the list of items pattern, the time order pattern, the example pattern, the comparison and/or contrast pattern, and the cause/effect pattern. What is the **main** pattern of organization used in this article? **Explain** why it is the major pattern. What other patterns are used? Give some examples.

Main pattern: _Listing._

Explain how the main pattern was used:
The author list different types of sub topic to be discussed.

Other pattern(s) used: _Cause/Effect._

Examples

Explain how the additional pattern(s) were used:
The author present the problem and he also gives the result or the outcome of the issue.

50

4. **If applicable: Give two examples that were used in the writing. Explain how they affected your understanding of the reading selection.**

The example(s) given	How example(s) contributed to your understanding
1. Cranberry weed killer	1. In the long run can cause malignant tumor
2. Systemic Insecticides	2. Causes the poison of plant nectars.

5. **If applicable: what is being compared and/or contrasted?**

Show two comparisons between items A and B:

A	B
Malathion - - Used by gardeners - house hold insecticide - mosquito spray.	DDT

Show two contrasts between items A and B:

A	B
Clordane	DDT

6. **Show two cause/effect relationships:**

Cause	Effect
1. Cranberry weed killer	Cause malignant tumor in the long run.
2. DDT	kille lice

7. **List three facts and three opinions from the article. Explain why it is either a fact or an opinion.**

	Explanation:
A.) fact: Herbercicel	A.) Causes metabolism to change in Animal temperature
B.) fact: Potentra tion	B.) The compound that destroys live enzmes
C.) fact: DDT	C.) ki

51

	Explanation:
A.) opinion How much DDT can be stored	A.)
B.) opinion: Pg. 29 Anyone...	B.)
C.) opinion: Pg. 28, Who's	C.)

8. **What is the author's purpose in this article? Is it to inform, persuade, or entertain? <u>Tell me how you arrived at that conclusion.</u>**

To inform the reader about the the dangers of toxic insecticides. persuade.

9. **What is the author's tone? <u>Explain your answer.</u>**

The authors tone is concern of the issue of threndible

10. **Discovering the ideas in writing that are <u>not stated directly</u> is called making inferences, or drawing conclusions. What inferences did you draw from the article you read? <u>Explain.</u>**

I find that the article is drawing an image of toxic chemicals causing unnessary death.

11. **Authors often use connotative language. Return to the reading selection and circle (in red or green) all connotative words. List 10 of those words here and explain how those words might affect the reader.**

sinster, doom, biocide, minapulation

How the connotative words above might affect the reader:

Paits a good picture Stirrs emotions

12. A good argument makes a point and then provides persuasive and logical evidence to back it up. However, a bad argument uses fallacies to support itself such as changing the subject, hasty generalization, circular reasoning, personal attack, straw man, false cause, false comparison, or either-or. Explain how the author supports his/her argument. <u>Does he/she use relevant and adequate support, or do fallacies exist? Explain.</u>

_____
_____
_____
_____
_____
_____
_____
_____
_____
_____
_____
_____
_____
_____
_____
_____
_____

13. The seven most common propaganda techniques are bandwagon, testimonial, transfer, plain folks, name calling, glittering generalities, and card staking. <u>Which techniques are used in this reading selection? Explain.</u>

_____
_____
_____
_____
_____
_____
_____
_____
_____
_____
_____
_____
_____
_____
_____
_____
_____

LOVE CANAL AND THE POISONING OF AMERICA

(From Laying Waste – The Poisoning Of America By Toxic Chemicals 1979)

Michael Brown

Niagara Falls is a city of unmatched natural beauty; it is also a tired industrial workhorse, beaten often and with a hard hand. A magnificent river— a strait, really—connecting Lake Erie to Lake Ontario flows hurriedly north, at a pace of a half-million tons a minute, widening into a smooth expanse near the city before breaking into whitecaps and taking its famous 186-foot plunge. Then it cascades through a gorge of overhung shale and limestone to rapids higher and swifter than anywhere else on the continent.

2   The falls attract long lines of newlyweds and other tourists. At the same time, the river provides cheap electricity for industry; a good stretch of its shore is now filled with the spiraled pipes of distilleries, and the odors of chlorine and sulfides hang in the air.

3   Many who live in the city of Niagara Falls work in chemical plants, the largest of which is owned by the Hooker Chemical Company, a subsidiary of Occidental Petroleum since the 1960s. Timothy Schroeder did not. He was a cement technician by trade dealing with the factories only if they needed a pathway poured, or a small foundation set. Tim and his wife,

I think it's great that the natural source is turn into energy that can be used to cut down cost of electricity bill.

Karen, lived in a ranch-style home with a brick and wood exterior at 460 99th Street. One of the Schroeders most cherished purchases was a Fiberglas pool, built into the ground and enclosed by a redwood fence.

4   Karen looked from a back window one morning in October 1974, noting with distress that the pool had suddenly risen two feet above the ground. She called Tim to tell him about it. Karen then had no way of knowing that this was the first sign of what would prove to be punishing family and economic tragedy.

5   Mrs. Schroeder believed that the cause of the uplift was the unusual groundwater flow of the area. Twenty-one years before, an abandoned hydroelectric canal directly behind their house had been backfilled with industrial rubble. The underground breaches created by this disturbance, aided by the marshland nature of the regions surficial layer, collected large volumes of rainfall and undermined the back yard. The Schroeders allowed the pool to remain in its precarious position until the following summer and then pulled it from the ground, intending to pour a new pool, cast in cement. This they were unable to do, for the gaping excavation immediately filled with what Karen called "chemical water," rancid liquids of yellow and orchid and blue. These same chemicals had mixed with the groundwater and flooded the entire yard, attacking the redwood posts with such a caustic bite that one day the fence simply collapsed. When the chemicals receded in the dry weather, they left the gardens and shrubs withered and scorched, as if by a brush fire.

How the Chemicals Got There

6   How the chemicals got there was no mystery. In the late 1930s, or perhaps early 1940s, the Hooker Company, whose many processes included the manufacture of pesticides, plasticizers, and caustic soda, began using the abandoned canal as a dump for at least 20,000 tons of waste residues—"still-bottoms," in the language of the trade.

7   Karen Schroeder's parents had been the first to experience problems with the canal's seepage. In 1959, her mother, Aileen Voorhees, encountered a strange black sludge bleeding through the basement walls. For the next twenty years, she and her husband, Edwin, tried various methods of halting the irritating intrusion, pasting the cinder-block wall with sealants and even constructing a gutter along the walls to intercept the inflow.

[margin notes, handwritten:]

Opinion

Goes to show how strong these chemical can be by the collapse of the hardood of redwood.

All that toxic waste was just an accident waiting to happen.

The amount of toxic waste is just massive.

55

Nothing could stop the chemical smell from permeating the entire household, and neighborhood calls to the city for help were fruitless. One day, when Edwin punched a hole in the wall to see what was happening, quantities of black liquid poured from the block. The cinder blocks were full of the stuff.

Birth Defects

8 More ominous than the Voorhees basement was an event that occurred at 11:12 P.M. on November 21, 1968, when Karen Schroeder gave birth to her third child, a seven-pound girl named Sheri. No sense of elation filled the delivery room. The child was born with a heart that beat irregularly and had a hole in it, bone blockages of the nose, partial deafness, deformed ear exteriors, and a cleft palate. Within two years, the Schroeders realized Sheri was also mentally retarded. When her teeth came in, a double row of them appeared on her lower jaw. And she developed an enlarged liver.

It's rare to see that all there birth defects affected towards one child.

9 The Schroeders considered these health problems, as well as illnesses among their other children, as acts of capricious genes—a vicious quirk of nature. Like Mrs. Schroeder's parents, they were concerned that the chemicals were devaluing their property. The crab apple tree and evergreen in the back were dead, and even the oak in front of the home was sick; one year, the leaves had fallen off on Father's Day.

Love Canal's Origin

10 The canal had been dug with much fanfare in the late nineteenth century by a flamboyant entrepreneur named William T. Love, who wanted to construct an industrial city with ready access to water power and major markets. The setting for Love's dream was to be a navigable power channel that would extend seven miles from the Upper Niagara before falling two hundred feet, circumventing the treacherous falls and at the same time providing cheap power. A city would be constructed near the point where the canal fed back into the river, and he promised it would accommodate half a million people.

Fact

Huge ideas and immagination, but too bad it didn't work out otherwise would have been a great resource.

11 So taken with his imagination were the state's leaders that they gave Love a free hand to condemn as much property as he liked, and to divert whatever amounts of water. Love's dream, however, proved grander than his resources, and he was eventually forced to abandon the project after a mile-long trench,

ten to forty feet deep and generally twenty yards wide, had been scoured perpendicular to the Niagara River. Eventually, the trench was purchased by Hooker.

Too Good to be True

12 Few of those who, in 1977, lived in the numerous houses that had sprung up by the site were aware that the large and barren field behind them was a burial ground for toxic waste. Both the Niagara County Health Department and the city said it was a nuisance condition, but no serious danger to the people. Officials of the Hooker Company refused comment, claiming only that they had no records of the chemical burials and that the problem was not their responsibility. Indeed, Hooker had deeded the land to the Niagara Falls Board of Education in 1953, for a token $1. With it the company issued no detailed warnings of the chemicals, only a brief paragraph in the quitclaim document that disclaimed company liability for any injuries or deaths which might occur at the site.

13 Though Hooker was undoubtedly relieved to rid itself of the contaminated land, the company was so vague about the hazards involved that one might have thought the wastes would cause harm only if touched, because they irritated the skin; otherwise, they were not of great concern. In reality, as the company must have known, the dangers of these wastes far exceeded those of acids or alkalines or inert salts. We now

knew that the drums Hooker had dumped in the canal contained a veritable witch's brew— compounds of truly remarkable toxicity. There were solvents that attacked the heart and liver, and residues from pesticides so dangerous that their commercial

Ironic for the Health Dept. to take the issue lightly.

Fact

sale was shortly thereafter restricted outright by the government; some of them were already suspected of causing cancer.

14   Yet Hooker gave no hint of that. When the board of education, which wanted the parcel for a new school, approached Hooker, B. Klaussen, at the time Hooker's executive vice president, said in a letter to the board. "Our officers have carefully considered your request. We are very conscious of the need for new elementary schools and realize that the sites must be carefully selected. We will be willing to donate the entire strip of property which we own between Colvin Boulevard and Frontier Avenue to be used for the erection of a school at a location to be determined…."

15   The board built the school and playground at the canal's midsection. Construction progressed despite the contractor's hitting a drainage trench that gave off a strong chemical odor and the discovery of a waste pit nearby. Instead of halting the work, the authorities simply moved the school eighty feet away. Young families began to settle in increasing numbers alongside the dump, many of them having been told that the field was to be a park and recreation area for their children.

16   Children found the "playground" interesting but at times painful. They sneezed, and their eyes teared. In the days when the dumping was still in progress, they. swam at the opposite end of the canal, occasionally arriving home with hard pimples all over their bodies. Hooker knew children were playing on its spoils. In 1958 three children were burned by exposed residues on the canal's surface, much of which, according to residents, had been covered with nothing more than fly ash and loose dirt. Because it wished to avoid legal repercussions, the company chose not to issue a public warning of the dangers it knew were there, nor to have its chemists explain to the people that their homes would have been better placed elsewhere.

17   The Love canal was simply unfit as a container for hazardous substances, poor even by the standards of the day, and now, in 1977, local authorities were belatedly finding that out. Several years of heavy snowfall and rain had filled the sparingly covered channel like a bathtub. The contents were overflowing at a frightening rate.

18   The city of Niagara Falls, I was assured, was planning a remedial drainage program to halt in some measure the chemical migration off the site. But no sense of urgency had been attached to the plan, and it was stalled in red tape. No one could agree on who should pay the bill— the city, Hooker, or the

Handwritten margin notes:
I can see that this article or story is taking a turn for the worst. Kids and a plot of contaminated land doesn't add up to be positive.

Dirt as a cover for a toxic contaminated waste seems a little crazy.

58

board of education— and engineers seemed confused over what exactly needed to be done.

19   Niagara Falls city Manager Donald O'Hara persisted in his view that, however displeasing to the eyes and nose, the Love Canal was not a crisis matter, mainly a question of aesthetics. O'Hara reminded me that Dr. Francis Clifford, county health commissioner, supported that opinion.

20   With the city, the board, and Hooker unwilling to commit themselves to a remedy, conditions degenerated in the area between 97th and 99th streets, until, by early 1978, the land was a quagmire of sludge that oozed from the canal's every pore. Melting snow drained the surface soot onto the private yards, while on the dump itself the ground had softened to the point of collapse, exposing the crushed tops of barrels. Beneath the surface, masses of sludge were finding their way out at a quickening rate, constantly forming springs of contaminated liquid. The Schroeder back yard, once featured in a local newspaper for its beauty, had reached the point where it was unfit even to walk upon. Of course, the Schroeders could not leave. No one would think of buying the property. They still owed on their mortgage and, with Tim's salary, could not afford

to maintain the house while they moved into a safer setting. They and their four children were stuck.

21   Apprehension about large costs was not the only reason the city was reluctant to help the Schroeders and the one hundred or so other families whose properties abutted the covered trench. The city may also have feared distressing Hooker. To an economically depressed area, the company provided desperately needed employment— as many as 3,000 blue-collar jobs and a substantial number of tax dollars. Hooker was speaking of building a $17 million headquarters in downtown Niagara Falls. So anxious were city officials to receive the new building that they and the state granted the company highly lucrative tax and loan incentives, and made available to the firm a prime parcel of property near the most popular tourist park on the American side.

Margin notes:
Toxic waste flowing into private yard, and for the company to just ignore it is completely irresponsible.

Fact

An Extremely Serious Problem

22 City Manager O'Hara and other authorities were aware of the nature of Hooker's chemicals. In fact, in the privacy of his office, O'Hara, after receiving a report on the chemicals tests at the canal, had informed the people at Hooker that it was an extremely serious problem. Even earlier, in 1976, the New York State Department of Environmental Conservation had been made aware that dangerous compounds were present in the basement sump pump of at least one 97th Street home, and soon after, its own testing had revealed that highly injurious halogenated hydrocarbons were flowing from the canal into adjoining sewers. Among them were the notorious PCBs; quantities as low as one part PCBs to a million parts normal water were enough to create serious environmental concerns; in the sewers of Niagara Falls,

the quantities of halogenated compounds were thousands of times higher. The other materials tracked, in sump pumps or sewers, were just as toxic as PCBs, or more so. Prime among the more hazardous ones was residue from hexachlorocyclopenta-diene, or C-56, which was deployed as an intermediate in the manufacture of several pesticides. In certain dosages, the chemical could damage every organ in the body.

23 While the mere presence of C-56 should have been cause for alarm, government remained inactive. Not until early 1978— a full eighteen months after C-56 was first detected— was testing conducted in basements along 97th and 99th streets to see if the chemicals had vaporized off the sump pumps and walls

This problem was not only known to the board of educators or the Health department, but it is also known to the NYC Stat Department and still the problem haven't be solve.

That alot of pesticides chemical to be dump into a canal that is not your average every day canal.

and were present in the household air.

24   While the basement tests were in progress, the rains of spring arrived at the canal, further worsening the situation. Heavier fumes rose above the barrels. More than before, the residents were suffering from headaches, respiratory discomforts, and skin ailments. Many of them felt constantly fatigued and irritable, and the children had reddened eyes. In the Schroeder home, Tim developed a rash along the backs of his legs. Karen could not rid herself of throbbing pains in her head. Their daughter, Laurie, seemed to be losing some of her hair.

25   The EPA test revealed that benzene, a known cause of cancer in humans, had been readily detected in the household air up and down the streets. A widely used solvent, benzene was known in chronic-exposure cases to cause headaches, fatigue, loss of weight, and dizziness followed by pallor nose-bleeds, and damage to the bone marrow.

26   No public announcement was made of the benzene hazard. Instead, officials appeared to shield the finding until they could agree among themselves on how to present it.

27   Dr. Clifford, the county health commissioner, seemed unconcerned by the detection of benzene in the air. His health department refused to conduct a normal study of the people's health, despite the air-monitoring results. For this reason, and because of the resistance growing among the local authorities, I went to the southern end of 99th Street to take an informal health survey of my own. I arranged a meeting with six neighbors, all of them instructed beforehand to list the illnesses they were aware of on their block, with names and ages specified for presentation at the session.

Serious Life-Threatening Illnesses Abound

28   The residents' list was startling. Though unafflicted before, they moved there, many people were now plagued with ear infections, nervous disorders, rashes, and headaches. One young man, James Gizzarelli, said he had missed four months of work owing to breathing troubles. His wife was suffering epileptic-like seizures which her doctor was unable to explain. Meanwhile, freshly applied paint was inexplicably peeling from the exterior of their house. Pets too were suffering, most seriously if they had been penned in the back yards nearest to the canal, constantly breathing air that smelled like mothballs and weedkiller. They lost their fur, exhibited skin lesions, and, while

---

Handwritten margin notes: Cause and Effect; Cause/Effect; cause/Effect; That's a long time off of work and his wife is suffering from epileptic seizures, unsure how these guys made a living.

still quite young, developed internal tumors. A great many cases of cancer were reported among the women, along with much deafness. On both 97th and 99th streets, traffic signs warned passing motorists to watch for deaf children playing near the road.

29   Evidence continued to mount that a large group of people, perhaps all of the one hundred families immediately by the canal, perhaps many more, were in imminent danger. While watching television, while gardening or doing a wash, in their sleeping hours, they were inhaling a mixture of damaging chemicals. Their hours of exposure were far longer than those of a chemical factory worker, and they wore no respirators or goggles. Nor could they simply open a door and escape. Helpessness and despair were the main responses to the blackened craters and scattered cinders behind their back yards.

30   But public officials often characterized the residents as hypochondriacs. Every agent of government had been called on the phone or sent pleas for help, but none offered aid.

31   Commissioner Clifford expressed irritation at my printed reports of illness, and disagreement began to surface in the newsroom on how the stories should be printed. "There's a high rate of cancer among my friends," Dr. Clifford argued. "It doesn't mean anything."

32   Yet as interest in the small community increased, further revelations shook the neighborhood. In addition to the benzene, eighty or more other compounds were found in the makeshift dump, ten of them potential carcinogens. The physiological effects they could cause were profound and diverse. At least fourteen of them could impact on the brain and central nervous system. Two of them, carbon tetrachloride and chlorobenzene, could readily cause narcotic or anesthetic consequences. Many others were known to cause headaches, seizures, loss of hair, anemia, or skin rashes. Together, the compounds were capable of inflicting innumerable illnesses, and no one knew what new concoctions were being formulated by their mixture underground.

Only Safe for 2.4 Minutes

33   Edwin and Aileen Voorhees had the most to be concerned about. When a state biophysicist analyzed the air content of their basement, he determined that the safe exposure time there was less than 2.4 minutes— the toxicity in the basement was

[Handwritten margin notes: "This really explains how bad the air was compared to the factory."; "Unreliable gov't that have no trust in its citizens, outrageous!"; "Fact"; "Cause/Effect"; "That barely even enough time to escape the air"]

thousands of times the acceptable limit for twenty-four-hour breathing. This did not mean they would necessarily become permanently ill, but their chances of contracting cancer, for example, had been measurably increased. In July, I visited Mrs. Voorhees for further discussion on her problems, and as we sat in the kitchen, drinking coffee, the industrial odors were apparent. Aileen, usually chipper and feisty, was visibly anxious. She stared down at the table, talking only in a lowered voice. Everything now looked different to her. The home she and Edwin had built had become their jail cell. Their yard was but a pathway through which toxicants entered the cellar walls. The field out back, that proposed "park," seemed destined to be the ruin of their lives.

34   On July 14 I received a call from the state health department with some shocking news. A preliminary review showed that women living at the southern end had suffered a high rate of miscarriages and had given birth to an abnormally high number of children with birth defects. In one age group, 35.3 percent had records of spontaneous abortions. That was far in excess of the norm. The odds against it happening by chance were 250 to one. These tallies, it was stressed, were "conservative" figures. Four children in one small section of the neighborhood had documentable birth defects, club feet, retardation, and deafness. Those who lived there the longest suffered the highest rates.

35   The data on miscarriages and birth defects, coupled with the other accounts of illness, finally pushed the state's bureaucracy into motion. A meeting was scheduled for August 2, at which time the state health commissioner, Dr. Robert Whalen, would formally address the issue. The day before the meeting, Dr. Nicholas Vianna, a state epidemiologist, told me that residents were also incurring some degree of liver damage. Blood analyses had shown hepatitis-like symptoms in enzyme levels. Dozens if not hundreds of people, apparently, had been adversely affected.

[Handwritten margin note: Cause/Effect of the toxic waste]

36   In Albany, on August 2, Dr. Whalen read a lengthy statements in which he urged the pregnant women and children under two years of age leave the southern end of the dump site immediately. He declared the Love Canal an official emergency, citing it as a "great and imminent peril to the health of the general public."

37   When Commissioner Whalen's words hit 97th and 99th streets, by way of one of the largest banner headlines in the Niagara *Gazette's* 125-year history, dozens of people massed on the streets, shouting into bullhorns and microphones to voice frustrations that had been accumula-ting for months. Many of them vowed a tax strike because their homes were rendered unmarketable and unsafe. They attacked their government for ignoring their welfare. A man of high authority, a physician with a title, had confirmed that their lives were in danger. Most wanted to leave the neighborhood immediately.

38   Terror and anger roiled together, exacerbated by Dr. Whalen's failure to provide a government-funded evacuation plan. His words were only a recommendation: individual families had to choose whether to risk their health and remain, or abandon their houses and, in so doing, write off a lifetime of work and savings.

A protest made in order for the the comissioners to take responsible action toward the issue.

Federal Disaster Area

39   On August 3, Dr. Whalen decided he should speak to the people. He arrived with Dr. David Axelrod, a deputy who had directed the state's investigation, and Thomas Frey, a key aide to Governor Hugh Carey.

40   At a public meeting, held in the 99th Street School auditorium, Frey was given the grueling task of controlling the crowd of 500 angry and frightened people. In an attempt to calm them, he announced that a meeting between the state and the White House had been scheduled for the following week. The state would propose that the Love Canal be classified a national disaster, thereby freeing federal funds. For now, however, he could promise no more. Neither could Dr. Whalen and his staff of experts. All they could say was what was already known: twenty-five organic compounds, some of them capable of causing cancer, were in their homes, and because young children were especially prone to toxic effects, they should be moved to another area.

41   Dr. Whalen's order had applied only to those living at the canal's southern end, on its immediate periphery. But families living across the street from the dump site, or at the northern portion, where the chemicals were not so visible at the surface, reported afflictions remarkably similar to those suffered by families whose yards abutted the southern end. Serious respiratory problems, nervous disorders, and rectal bleeding were reported by many who were not covered by the order.

42   Throughout the following day, residents posted signs of protest on their front fences or porch posts. "Love Canal Kills," they said, or "Give Me Liberty I've Got Death." Emotionally exhausted and uncertain about their future, men stayed home from work, congregating on the streets or comforting their wives. By this time the board of education had announced it was closing the 99th Street School for the following year, because of its proximity to the exposed toxicants. Still, no public relief was provided for the residents.

43   Another meeting was held that evening, at a fire hall on 102 Street. It was unruly, but the people, who had called the session in an effort to organize themselves, managed to form an alliance, the Love Canal Homeowners Association, and to elect as president Lois Gibbs, a pretty, twenty-seven-year-old woman with jet-black hair who proved remarkably

Finally after a number of voice from the frightning citizens gov't finaly take action)

Cause Effect

adept at dealing with experienced politicians and at keeping the matter in the news. After Mrs. Gibbs' election, Congressman John LaFalce entered the hall and announced, to wild applause, that the Federal Disaster Assistance Administration would be represented the next morning, and that the state's two senators, Daniel Patrick Moynihan and Jacob Javits, were working with him in an attempt to get funds from Congress.

44   With the Love Canal story now attracting attention from the national media, the Governor's office announced that Hugh Carey would

be at the 99th Street School on August 7 to address the people. Decisions were being made in Albany and Washington. Hours before the Governor's arrival, a sudden burst of "urgent" reports from Washington came across the newswires. President Jimmy Carter had officially declared the Hooker dump site a national emergency.

45   Hugh Carey was applauded on his arrival. The Governor announced that the state, through its Urban Development Corporation,

planned to purchase, at fair market value, those homes rendered uninhabitable by the marauding chemicals. He spared no promises. "You will not have to make mortgage payments on homes you don't want or cannot occupy. Don't worry about the banks. The state will take care of them." By the standards of Niagara Falls, where the real estate market was

depressed, the houses were middle-class range, worth from $20,000 to $40,000 apiece. The state would assess each house and purchase it, and

also pay the costs of moving, temporary housing during the transition period, and special items not covered by the usual real estate assessment, such as installation of telephones.

46   First in a trickle and them, by September in droves, the families gathered their belongings and carted them away. Moving vans crowded

97th and 99th streets. Linesmen went from house to house disconnecting the telephones and electrical wires, while carpenters pounded plywood over the windows to keep vandals away. By the following spring, 237 families were gone; 170 of them had moved into new houses. In time the state erected around a six-block residential area a green chain-link fence, eight feet in height, clearly demarcating the contamination zone.

47   In October 1978, the long-awaited remedial drainage program began at the south end. Trees were uprooted, fences

Nice to see some responsible gov't taking much needed action to help out the victims

About time they notice the danger of the chemical waste

66

and garages torn down, and swimming pools removed from the area. So great were residents' apprehensions that dangerous fumes would be released over the surrounding area that the state, at a cost of $500,000, placed seventy-five buses at emergency evacuation pickup spots during the months of work, in the event that outlying homes had to be vacated quickly because of an explosion. The plan was to construct drain tiles around the channel's

periphery, where the back yards had been located, in order to divert leakage to seventeen-foot-deep wet wells from which contaminated groundwater could be drawn and treated by filtration through activated carbon. (Removing the chemicals themselves would have been financially prohibitive, perhaps costing as much as $100 million--and even then the materials would have to be buried elsewhere.) After the trenching was complete, and the sewers installed, the canal was to be covered by a sloping mound of clay and planted with grass. One day, city officials hoped, the wasteland would become a park.

48   In spite of the corrective measures and the enormous effort by the state health department, which took thousands of blood samples from past and current residents and made uncounted analyses of soil, water, and air, the full range of the effects remained unknown. In neighborhoods immediately outside the official "zone of contamination," more than 500 families were left near the desolate setting, their health still in jeopardy. The state announced it would buy no more homes.

49   The first public indication that chemical contamination had probably reached streets to the east and west of 97th and 99th streets, and to the north and south as well, came on August 11, 1978, when sump-pump samples I had taken from 100th and 101st streets, analyzed in a laboratory, showed the trace presence of a number of chemicals found in the canal itself, including lindane, a restricted pesticide that had been suspected of causing cancer in laboratory animals. While probing 100th Street, I had knocked on the door of Patricia Pino, thirty-four, a blond divorcee with a young son and daughter. I had noticed that some of the leaves on a large tree in front of her house exhibited a black oiliness much like that on the trees and shrubs of 99th Street; she was located near what had been a drainage swale.

50   After I had extracted a jar of sediment from her sump pump for the analysis, we conversed about her family situation and what the trauma now unfolding meant to them. Ms. Pino was extremely depressed and embittered. Both of her children

had what appeared to be slight liver abnormalities, and her son had been plagued with "non-specific" allergies, teary eyes, sinus trouble, which improved markedly when he was sent away from home. Patricia told of times, during the heat of summer, when fumes were readily noticeable in her basement and sometimes even upstairs. She herself had been treated for a possibly cancerous condition on her cervix. But, like others, her family was now trapped.

51   On September 24, 1978, I obtained a state memorandum that said chemical infiltration of the outer regions was significant indeed. The letter, sent from the state laboratories to the U.S. Environmental Protection Agency said, "Preliminary analysis of soil samples demonstrates extensive migration of potentially toxic materials outside the immediate canal area." There it was, in the state's own words. Not long afterward, the state medical investigator. Dr, Nicholas Vianna, reported indications that residents from 93rd to 103rd streets might also have incurred liver damage.

Death of John Allen Kenny

52   On October 4, a young boy, John Allen Kenny, who lived quite a distance north of the evacuation zone, died. The fatality was due to the failure of another organ that can be readily affected by toxicants, the kidney. Naturally, suspicions were raised that his death was in some way related to a creek that still flowed behind his house and carried, near an outfall, the odor of chlorinated compounds. Because the creek served as a catch basin for a portion of the Love Canal, the state studied an autopsy of the boy. No conclusions were reached. John Allen's parents, Norman, a chemist, and Luella, a medical research assistant, were unsatisfied with the state's investigation, which they felt was "superficial." Luella said, "He played in the creek all the time. There had been restrictions on the older boys, but he was the youngest and played with them when they were old enough to go to the creek. We let him do what the other boys did. He died of nephrosis. Proteins were passing through his urine. Well, in reading the literature, we discovered that chemicals can trigger this. There was no evidence of infection, which there should have been, and there was damage to his thymus and brain. He also had nosebleeds and headaches, and dry heaves. So our feeling is that chemicals probably triggered it."

53   The likelihood that water-carried chemicals had escaped

68

from the canal's deteriorating bounds and were causing problems quite a distance from the site was not lost upon the Love Canal Homeowners Association and its president, Lois Gibbs, who was attempting to have additional families relocated. Because she lived on 101st Street, She was one of those left behind, with no means of moving despite persistent medical difficulties in her six-year-old son, Michael, who had been operated on twice for urethral strictures. [Mrs. Gibbs' husband, a worker at a chemical plant brought home only $150 a week, she told me, and when they subtracted from that the $90 a week for food and other necessities, clothing costs for their two children, $215 a month for mortgage payments and taxes, utility and phone expenses, and medical bills, they had hardly enough cash to buy gas and cigarettes, let alone vacate their house.]

54   Assisted by two other stranded residents, Marie Pozniak and Grace McCoulf, and with the professional analysis of a Buffalo scientist name Beverly Paigen, Lois Gibbs mapped out the swale and creekbed areas, many of them long ago filled, and set about interviewing the numerous people who lived on or near formerly wet ground. The survey indicated that these people were suffering from an abnormal number of kidney and bladder aggravations and problems of the reproductive system. In a report to the state, Dr. Paigen claimed to have found, in 245

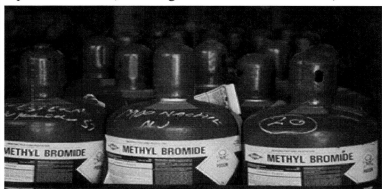

homes outside the evacuation zone, thirty-four miscarriages, eighteen birth defects, nineteen nervous breakdowns, ten cases of epilepsy, and high rates of hyperactivity and suicide.

55   In their roundabout way, the state health experts, after an elaborate investigation, confirmed some of the homeowners' worst fears. On February 8, 1979, Dr. David Axelrod, who by then had been appointed health commissioner, and whose excellence as a scientist was widely acknowledged, issued a new order that officially extended the health emergency of the

69

previous August, citing high incidents of birth deformities and miscarriages in the areas where creeks and swales had once flowed, or where swamps had been. With that, the state offered to evacuate temporarily those families with pregnant women or children under the age of two from the outer areas of contamination, up to 103rd Street. But no additional homes would be purchased; nor was another large-scale evacuation, temporary or otherwise, under consideration. Those who left under the new plan would have to return when their children passed the age limit.

56   Twenty-three families accepted the state's offer. Another seven families, ineligible under the plan but of adequate financial means to do so, simply left their homes and took the huge loss of investment. Soon boarded windows speckled the outlying neighborhoods.

Toxicity Beyond Imagination

57   The previous November and December, not long after the evacuation of 97th and 99th streets, I became interested in the possibility that Hooker might have buried in the Love Canal waste residues from the manufacture of what is known as 2,3,5-trichlorophenol. My curiosity was keen because I knew that this substance, which Hooker produced for the manufacture of the antibacterial agent hexachlorophene, and which was also used to make defoliants such as Agent Orange, the herbicide employed in Vietnam, carries with it an unwanted by-product technically called 2,3,7,8-tetrachlorodibenzo-para-dioxin, or tetradioxin. The potency of dioxin of this isomer is nearly beyond imagination. Although its toxicological effect are not fully known, the few experts on the subject estimate that if three ounces were evenly distributed and subsequently ingested among a million people, or perhaps more than that, all of them would die. It compares in toxicity to the botulinum toxin. On skin contact, dioxin causes a disfiguration called "chloracne," which begins as pimples, lesions, and eysts, but can lead to calamitous internal damage. Some scientists suspect that dioxin causes cancer, perhaps even malignancies that occur, in galloping fashion, within a short time of contact. At least two (some estimates went as high as eleven) pounds of dioxin were dispersed over Seveso, Italy, in 1976, after an explosion at a trichlorophenol plant: dead animals littered the streets, and more than 300 acres of land were immediately evacuated. In Vietnam,

the spraying of Agent Orange, because of the dioxin contaminant, was banned in 1970, when the first effects on human beings began to surface, including dioxin's powerful teratogenic, or fetus-deforming, effects.

58   I posed two questions concerning trichlorophenol: Were wastes from the process buried in the canal? If so, what were the quantities?

59   On November 8, before Hooker answered my queries, I learned that, indeed, trichlorophenol had been found in liquids pumped from the remedial drain ditches. No dioxin had been found yet, and some officials, ever wary of more emotionalism among the people, argued that, because the compound was not soluble in water, there was little chance it had migrated off-site. Officials at Newco Chemical Waste Systems, a local waste disposal firm, at the same time claimed that if dioxin had been there, it had probably been photolytically destroyed. Its half-life, they contended, was just a few short years.

60   I knew form Whiteside, however, that in every known case, waste from 2,4,5,-trichlorophenol carried dioxin with it. I also knew that dioxin could become soluble in groundwater and migrate into the neighborhood upon mixing with solvents such as benzene. Moreover, because it had been buried, sunlight would not break it down.

61   On Friday, November 10, I called Hooker again to urge that they answer my questions. Their spokesman, Bruce Davis, came to the phone and, in a controlled tone, gave me the answer: His firm had indeed buried trichlorophenol in the canal--200 tons of it.

62   Immediately I called Whiteside. His voice took on an urgent tone. According to his calculation, if 200 tons of trichlorophenol were there, in all likelihood they were accompanied by 130 pounds of tetra dioxin, an amount equaling the estimated total content of dioxin in the thousands of tons of Agent Orange rained upon Vietnamese jungles. The seriousness of the crisis had

deepened, for now the Love Canal was not only a dump for highly dangerous solvents and pesticides; it was also the broken container for one of the most toxic substances ever synthesized by man.

63   I reckoned that the main danger was to those working on the remedial project, digging in the trenches. The literature on dioxin indicated that, even in quantities at times too small to detect, the substance possessed vicious characteristics. In one case, workers in a trichlorophe-nol plant had developed chloracne, although the substance could not be traced on the equipment with which they worked. The mere tracking of minuscule amounts of dioxin on a pedestrian's shoes in Seveso led to major concerns, and, according to Whiteside, a plant in Amsterdan, upon being found contaminated with dioxin had been "dismantled, brick by brick, and the material embedded in concrete, loaded at a specially constructed dock, on ships, and dumped at sea, in deep water near the Azores." Workers in trichlorophenol plants had died of cancer or severe liver damage, or had suffered emotional and sexual disturbances.

64   Less than a month after the first suspicions arose, on the evening of December 9, I received a call from Dr. Axelrod. "We found it. The dioxin. In a drainage trench behind 97th Street. It was in the part-per-trillion-range."

65   The state remained firm in its plans to continue the construction, and, despite the ominous new findings, no further evacuations were announced. During the next several weeks, small incidents of vandalism occurred along 97th and 99th streets. Tacks were spread on the road, causing numerous flat tires on the trucks. Signs of protest were hung in the school. Meetings of the Love Canal Homeowners Association became more vociferous. Christmas was near, and in the association's office at 99th Street School, a holiday tree was decorated with bulbs arranged to spell "DIOXIN."

66   The Love Canal people chanted and cursed at meetings with the state officials, cried on the telephone, burned an effigy of the health commissioner, traveled to Albany with a makeshift child's coffin, threatened to hold officials hostage, sent letters and telegrams to the White House, held days of mourning and nights of prayer. On Mother's Day this year, they marched down the industrial corridor and waved signs denouncing Hooker, which had issued not so much as a statement of remorse. But no happy ending was in store for them. The federal government was clearly not planning to come to their rescue, and the state

72

felt it had already done more than its share. City Hall was silent and remains silent today. Some residents still hoped that, miraculously, an agency of government would move them. All of them watched with anxiety as each newborn came to the neighborhood, and they looked at their bodies for signs of cancer.

67   One hundred and thirty families from the Love Canal area began leaving their homes last August and September, seeking temporary refuge in local hotel rooms under a relocation plan funded by the state which had been implemented after fumes became so strong, during remedial trenching operations, that the United Way abandoned a care center it had opened in the neighborhood.

68   As soon as remedial constructions is complete, the people will probably be forced to return home, as the state will no longer pay for their lodging. Some have threatened to barricade themselves in the hotels. Some have mentioned violence. Anne Hillis of 102nd Street, who told reporters her first child had been born so badly decomposed that doctors could not determine its sex, was so bitter that she threw table knives and a soda can at the state's on-site coordinator.

69   In October, Governor Carey announced that the state probably would buy and additional 200 to 240 homes, at an expense of some $5 million. In the meantime, lawyers have prepared lawsuits totaling about $2.65 billion and have sought court action for permanent relocation. Even if the latter action is successful, and they are allowed to move, the residents' plight will not necessarily have ended. The psychological scars are bound to remain among them and their children, along with the knowledge that, because they have already been exposed, they may never fully escape the Love Canal's insidious grasp.

The questions that follow may be used for further discussion of the reading selection or as topics for essay writing.

1. Michael Brown wrote **_Love Canal_** in a very straightforward manner. He utilized time to place all of the events in their proper perspective. Create a timeline showing the progression of events from the earliest date to the end of the article.

2. List ten of the chemicals found buried in Love Canal.

3. Search the Internet for information on other toxic waste sites. Write a paragraph or more discussing your findings.

4. Search the Internet for information on schools built on toxic waste sites. Discuss your findings in a paragraph or more.

5. _____
   _____
   _____
   _____
   _____
   _____
   _____
   _____

6. _____
   _____
   _____
   _____
   _____
   _____
   _____

Applying Reading Skills
(Neatly **PRINT** all answers using ink <u>not</u> pencil)

Title of the Reading Selection: _____

1. **What is the author's overall main idea, (central point, or thesis)?**

   To inform the reader about the toxic waste and it's impact on human lives.

2. **There are two kinds of supporting details--major and minor. Major details are the primary points that support the main idea and minor details expand major details. List <u>three</u> details and explain how they support the author's primary point?**

Details used	Explanation of how they support the thesis
1. 20,000 tons of toxic waste was dump	

Details used	Explanation of how they support the thesis
2. Birth defects	

Details used	Explanation of how they support the thesis
3. I love vision of the Canal to be a community of low cost power	insufficient resource

3. **The five major patterns of organization are the list of items pattern, the time order pattern, the example pattern, the comparison and/or contrast pattern, and the cause/effect pattern. What is the <u>main</u> pattern of organization used in this article? <u>Explain</u> why it is the major pattern. What other patterns are used? Give some examples.**

Main pattern: _Cause/Effect_

Explain how the main pattern was used: _____

Other pattern(s) used: _Example_

Explain how the additional pattern(s) were used: _____

_____

75

4. If applicable: Give <u>two</u> examples that were used in the writing. <u>Explain</u> how they affected your understanding of the reading selection.

The example(s) given	How example(s) contributed to your understanding
1.	1.
2.	2.

5. If applicable: what is being compared and/or contrasted?

Show <u>two</u> comparisons between items A and B:

A	B

Show <u>two</u> contrasts between items A and B:

A	B

6. Show <u>two</u> cause/effect relationships:

Cause	Effect
1. 80-86	head aches
	respiratory discomforts
2. Benzene	cancer

7. List <u>three</u> facts and <u>three</u> opinions from the article. <u>Explain why</u> it is either a fact or an opinion.

	Explanation:
A.) fact: Carcinogens	A.) Found in the toxic waste
B.) fact: Hooker deeded the land	B.) To the Niagra Falls (BOE)
C.) fact:	C.)

76

	Explanation:
A.) opinion _Mrs. Schroeder_	A.) _unusuall ground water flow thet cause an uplife_
B.) opinion: _Govt_	B.) _thought it wasn't dangerous._
C.) opinion:	C.)

8. **What is the author's purpose in this article? Is it to inform, persuade, or entertain? <u>Tell me how you arrived at that conclusion.</u>**

To inform the reader about the tragedy cause by the the toxic water

9. **What is the author's tone? <u>Explain your answer.</u>**

cautionary, bitter, informative

10. **Discovering the ideas in writing that are <u>not stated directly</u> is called making inferences, or drawing conclusions. What inferences did you draw from the article you read? <u>Explain.</u>**

I thought the article was going the be the dangerous factor of the canel

11. **Authors often use connotative language. Return to the reading selection and circle (in red or green) all connotative words. List 10 of those words here and explain how those words might affect the reader.**

deformed, burned, collapse crush seizures, bleeding

How the connotative words above might affect the reader:

The connotative helps the reader to pick up how sever the problem the auth is trying to convey.

77

12. A good argument makes a point and then provides persuasive and logical evidence to back it up. However, a bad argument uses fallacies to support itself such as changing the subject, hasty generalization, circular reasoning, personal attack, straw man, false cause, false comparison, or either-or. Explain how the author supports his/her argument. <u>Does he/she use relevant and adequate support, or do fallacies exist? Explain.</u>

_____
_____
_____
_____
_____
_____
_____
_____
_____
_____
_____
_____
_____
_____
_____
_____
_____

13. The seven most common propaganda techniques are bandwagon, testimonial, transfer, plain folks, name calling, glittering generalities, and card staking. <u>Which techniques are used in this reading selection? Explain.</u>

_____
_____
_____
_____
_____
_____
_____
_____
_____
_____
_____
_____
_____
_____
_____
_____
_____

Landmines

Lawrence Scheg

As a child back in the 1950's, I ran with the other neighborhood kids into the white clouds of smoke billowing from the back of the spray truck. I didn't realize then how dangerous it was to inhale that smoke – it was DDT. Many years later, Rachel Carson's book *Silent Spring* would detail the adverse effects of DDT. Its use would be banned in the United States, but, as naïve children, we had already subjected our bodies to its poisonous effects.

How the author got into researching

I also didn't realize the toxic effects of the fluoride that was added to our drinking water in Rochester, New York. I felt nauseous when I drank the water so I tried to avoid drinking it. I thought that maybe there were bacteria, or something like that, in the pipes causing my ill feelings.

Nor did I think much about the harmful effects of fluoride as I brushed it on my teeth. It would be many years before the full knowledge of its dangers would be discovered.

Worrying about chemicals wasn't a priority during those early years.

When I was ten years old, I developed a sudden case of appendicitis. My mother called the doctor on a Sunday (they made house calls in those days!) but he didn't arrive until Wednesday evening. My appendix burst and I almost died as the poison traveled throughout my body. I didn't give it too much thought at the time, but would later wonder if a "bad" diet hadn't nearly killed me.

During my college years, I suffered from stomach pain and the doctors put me on a "bland" diet. When I let the water in a glass sit over night, I soon discovered that rust, slime, and who knows what else, settled to the bottom of the glass. I told the campus doctor about that and was told that that "stuff" was harmless. For the second time in my life, I avoided water. I also was able to leave the "bland" diet behind by not drinking that "safe" water anymore.

During the 1970's, I read Rachel Carson's book *Silent Spring*. It gave me an entirely new and enlightened perspective on the world we live in, and many of the chemicals that occupy this world. I was grateful for her powerful book and felt that because of her writing most of the dangerous chemicals were no longer being sold or used. I was very wrong about thinking that those chemicals were no longer a threat, and would not realize how wrong I was until several years later.

As the late 1970's approached, I was again taken ill. I thought that I must have been cursed with a weak body to be so sick. It looked like I was going to die. Three doctors, who did not know one another, and had no communication with one another, told me they were baffled by my illness and should just go home and die.

I thought that that was a rather cold way of dealing with my problem and I was not ready to die. I was only 27 years old, had a 4 year old son, and hoped for a future. I wanted to live, but I was very sick and very weak.

I decided to research my problem. I went to the libraries, bookstores, and health food stores in search of an answer. I mainly began to build my body back up by mega-vitamin therapy and very short walks that eventually turned into longer walks and then into jogging.

I also learned that a great amount of my weakness was due to allergies. My worst allergies were to dogs and cats and bug bites. These weakened my system and then I began to develop allergies to most foods, ink smells, chalk dust, regular dust, molds, food colorings, and the list went on and on.

My "recovery" took about 18 months. From my worst allergies I have never totally recovered, but I have learned to live with my disability.

Why have I shared all of this with you? To let you know that the chemicals that I was exposed to, and the effects they had on me, are very small when compared to the chemical dangers that exist in our "modern" world.

I hesitate to write this for fear of being called an alarmist, or a paranoid person, or a health nut (that's an oxymoron), or whatever other derogatory term someone may come up with. But as I hesitate, I also think of the many brave persons who have written controversial works before me and I cannot remain silent.

As a critical reader, you should check into every item that I write about in this next section. Start with the Internet because it is one of the few places in this world where money and censorship do not reign. Then, let your search take you to medical journals, news reports, books, and wherever else you need to journey to complete your search for knowledge.

With that said, I will continue my discussion and will just briefly mention some of the dangers that exist in our world today. I will leave the more extensive research for you to complete at a later date – it would fill hundreds, if not thousands, of pages.

Aspartame

In 1996, I met my wife. She has been a diabetic since she was 8 years old. One afternoon at lunch I watched her pour some artificial sweetener into her coffee. Earlier she had been telling me about her joint pains, numbness in her arms, migraines, and vision problems. She was only 26 years old and suffering such poor health!

I looked at her and said, "I don't know anything about that stuff that you are pouring into your coffee but you know they once pulled an artificial sweetener from the market because it was suspected of causing cancer.

Maybe that blue packet has something to do with your illnesses." She politely dismissed my thoughts and consumed her coffee. She also continued to suffer her symptoms.

About six months later, I was having lunch in Santa Barbara, and as I read through a newspaper, I came upon an article discussing the dangers of Aspartame. The article confirmed what I had suspected – that "stuff" was dangerous and related to her illnesses. I showed the article to my wife Christy and she stopped consuming the Aspartame products. All of her symptoms disappeared and never returned. It has been over six years since she stopped using Aspartame products. The doctors were attributing her symptoms to her diabetes - clearly she still has diabetes - but no longer has those symptoms.

Since 1996, I have continued to research Aspartame and the evidence against it is overwhelming. I have found it in baby vitamins, gum (even gum sweetened with sugar), yogurt, and it exists in over 5000 other products. I believe it is a danger to everyone's health and should be avoided.

Fluoride

Drug Facts		Drug Facts (continued)	
Active ingredient	Purpose	**Directions** • do not swallow • supervise children as necessary until capable of using without supervision	
Sodium monofluorophosphate (0.8%).............	artificially toothpaste	adults and children 2 years and older	brush teeth thoroughly after meals or at least twice a day, or use as directed by a dentist or physician
Use aids in the prevention of dental decay		children under 6 years	instruct in good brushing and rinsing habits (to minimize swallowing)
Warnings		children under 2 years	ask a dentist or physician
Keep out of reach of children under 6 years of age. If more than used for brushing is accidentally swallowed, get medical help or contact a Poison Control Center right away.		**Inactive ingredients:** sorbitol, water, hydrated silica, PEG-32, sodium lauryl sulfate, SD alcohol 38-B, flavor, cellulose gum, sodium saccharin, titanium dioxide.	
		Questions or Comments? Call 1-800-786-5135 Monday - Friday 8am - 5pm	

The label above says,

" **Warnings** *Keep out of reach of children under 6 years of age. If more than used for brushing is accidentally swallowed, get medical help or contact a Poison Control Center right away."*

The recommended amount that should be used for brushing, according to most dentists, is the size of a pea. Have you ever seen anyone use an amount that small?

Under the "Directions" heading it says,

Directions Do not swallow …

Fluoride is still a menace in most parts of the country. Even if it is not added to your local water supply, (and not having it added is extremely rare) it may find its way into your body through toothpaste, soda drinks, juice, beer, wine, ice cubes, canned foods, and so forth. All of your doubts about its danger can be cleared up by reading the poison warning required on the side of every box of fluoridated toothpaste sold in this country.

Non-fluoridated toothpaste may be purchased at many health food stores, health food sections of supermarkets, or online at www.SierraPublishing.com under Dr. Mom's Health Products in the shopping section.

As can be seen by the picture above, my son Brian was the September 2004 winner of our dentist's "No Cavity" contest. Brian does not use fluoridated toothpaste, rarely drinks soda, and flosses with a plastic floss stick. Those three items are what I consider to be the best way to prevent cavities – not poisoning our bodies with fluoride in the water and toothpaste.

Acesulfame-k

Acesulfame-k is an artificial sweetener closely related to Aspartame. It was developed in Germany and recently I have found it in Gum along with sugar and Aspartame. I have also found it added to Pedialite type products to replace Aspartame.

Rbst or Rbgh

Rbst is a growth hormone that is injected into cows to make them produce more milk. It has a bad effect on the cows and it has been blamed for everything from allergies to cancer.

Sucralose

Sucralose, while it seems to not be as dangerous as Aspartame, it still has a long list of possible side effects. Many persons report gastrointestinal distress and other ailments resulting from the use of this product. One of the trade names is Splenda.

Citric Acid

Citric acid is added to a wide variety of food products including sodas, yogurts, candies, spaghetti sauces, tea, juices, and much more. It has been claimed by some to upset the natural balance of digestive acids in the body and may lead to, or aggravate, stomach problems such as Acid Reflux Disease. It may weaken, shrink, or destroy the esophagus. The victim of this additive may then have a difficult time swallowing food, or even water, and feel like they are choking.

Atrazine

A weed killer used extensively in the United States is being blamed for some rather strange birth defects such as animals being born with multiple sex organs!

Accutane

Accutane is an ingredient in some acne medicines. It is known to cause birth defects. It is also an ingredient in some pesticides and may be at least partly responsible for many of the **deformed frogs** that have suddenly begun to appear around the world.

MTBE

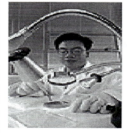

MTBE is an additive that was added to gasoline in some parts of the country. It has been alleged to cause everything from allergy problems to sudden death in otherwise healthy joggers.

Microwave ovens

Microwave ovens are so common yet their safety is called into question for many reasons. A quick search of information on the web will probably convince you that

Bizzare info don't want that to happen to the humans.

84

it is time to unplug yours and throw it away.

Cell Phones

I own and occasionally use a cell phone - but only occasionally. The research, even by most of the cell phone companies, points to some real health dangers here. Everything from increased tiredness to brain tumors has been attributed to cell phone use.

I used a cell phone extensively when I was traveling a lot during the years 1995 to 1996. I also developed a severe headache that would not go away. It lasted for about 45 days until I suspected my cell phone might be causing the pain and I stopped using it. The headaches disappeared shortly after that. I didn't use a cell phone again until shortly after 9/11 when I decided that in certain instances they could be quite useful and necessary.

Another danger associated with cell phones is their use by drivers of motor vehicles. Some States are banning their use by drivers. The number of accidents and deaths caused by cell phone use is growing as cell phone use increases. It could become a problem similar in magnitude to driving under the influence of alcohol.

SSRI Drugs

Luvox (and drugs of like kind – termed SSRI drugs) is an antidepressant drug that seems to cause severe mood changes and problems of rage in about 4% of the people taking it – that equals about 80,000 individuals (mostly children and teenagers). It, or similar drugs, have been connected to seven out of twelve school shootings (including Columbine).

Some of the common trade names are: Luvox, Celexa, Paxil, Zoloft, Prozac, and an especially dangerous one (according to many experts), Effexor.

Over five million teenagers are taking these drugs and, in 2004, the FDA ordered new warnings to be added to the labels of these drugs when prescribed to young people. Adult's prescription bottles are not required to carry the new warnings – even though they may suffer similar side effects.

Drugs don't be need to give to teenagers, to deal with it in a natural way

Our Dangerous New World

As can be seen from the brief information given above, we live in a dangerous world of chemicals that neither Rachel Carson, nor Michael Brown, nor probably anyone else could have predicted. It is like walking through a world of landmines – one false step could take away your health or your life, or the health or life of someone you love.

We don't need to be paranoid, but we do need to walk with wisdom and knowledge.

Why is the world this way? Why doesn't our government protect us from these dangers? Is it ignorance on the part of the purveyors of these toxins, or is it greed, or is it something even more sinister such as a conspiracy of some sort? We each have to search for the answers to those questions but more importantly we each have to protect ourselves and our loved ones from the dangers that exist.

We have perhaps the best government that has ever existed and I believe Jefferson and the Founders of this country would tell us to work to change it – not to destroy it. I believe Thoreau would have us continue to imagine what better form of government we could evolve it into. Yes, the problems exist, yes, the corruption exists, yes, the greed exists so bad that men and women would watch others die while they fill their bank accounts, yes, perhaps conspiracies also exist – but this has never been a perfect world occupied by perfect people. Sometimes the battles are fought through dirt, mud, towns and cities. Sometimes the battles (remember Martin Luther King Jr.) are fought in the courts, protested in the streets, and economically decided at the point of sale.

Many years ago a rock band named Quicksilver (later Quicksilver Messenger Service) sang a song written by Jesse Oris Farrow entitled *What About Me?* The first few lines of that song have been drifting through my mind for several months now – even though it has been over 20 years since I last listened to that song:

86

You've poisoned my sweet water
You've cut down my green trees
The food you fed my children
Was the cause of their disease

My world is slowly falling down
And the air's not fit to breathe
And those of us who carry on
We have to do something …

These lyrics address the problem, but this generation must decide how it will address the solution. "Landmines" are not easy to avoid. They lie in wait to destroy the strong as well as the weak. Sometimes they disable and disfigure. Sometimes they kill. But landmines can be sought out, identified, defused, or destroyed. We don't have to live with landmines. We don't have to live with unnecessary chemicals in our air, food, water, and bodies.

The questions that follow may be used for further discussion of the reading selection or as topics for essay writing.

1. Do an Internet search on one of the chemicals, drugs, or any other topic mentioned in this article. Paste your research into a download template (from the CD Rom) and discuss your findings.

2. Look up Fluoride and the Atomic bomb on the Internet. Discuss your findings in a paragraph or more.

3. Research Luvox and other SSRI drugs. Discuss your findings in a well written essay.

4. The author refers to Thomas Jefferson and Martin Luther King Jr. in this selection. Why does he do that?

5. The Author entitled this selection *"Landmines"*. Discuss why he chose that title.

6. The author ends this selection with a reference to a song. Discuss the meaning of the song as it relates to the rest of the article.

7. What do you think finally convinced the author's wife to stop using artificial sweeteners? Was her first reaction (at lunch) typical of how most people would react?

8._____
_____
_____
_____
_____

9._____
_____
_____
_____
_____

Applying Reading Skills

Title of the Reading Selection: _____

1. **What is the author's overall main idea, (central point, or thesis)?**

    Our world is filled with dangers that we
    need to be aware of.

2. **There are two kinds of supporting details--major and minor. Major details are the primary points that support the main idea and minor details expand major details. List <u>three</u> details and explain how they support the author's primary point?**

	Details used	Explanation of how they support the thesis
1.	Flouride Citric Acid	Dargers to Health

	Details used	Explanation of how they support the thesis
2.	Rbst	Bad effect on Cow

	Details used	Explanation of how they support the thesis
3.	CEll phone	

3. **The five major patterns of organization are the list of items pattern, the time order pattern, the example pattern, the comparison and/or contrast pattern, and the cause/effect pattern. What is the <u>main</u> pattern of organization used in this article? <u>Explain</u> why it is the major pattern. What other patterns are used? Give some examples.**

Main pattern: _Listing Pattern_

Explain how the main pattern was used:
Listed the main notes he used to get his point across

Other pattern(s) used: _Examples_

Explain how the additional pattern(s) were used:

_____

_____

89

4. **If applicable: Give two examples that were used in the writing. Explain how they affected your understanding of the reading selection.**

The example(s) given	How example(s) contributed to your understanding
1. Toxic effect of Flouride	1. Became nauseous
2. Aspartame - wife	2.
3. Cell phone - severe headache.	

5. **If applicable: what is being compared and/or contrasted?**

Show two comparisons between items A and B:

A	B
landmines	harmful chemicals
Sucralose	Aspartame

Show two contrasts between items A and B:

A	B
Government	Charges of Government
Users of flouride toothpaste	Non Users
1950's	today

6. **Show two cause/effect relationships:**

Cause	Effect
1. Bad diet	stomach pain
2. Flouride	Nausea
Artificial Sweetener	joint pain

7. **List three facts and three opinions from the article. Explain why it is either a fact or an opinion.**

	Explanation:
A.) fact: Inhale DDT smoke	A.) During childhood suffering
B.) fact: Appendicitis	B.) surgery was needed.
C.) fact:	C.)

A.) opinion For the gov't to change in to better *news*	A.)
B.) opinion:	B.)
C.) opinion: Cell phone	C.)

8. **What is the author's purpose in this article? Is it to inform, persuade, or entertain? <u>Tell me how you arrived at that conclusion.</u>**

To inform about the many dangers out in this world / persuade

9. **What is the author's tone? <u>Explain your answer.</u>**

Concern, urgency, informative, the author is really clear and straight to the point about the critical danger of different topics

10. **Discovering the ideas in writing that are <u>not stated directly</u> is called making inferences, or drawing conclusions. What inferences did you draw from the article you read? <u>Explain.</u>**

I thought that the article was about the different danger that readers need to be cautious.

11. **Authors often use connotative language. Return to the reading selection and circle (in red or green) all connotative words. List 10 of those words here and explain how those words might affect the reader.**

toxic, nauseous, joint pains, numbness, migraines, allergies, cancel, death.

How the connotative words above might affect the reader:

The connotative paints a picture in the readers mind of how it projects urgency of charge needed in the gourment.

12. **A good argument makes a point and then provides persuasive and logical evidence to back it up. However, a bad argument uses fallacies to support itself such as changing the subject, hasty generalization, circular reasoning, personal attack, straw man, false cause, false comparison, or either-or. Explain how the author supports his/her argument.** <u>**Does he/she use relevant and adequate support, or do fallacies exist?**</u> **Explain.**

Yes the author brought out strong examples that have been proved that their are landmines that can easily destroy our health The varieties of the example shows it is clear that we are not cautious enough for our heath.

13. **The seven most common propaganda techniques are bandwagon, testimonial, transfer, plain folks, name calling, glittering generalities, and card staking.** <u>**Which techniques are used in this reading selection?**</u> **Explain.**

Testimony is the main technique use in the article to convey his main idea. He shared about his life as a child and the dangers he faced, including his coise with a bad health.

92

Theme 2
Government and Politics

How Should a Ruler rule? Where does the Ruler's power come from? What rights should the citizens of a country possess? Why, when and how should a government be changed? What is the duty of the government to the governed?

The first theme presents three writings that have influenced the world for centuries and continue to influence the world even today. You will explore the minds of three men who still influence our world from the grave. They have left an indelible mark on history, politics, and government. Without their writings, our world would be a very different place. Through reading and analyzing their writings, you will more fully understand how our world functions and possibly develop a deeper understanding of its present and future direction.

The Qualities of the Prince

Niccolo Machiavelli

The Art of War

A prince, therefore, must not have any other object nor any other thought, nor must he take anything as his profession but war, its institutions, and its discipline; because that is the only profession which befits one who commands; and it is of such importance that not only does it maintain those who were born princes, but many times it enables men of private station to rise to that position; and, on the other hand, it is evident that when princes have given more thought to personal luxuries than to arms, they have lost their state. And the first way to lose it is to neglect this art; and the way to acquire it is to be well versed in this art.

2   Francesco Sforza became Duke of Milan from being a private citizen because he was armed; his sons, since they avoided the inconveniences of arms, became private citizens after having been dukes. For, among the other bad effects it causes, being disarmed makes you despised; this is one of those infamies a prince should guard himself against, as will be treated below: for between an armed and an unarmed man there is no comparison whatsoever, and it is not reasonable for an armed man to obey an unarmed man willingly, nor that an unarmed man should be safe among armed servants; since, when the former is suspicious and the latter are contemptuous, it is impossible for them to work well together. And therefore, a prince who does not understand military matters, besides the other misfortunes already noted, cannot be esteemed by his own soldiers, nor can he trust them.

3   He must, therefore, never raise his thought from this exercise of war, and in peacetime he must train himself more than in time of war; this can be done in two ways: one by action, the other by the mind. And as far as actions are concerned, besides keeping his soldiers well disciplined and trained, he must always be out hunting, and must accustom his body to hardships in this manner; and he must also learn the nature of the terrain, and know how mountains slope, how valleys open, how plains lie, and understand the nature of rivers

Handwritten note in margin: Can't believe that this principle was implemented and the class that is unarmed would be treat unequal just because they didn't have the means to own weapons.

and swamps; and he should devote much attention to such activities. Such knowledge is useful in two ways: first, one learns to know one's own country and can better understand how to defend it; second, with the knowledge and experience of the terrain, one can easily comprehend the characteristics of any other terrain that it is necessary to explore for the first time; for the hills, valleys, plains, rivers, and swamps of Tuscany, for instance, have certain similarities to those of other provinces; so that by knowing the lay of the land in one province one can easily understand it in others. And a prince who lacks this ability lacks the most important quality in a leader; because this skill teaches you to find the enemy, choose a campsite, lead troops, organize them for battle, and besiege towns to your own advantage.

4   Philopoemon, Prince of the Achaeans, among the other praises given to him by writers, is praised because in peacetime he thought of nothing except the means of waging war; and when he was out in thecountry with his friends, he often stopped and reasoned with them: "If the enemy were on that hilltop and we were here with our army, which of the two of us would have the advantage? How could we attack them without breaking formation? If we wanted to retreat, how could we do this? If they were to retreat, how could we pursue them?" And he proposed to them, as they rode along, all the contingencies that can occur in an army; he heard their opinions, expressed his own, and backed it up with arguments; so that, because of these continuous deliberations, when leading his troops no unforeseen incident could arise for which he did not have the remedy.

The Training of the Mind

5   But as for the exercise of the mind, the prince must read histories and in them study the deeds of great men; he must see how they conducted themselves in wars; he must examine the reasons for their victories and for their defeats in order to avoid the latter and to imitate the former; and above all else he must do as some distinguished man before him has done, who elected to imitate someone who had been praised and honored before him, and always keep in mind his deeds and actions; just as it is reported that Alexander the Great imitated Achilles; Caesar, Alexander; Scipio, Cyrus. And anyone who reads the life of Cyrus written by Xenophon then realizes how important in the life of Scipio that imitation was to his glory and how much, in purity, goodness, humanity, and generosity, Scipio conformed to those characteristics of Cyrus that Xenophon had written

knowing the terrain was mentioned quite a bit in this paragraph, this might be one of the United States downfall in the Vietnam War. Of course this is just an opinion, but it does make sense if the soldiers understood the terrains, maybe they would know where the captured and defend there ground.

So, being a prince is just a role played for the acceptance of the people, yet instead when the real personality is hidden from within.

about.

6   Such methods as these a wise prince must follow, and never in peaceful times must he be idle; but he must turn them diligently to his advantage in order to be able to profit from them in times of adversity, so that, when Fortune changes, she will find him prepared to withstand such times.

How to Treat Your Subjects and Friends

7   Now there remains to be examined what should be the methods and procedures of a prince in dealing with his subjects and friends. And because I know that many have written about this, I am afraid that by writing about it again I shall be thought of as presumptuous, since in discussing this material I depart radically from the procedures of others. But since my intention is to write something useful for anyone who understands it, it seemed more suitable to me to search after the effectual truth of the matter rather than its imagined one. And many writers have imagined for themselves republics and principalities that have never been seen nor known to exist in reality; for there is such a gap between how one lives and how one ought to live that anyone who abandons what is done for what ought to be done learns his ruin rather than his preservation: for a man who wishes to make a vocation of being good at all times will come to ruin among so many who are not good. Hence it is necessary for a prince who wishes to maintain his position to learn how not to be good, and to use this knowledge or not to use it according to necessity.

8   Leaving aside, therefore, the imagined things concerning a prince, and taking into account those that are true, I say that all men, when they are spoken of, and particularly princes, since they are placed on a higher level, are judged by some of these qualities which bring them either blame or praise. And this is why one is considered generous, another miserly (to use a Tuscan word, since "avaricious" in our language is still used to mean one who wishes to acquire by means of theft; we call "miserly" one who excessively avoids using what he has); one is considered a giver, the other rapacious; one cruel, another merciful; one treacherous, another faithful; one effeminate and cowardly, another bold and courageous; one humane, another haughty; one lascivious, another chaste; one trustworthy, another cunning; one harsh, another lenient; one serious, another frivolous; one religious, another unbelieving; and the

like. And I know that everyone will admit that it would be a very praiseworthy thing to find in a prince, of the qualities mentioned above, those that are held to be good, but since it is neither possible to have them nor to observe them all completely, because human nature does not permit it, a prince must be prudent enough to know how to escape the bad reputation of those vices that would lose the state for him, and must protect himself from those that will not lose it for him, if this is possible; but if he cannot, he need not concern himself unduly if he ignores these less serious vices. And, moreover, he need not worry about incurring the bad reputation of those vices without which it would be difficult to hold his state; since, carefully taking everything into account, one will discover that something which appears to be a virtue, if pursued, will end in his destruction; while some other thing which seems to be a vice, if pursued, will result in his safety and his well-being.

Generosity or Miserliness?

9 Beginning, therefore, with the first of the above-mentioned qualities, I say that it would be good to be considered generous; nevertheless, generosity used in such a manner as to give you a reputation for it will harm you; because if it is employed virtuously and as one should employ it, it will not be recognized and you will not avoid the reproach of its opposite. And so, if a prince wants to maintain his reputation for generosity among men, it is necessary for him not to neglect any possible means of lavish display; in so doing such a prince will always use up all his resources and he will be obliged, eventually, if he wishes to maintain his reputation for generosity, to burden the people with excessive taxes and to do everything possible to raise funds. This will begin to make him hateful to his subjects, and, becoming impoverished, he will not be much esteemed by anyone; so that, as a consequence of his generosity, having offended many and rewarded few, he will feel the effects of any slight unrest and will be ruined at the first sign of danger; recognizing this and wishing to alter his policies, he immediately runs the risk of being reproached as a miser.

10 A prince, therefore, unable to use this virtue of generosity in a manner which will not harm himself if he is known for it, should, if he is wise, not worry about being called a miser; for with time he will come to be considered more generous once it

is evident that, as a result of his parsimony, his income is sufficient, he can defend himself from anyone who makes war against him, and he can undertake enterprises without overburdening his people, so that he comes to be generous with all those from whom he takes nothing, who are countless, and miserly with all those to whom he gives nothing, who are few. In our times we have not seen great deeds accomplished except by those who were considered miserly; all others were done away with. Pope Julius II, although he made use of his reputation for generosity in order to gain the papacy, then decided not to maintain it in order to be able to wage war; the present King of France has waged many wars without imposing extra taxes on his subjects, only because his habitual parsimony has provided for the additional expenditures; the present King of Spain, if he had been considered generous, would not have engaged in nor won so many campaigns.

11   Therefore, in order not to have to rob his subjects, to be able to defend himself, not to become poor and contemptible, and not to be forced to become rapacious, a prince must consider it of little importance if he incurs the name of miser, for this is one of those vices that permits him to rule. And if someone were to say: Caesar with his generosity came to rule the empire, and many others, because they were generous and known to be so, achieved very high positions; I reply: you are either already a prince or you are on the way to becoming one; in the first instance such generosity is damaging; in the second it is very necessary to be thought generous. And Caesar was one of those who wanted to gain the principality of Rome; but if, after obtaining this, he had lived and had not moderated his expenditures, he would have destroyed that empire. And if someone were to reply: there have existed many princes who have accomplished great deeds with their armies who have been reputed to be generous; I answer you: a prince either spends his own money and that of his subjects or that of others; in the first case he must be economical; in the second he must not restrain any part of his generosity. And for that prince who goes out with his soldiers and lives by looting, sacking, and ransoms, who controls the property of others, such generosity is necessary; otherwise he would not be followed by his troops. And with what does not belong to you or to your subjects you can be a more liberal giver, as were Cyrus, Caesar, and Alexander; for spending the wealth of others does not lessen your reputation but adds to it; only the spending of your

own is what harms you. And there is nothing that uses itself up faster than generosity, for as you employ it you lose the means of employing it, and you become either poor or despised or, in order to escape poverty, rapacious and hated. And above all other things a prince must guard himself against being despised and hated; and generosity leads you to both one and the other. So it is wiser to live with the reputation of a miser, which produces reproach without hatred, than to be forced to incur the reputation of rapacity, which produces reproach along with hatred, because you want to be considered as generous.

To Be Merciful or Cruel?

12   Proceeding to the other qualities mentioned above, I say that every prince must desire to be considered merciful and not cruel; nevertheless, he must take care not to misuse this mercy. Cesare Borgia was considered cruel; nonetheless, his cruelty had brought order to Romagna, united it, restored it to peace and obedience. If we examine this carefully, we shall see that he was more merciful than the Florentine people, who, in order to avoid being considered cruel, allowed the destruction of Pistoia. Therefore, a prince must not worry about the reproach of cruelty when it is a matter of keeping his subjects united and loyal; for with a very few examples of cruelty he will be more compassionate than those who, out of excessive mercy, permit disorders to continue, from which arise murders and plundering; for these usually harm the community at large, while the executions that come from the prince harm one individual in particular. And the new prince, above all other princes, cannot escape the reputation of being called cruel, since new states are full of dangers. And Virgil, through Dido, states; "My difficult condition and the newness of my rule make me act in such a manner, and to set guards over my land on all sides."

13   Nevertheless, a prince must be cautious in believing and in acting, nor should he be afraid of his own shadow; and he should proceed in such a manner, tempered by prudence and humanity, so that too much trust may not render him imprudent nor too much distrust render him intolerable.

101

Better to be Loved than Feared?

14   From this arises an argument: whether it is better to be loved than to be feared, or the contrary. I reply that one should like to be both one and the other; but since it is difficult to join them together, it is much safer to be feared than to be loved when one of the two must be lacking. For one can generally say this about men: that they are ungrateful, fickle, simulators and deceivers, avoiders of danger, greedy for gain; and while you work for their good they are completely yours, offering you their blood, their property, their lives, and their sons, as I said earlier, when danger is far away; but when it comes nearer to you they turn away. And that prince who bases his power entirely on their words, finding himself stripped of other preparations, comes to ruin; for friendships that are acquired by a price and not by greatness and nobility of character are purchased but are not owned, and at the proper moment they cannot be spent. And men are less hesitant about harming someone who makes himself loved than one who makes himself feared because love is held together by a chain of obligation which, since men are a sorry lot, is broken on every occasion in which their own self-interest is concerned; but fear is held together by a dread of punishment which will never abandon you.

15   A prince must nevertheless make himself feared in such a manner that he will avoid hatred, even if he does not acquire love; since to be feared and not to be hated can very well be combined; and this will always be so when he keeps his hands off the property and the women of his citizens and his subjects. And if he must take someone's life, he should do so when there is proper justification and manifest cause; but, above all, he should avoid the property of others; for men forget more quickly the death of their father than the loss of their patrimony. Moreover, the reasons for seizing their property are never lacking; and he who begins to live by stealing always finds a reason for taking what belongs to others; on the contrary, reasons for taking a life are rarer and disappear sooner.

16   But when the prince is with his armies and has under his command a multitude of troops, then it is absolutely necessary that he not worry about being considered cruel; for without that reputation he will never keep an army united or prepared for any combat. Among the praiseworthy deeds of Hannibal is

counted this: that, having a very large army, made up of all kinds of men, which he commanded in foreign lands, there never arose the slightest dissention, neither among themselves nor against their prince, both during his good and his bad fortune. This could not have arisen from anything other than his inhuman cruelty, which, along with his many other abilities, made him always respected and terrifying in the eyes of his soldiers; and without that, to attain the same effect, his other abilities would not have sufficed. And the writers of history, having considered this matter very little, on the one hand admire these deeds of his and on the other condemn the main cause of them.

17   And that it be true that his other abilities would not have been sufficient can be seen from the example of Scipio, a most extraordinary man not only in his time but in all recorded history, whose armies in Spain rebelled against him; this came about from nothing other than his excessive compassion, which gave to his soldiers more liberty than military discipline allowed. For this he was censured in the senate by Fabius Maximus, who called him the corruptor of the Roman militia. The Locrians, having been ruined by one of Scipio's officers, were not avenged by him, nor was the arrogance of that officer corrected, all because of his tolerant nature; so that someone in the senate who tried to apologize for him said that there were many men who knew how not to err better than they knew how to correct errors. Such a nature would have, in time, damaged Scipio's fame and glory if he had maintained it during the empire; but, living under the control of the senate, this harmful characteristic of his not only concealed itself but brought him fame.

18   I conclude, therefore, returning to the problem of being feared and loved, that since men love at their own pleasure and fear at the pleasure of the prince, a wise prince should build his foundation upon that which belongs to him, not upon that which belongs to others: he must strive only to avoid hatred, as has been said.

Integrity or Deceit?

19   How praiseworthy it is for a prince to keep his word and to live by integrity and not by deceit everyone knows; nevertheless, one sees from the experience of our times that the princes who have accomplished great deeds are those who have

cared little for keeping their promises and who have known how to manipulate the minds of men by shrewdness; and in the end they have surpassed those who laid their foundations upon honesty.

20   You must, therefore, know that there are two means of fighting: one according to the laws, the other with force; the first way is proper to man, the second to beasts; but because the first, in many cases, is not sufficient, it becomes necessary to have recourse to the second. Therefore, a prince must know how to use wisely the natures of the beast and the man. This policy was taught to princes allegorically by the ancient writers, who described how Achilles and many other ancient princes were given to Chiron the Centaur to be raised and taught under his discipline. This can only mean that, having a half-beast and half-man as a teacher, a prince must know how to employ the nature of the one and the other; and the one without the other cannot endure.

21   Since, then, a prince must know how to make good use of the nature of the beast, he should choose from among the beasts the fox and the lion; for the lion cannot defend itself from traps and the fox cannot protect itself from wolves. It is therefore necessary to be a fox in order to recognize the traps and a lion in order to frighten the wolves. Those who play only the part of the lion do not understand matters. A wise ruler, therefore, cannot and should not keep his word when such an observance of faith would be to his disadvantage and when the reasons which made him promise are removed. And if men were all good, this rule would not be good; but since men are a sorry lot and will not keep their promises to you, you likewise need not keep yours to them. A prince never lacks legitimate reasons to break his promises. Of this one could cite an endless number of modern examples to show how many pacts, how many promises have been made null and void because of the infidelity of princes; and he who has known best how to use the fox has come to a better end. But it is necessary to know how to disguise this nature well and to be a great hypocrite and a liar: and men are so simpleminded and so controlled by their present necessities that one who deceives will always find another who will allow himself to be deceived.

22   I do not wish to remain silent about one of these recent instances. Alexander VI did nothing else, he thought about nothing else, except to deceive men, and he always found the occasion to do this. And there never was a man who had more

forcefulness in his oaths, who affirmed a thing with more promises, and who honored his word less; nevertheless, his tricks always succeeded perfectly since he was well acquainted with this aspect of the world.

Reality or Appearance?

23   Therefore, it is not necessary for a prince to have all of the above-mentioned qualities, but it is very necessary for him to appear to have them. Furthermore, I shall be so bold as to assert this: that having them and practicing them at all times is harmful; and appearing to have them is useful; for instance, to seem merciful, faithful, humane, forthright, religious, and to be so; but his mind should be disposed in such a way that should it become necessary not to be so, he will be able and know how to change to the contrary. And it is essential to understand this: that a prince, and especially a new prince, cannot observe all those things by which men are considered good, for in order to maintain the state he is often obliged to act against his promise, against charity, against humanity, and against religion. And therefore, it is necessary that he have a mind ready to turn itself according to the way the winds of Fortune and the changeability of affairs require him; and, as I said above, as long as it is possible, he should not stray from the good, but he should know how to enter into evil when necessity commands.

24   A prince, therefore, must be very careful never to let anything slip from his lips which is not full of the five qualities mentioned above: he should appear, upon seeing and hearing him, to be all mercy, all faithfulness, all integrity, all kindness, all religion. And there is nothing more necessary than to seem to possess this last quality. And men in general judge more by their eyes than their hands; for everyone can see but few can feel. Everyone sees what you seem to be, few perceive what you are, and those few do not dare to contradict the opinion of the many who have the majesty of the state to defend them; and in the actions of all men, and especially of princes, where there is no impartial arbiter, one must consider the final result. Let a prince therefore act to seize and to maintain the state; his methods will always be judged honorable and will be praised by all; for ordinary people are always deceived by appearances and by the outcome of a thing; and in the world there is nothing but ordinary people; and there is no room for the few, while the many have a place to lean on. A certain prince of the present

day, whom I shall refrain from naming, preaches nothing but peace and faith, and to both one and the other he is entirely opposed; and both, if he had put them into practice, would have cost him many times over either his reputation or his state.

Additional Qualities of the Prince and Avoiding Conspiracies

25   But since, concerning the qualities mentioned above, I have spoken about the most important, I should like to discuss the others briefly in this general manner: that the prince, as was noted above, should think about avoiding those things which make him hated and despised; and when he has avoided this, he will have carried out his duties and will find no danger whatsoever in other vices. As I have said, what makes him hated above all else is being rapacious and a usurper of the property and the women of his subjects; he must refrain from this; and in most cases, so long as you do not deprive them of either their property or their honor, the majority of men live happily; and you have only to deal with the ambition of a few, who can be restrained without difficulty and by many means. What makes him despised is being considered changeable, frivolous, effeminate, cowardly, irresolute; from these qualities a prince must guard himself as if from a reef, and he must strive to make everyone recognize in his actions greatness, spirit, dignity, and strength; and concerning the private affairs of his subjects, he must insist that his decision be irrevocable; and he should maintain himself in such a way that no man could imagine that he can deceive or cheat him.

26   That prince who projects such an opinion of himself is greatly esteemed; and it is difficult to conspire against a man with such a reputation and difficult to attack him, provided that he is understood to be of great merit and revered by his subjects. For a prince must have two fears: one, internal, concerning his subjects; the other, external, concerning foreign powers. From the latter he can defend himself by his good troops and friends; and he will always have good friends if he has good troops; and internal affairs will always be stable when external affairs are stable, provided that they are not already disturbed by a conspiracy; and even if external conditions change, if he is properly organized and lives as I have said and does not lose control of himself, he will always be able to with-stand every attack, just as I said that Nabis the Spartan did. But

concerning his subjects, when external affairs do not change, he has to fear that they may conspire secretly: the prince secures himself from this by avoiding being hated or despised and by keeping the people satisfied with him; this is a necessary matter, as was treated above at length. And one of the most powerful remedies a prince has against people conspiracies is not to be hated by the masses; for a man who plans a conspiracy always believes that he will satisfy the people by killing the prince; but when he thinks he might anger them, he cannot work up the courage to undertake such a deed; for the problems on the side of the conspirators are countless. And experience demonstrates that conspiracies have been many but few have been concluded successfully; for anyone who conspires cannot be alone, nor can he find companions except from amongst those whom he believes to be dissatisfied; and as soon as you have uncovered your intent to one dissatisfied man, you give him the means to make himself happy, since he can have everything he desires by uncovering the plot; so much is this so that, seeing a sure gain on the one hand and one doubtful and full of danger on the other, if he is to maintain faith with you he has to be either an unusually good friend or a completely determined enemy of the prince. And to treat the matter briefly, I say that on the part of the conspirator there is nothing but fear, jealousy, and the thought of punishment that terrifies him; but on the part of the prince there is the majesty of the principality, the laws, the defenses of friends and the state to protect him; so that, with the good will of the people added to all these things, it is impossible for anyone to be so rash as to plot against him. For, where usually a conspirator has to be afraid before he executes his evil deed, in this case he must be afraid, having the people as an enemy, even after the crime is performed, nor can he hope to find any refuge because of this.

27   One could cite countless examples on this subject; but I want to satisfy myself with only one which occurred during the time of our fathers. Messer Annibale Bentivoglio, prince of Bologna and grandfather of the present Messer Annibale, was murdered by the Canneschi family, who conspired against him; he left behind no heir except Messer Giovanni, then only a baby. As soon as this murder occurred, the people rose up and killed all the Canneschi. This came about because of the good will that the house of the Bentivoglio enjoyed in those days; this good will was so great that with Annibale dead, and there being no one of that family left in the city who could rule

Bologna, the Bolognese people, having heard that in Florence there was one of the Bentivoglio blood who was believed until that time to be the son of a blacksmith, went to Florence to find him, and they gave him the control of that city; it was ruled by him until Messer Giovanni became of age to rule.

28   I conclude, therefore, that a prince must be little concerned with conspiracies when the people are well disposed toward him; but when the populace is hostile and regards him with hatred, he must fear everything and everyone. And well-organized states and wise princes have, with great diligence, taken care not to anger the nobles and to satisfy the common people and keep them contented; for this is one of the most important concerns that a prince has.

The questions that follow may be used for further discussion of the reading selection or as topics for essay writing.

1. Niccolo Machiavelli asserted that most people are easily deceived and he suggested this as a necessary manner in which to rule. Do you agree or disagree with him, and please explain your answer.

2. Do we have politicians today who seem to be "Machiavellian" in their approach to politics? If so, give clear examples to support your opinion.

3. Using the Internet, your library, and other sources, conduct some more research into the life and thinking of Niccolo Machiavelli.

4. Machiavelli states that "being disarmed makes you despised." Discuss how that relates to the relationships among nations, and the leaders of those nations in our modern world.

5. How valuable is Machiavelli's advice to our current society and leaders? Explain your answer using strong examples.

6. Do the "ends" justify the "means"? Is questionable, or unethical, behavior acceptable in achieving a goal?

7. _____
   _____
   _____
   _____
   _____
   _____

8. _____
   _____
   _____
   _____
   _____
   _____

Applying Reading Skills

Title of the Reading Selection: _____

1. What is the author's overall main idea, (central point, or thesis)?

_____

_____

2. There are two kinds of supporting details--major and minor. Major details are the primary points that support the main idea and minor details expand major details. List <u>three</u> details and explain how they support the author's primary point?

Details used	Explanation of how they support the thesis
1.	

Details used	Explanation of how they support the thesis
2.	

Details used	Explanation of how they support the thesis
3.	

3. The five major patterns of organization are the list of items pattern, the time order pattern, the example pattern, the comparison and/or contrast pattern, and the cause/effect pattern. What is the <u>main</u> pattern of organization used in this article? <u>Explain</u> why it is the major pattern. What other patterns are used? Give some examples.

Main pattern: _____

Explain how the main pattern was used:

_____

Other pattern(s) used: _____

Explain how the additional pattern(s) were used:

_____

_____

110

4. If applicable: Give <u>two</u> examples that were used in the writing. <u>Explain</u> how they affected your understanding of the reading selection.

The example(s) given	How example(s) contributed to your understanding
1.	1.
2.	2.

5. If applicable: what is being compared and/or contrasted?

Show <u>two</u> comparisons between items A and B:

A	B

Show <u>two</u> contrasts between items A and B:

A	B

6. Show <u>two</u> cause/effect relationships:

Cause	Effect
1.	
2.	

7. List <u>three</u> facts and <u>three</u> opinions from the article. <u>Explain why</u> it is either a fact or an opinion.

	Explanation:
A.) fact:	A.)
B.) fact:	B.)
C.) fact:	C.)

	Explanation:
A.) opinion	A.)
B.) opinion:	B.)
C.) opinion:	C.)

8. What is the author's purpose in this article? Is it to inform, persuade, or entertain? <u>Tell me how you arrived at that conclusion.</u>

_____
_____
_____

9. What is the author's tone? <u>Explain your answer.</u>

_____
_____
_____

10. Discovering the ideas in writing that are <u>not stated directly</u> is called making inferences, or drawing conclusions. What inferences did you draw from the article you read? <u>Explain</u>.

_____
_____
_____

11. Authors often use connotative language. Return to the reading selection and circle (in red or green) all connotative words. List 10 of those words here and explain how those words might affect the reader.

_____
_____
_____
_____

How the connotative words above might affect the reader:

_____
_____
_____
_____
_____
_____
_____

112

12. A good argument makes a point and then provides persuasive and logical evidence to back it up. However, a bad argument uses fallacies to support itself such as changing the subject, hasty generalization, circular reasoning, personal attack, straw man, false cause, false comparison, or either-or. Explain how the author supports his/her argument. <u>Does he/she use relevant and adequate support, or do fallacies exist?</u> <u>Explain.</u>

_____
_____
_____
_____
_____
_____
_____
_____
_____
_____
_____
_____
_____
_____
_____
_____

13. The seven most common propaganda techniques are bandwagon, testimonial, transfer, plain folks, name calling, glittering generalities, and card staking. <u>Which techniques are used in this reading selection? Explain.</u>

_____
_____
_____
_____
_____
_____
_____
_____
_____
_____
_____
_____
_____
_____
_____

The Declaration of Independence
July 4, 1776

THOMAS JEFFERSON

The Unanimous Declaration
of the
Thirteen United States of America

When in the Course of human events, it becomes necessary for one people to dissolve the political bands which have connected them with another, and to assume among the Powers of the earth, the separate and equal station to which the Laws of Nature and of Nature's God entitle them, a decent respect to the opinions of mankind requires that they should declare the causes which impel them to the separation.

2 We hold these truths to be self-evident, that all men are created equal, that they are endowed by their Creator with certain unalienable Rights, that among these are Life, Liberty and the pursuit of Happiness. That to secure these rights, Governments are instituted among Men, deriving their just powers from the consent of the governed. That whenever any Form of Government becomes destructive of these ends, it is the Right of the People to alter or to abolish it, and to institute new Government, laying its foundation on such principles and organizing its powers in such form, as to them shall seem most likely to effect their Safety and Happiness. Prudence, indeed, will dictate that Governments long established should not be changed for light and transient causes; and accordingly all experience hath shown, that mankind are more disposed to suffer, while evils are sufferable, than to right themselves by abolishing the forms to which they are accustomed. But when a long train of abuses and usurpations, pursuing invariably the same Object evinces a design to reduce them under absolute

Despotism, it is their right, it is their duty, to throw off such Government, and to provide new Guards for their future security.--Such has been the patient sufferance of these Colonies; and such is now the necessity which constrains them to alter their former Systems of Government. The history of the present King of Great Britain is a history of repeated injuries and usurpations, all having in direct object the establishment of an absolute Tyranny over these States. To prove this, let Facts be submitted to a candid world.

3 He has refused his Assent to Laws, the most wholesome and necessary for the public good.

4 He has forbidden his Governors to pass Laws of immediate and pressing importance, unless suspended in their operation till his Assent should be obtained; and when so suspended, he has utterly neglected to attend to them.

5 He has refused to pass other laws for the accommodation of large districts of people, unless those people would relinquish the right of Representation in the Legislature, a right inestimable to them and formidable to tyrants only.

6 He has called together legislative bodies at places unusual, uncomfortable, and distant from the depository of their Public Records, for the sole purpose of fatiguing them into compliance with his measures.

7 He has dissolved Representative Houses repeatedly, for opposing with manly firmness his invasions on the rights of the people.

8 He has refused for a long time, after such dissolutions, to cause others to be elected; whereby the Legislative Powers, incapable of Annihilation, have returned to the People at large for their exercise; the State remaining in the mean time exposed to all the dangers of invasion from without, and convulsions within.

9 He has endeavoured to prevent the population of these States; for that purpose obstructing the Laws for Naturalization of Foreigners; refusing to pass others to encourage their migration hither, and raising the conditions of new Appropriations of Lands.

10 He has obstructed the Administration of Justice, by refusing his Assent to Laws for establishing Judiciary Powers.

11 He has made Judges dependent on his Will alone, for the tenure of their offices, and the amount and payment of their salaries.

12 He has erected a multitude of New Offices, and sent hither

swarms of Officers to harass our People, and eat out their substance.

13 He has kept among us, in times of peace, Standing Armies without the Consent of our legislature.

14 He has affected to render the Military independent of and superior to the Civil Power.

15 He has combined with others to subject us to a jurisdiction foreign to our constitution, and unacknowledged by our laws; giving his Assent to their acts of pretended Legislation:

16 For quartering large bodies of armed troops among us:

17 For protecting them, by a mock Trial, from Punishment for any Murders which they should commit on the Inhabitants of these States:

18 For cutting off our Trade with all parts of the world:

19 For imposing taxes on us without our Consent:

20 For depriving us in many cases, of the benefits of Trial by Jury:

21 For transporting us beyond Seas to be tried for pretended offences:

22 For abolishing the free System of English Laws in a neighbouring Province, establishing therein an Arbitrary government, and enlarging its Boundaries so as to render it at once an example and fit instrument for introducing the same absolute rule into these Colonies:

23 For taking away our Charters, abolishing our most valuable Laws, and altering fundamentally the Forms of our Governments:

24 For suspending our own Legislatures, and declaring themselves invested with Power to legislate for us in all cases whatsoever.

25 He has abdicated Government here, by declaring us out of his Protection and waging War against us.

26 He has plundered our seas, ravaged our Coasts, burnt our towns, and destroyed the lives of our people.

27 He is at this time transporting large armies of foreign mercenaries to compleat the works of death, desolation and tyranny, already begun with circumstances of Cruelty & perfidy scarcely paralleled in the most barbarous ages, and totally unworthy the Head of a civilized nation.

28 He has constrained our fellow Citizens taken Captive on the high Seas to bear Arms against their Country, to become the executioners of their friends and Brethren, or to fall themselves by their Hands.

29 He has excited domestic insurrections amongst us, and has endeavoured to bring on the inhabitants of our frontiers, the merciless Indian Savages, whose known rule of warfare, is an undistinguished destruction of all ages, sexes and conditions.

30 In every stage of these Oppressions We have Petitioned for Redress in the most humble terms: Our repeated Petitions have been answered only by repeated injury. A Prince, whose character is thus marked by every act which may define a Tyrant, is unfit to be the ruler of a free People.

31 Nor have We been wanting in attention to our British brethren. We have warned them from time to time of attempts by their legislature to extend an unwarrantable jurisdiction over us. We have reminded them of the circumstances of our emigration and settlement here. We have appealed to their native justice and magnanimity, and we have conjured them by the ties of our common kindred to disavow these usurpations, which, would inevitably interrupt our connections and correspondence. They too have been deaf to the voice of justice and of consanguinity. We must, therefore, acquiesce in the necessity, which denounces our Separation, and hold them, as we hold the rest of mankind, Enemies in War, in Peace Friends.

32 We, therefore, the Representatives of the United States of America, in General Congress, Assembled, appealing to the Supreme Judge of the world for the rectitude of our intentions, do, in the Name, and by Authority of the good People of these Colonies, solemnly publish and declare, That these United Colonies are, and of Right ought to be Free and Independent States, that they are Absolved from all Allegiance to the British Crown, and that all political connection between them and the State of Great Britain, is and ought to be totally dissolved; and that as Free and Independent States, they have full Power to levy War, conclude Peace, contract Alliances, establish Commerce, and to do all other Acts and Things which Independent States may of right do. And for the support of this Declaration, with a firm reliance on the Protection of Divine Providence, we mutually pledge to each other our Lives, our Fortunes and our sacred Honor.

The questions that follow may be used for further discussion of the reading selection or as topics for essay writing.

1. One main reason for the writing of the Declaration of Independence was so that people would not forget the real, and very serious reasons for the Colonies breaking away from Great Britain. Do you think that most people in the United States have ever taken the time to read, discuss, and study the document? Is the Declaration still influencing our society today? Explain.

2. The Founders ideas are radically different from those of Machiavelli. Compare, contrast, and discuss their ideas on governing.

3. The Founders pledged their Lives, Fortunes, and Sacred Honor to one another. What does this say about these individuals?

4. Jefferson often uses capitalization throughout the writing to draw emphasis to certain words (much as we would use the Bold function on our computer). Reread the Declaration and notice the clarifying and strengthening effect it has on your understanding of the document.

5. How many abuses toward the colonists can you count in the document? Were you surprised at the number? Were the colonists right in breaking away from Great Britain?

6. Why did Jefferson use the words "Divine Providence", "Nature's God", "Creator", "Judge of the World", "Laws of Nature"? What is the overall effect of these words on the document?

7. Study the Constitution and the Bill of Rights. Can you see how many of the abuses were noted and laws were made to protect the citizens of the United States from similar abuses in the future? Explain by using a cause and effect approach to your discussion and/or writing.

8. _____
    _____
    _____
    _____
    _____
    _____

Applying Reading Skills
(Neatly **PRINT** all answers using ink <u>not</u> pencil)

Title of the Reading Selection: _____

1. **What is the author's overall main idea, (central point, or thesis)?**

   _____

   _____

2. **There are two kinds of supporting details--major and minor. Major details are the primary points that support the main idea and minor details expand major details. List <u>three</u> details and explain how they support the author's primary point?**

Details used	Explanation of how they support the thesis
1.	

Details used	Explanation of how they support the thesis
2.	

Details used	Explanation of how they support the thesis
3.	

3. **The five major patterns of organization are the list of items pattern, the time order pattern, the example pattern, the comparison and/or contrast pattern, and the cause/effect pattern. What is the <u>main</u> pattern of organization used in this article? <u>Explain</u> why it is the major pattern. What other patterns are used? Give some examples.**

Main pattern: _____

Explain how the main pattern was used:

   _____

Other pattern(s) used: _____

Explain how the additional pattern(s) were used:

   _____

   _____

119

4. If applicable: Give <u>two</u> examples that were used in the writing. <u>Explain</u> how they affected your understanding of the reading selection.

The example(s) given	How example(s) contributed to your understanding
1.	1.
2.	2.

5. If applicable: what is being compared and/or contrasted?

Show <u>two</u> comparisons between items A and B:

A	B

Show <u>two</u> contrasts between items A and B:

A	B

6. Show <u>two</u> cause/effect relationships:

Cause	Effect
1.	
2.	

7. List <u>three</u> facts and <u>three</u> opinions from the article. <u>Explain why</u> it is either a fact or an opinion.

	Explanation:
A.) fact:	A.)
B.) fact:	B.)
C.) fact:	C.)

	Explanation:
A.) opinion	A.)
B.) opinion:	B.)
C.) opinion:	C.)

8. **What is the author's purpose in this article? Is it to inform, persuade, or entertain? <u>Tell me how you arrived at that conclusion.</u>**

_____

_____

_____

9. **What is the author's tone? <u>Explain your answer.</u>**

_____

_____

_____

10. **Discovering the ideas in writing that are <u>not stated directly</u> is called making inferences, or drawing conclusions. What inferences did you draw from the article you read? <u>Explain.</u>**

_____

_____

_____

11. **Authors often use connotative language. Return to the reading selection and circle (in red or green) all connotative words. List 10 of those words here and explain how those words might affect the reader.**

_____

_____

_____

_____

_____

How the connotative words above might affect the reader:

_____

_____

_____

_____

_____

_____

12. A good argument makes a point and then provides persuasive and logical evidence to back it up. However, a bad argument uses fallacies to support itself such as changing the subject, hasty generalization, circular reasoning, personal attack, straw man, false cause, false comparison, or either-or. Explain how the author supports his/her argument. <u>Does he/she use relevant and adequate support, or do fallacies exist?</u> <u>Explain</u>.

13. The seven most common propaganda techniques are bandwagon, testimonial, transfer, plain folks, name calling, glittering generalities, and card staking. <u>Which techniques are used in this reading selection? Explain</u>.

A working <u>DRAFT</u> of the:

Declaration of Independence

Thomas Jefferson

When in the course of human events it becomes necessary for a people to advance from that subordination in which they have hitherto remained, and to assume among the powers of the earth the equal and independant station to which the laws of nature and of nature's god entitle them, a decent respect to the opinions of mankind requires that they should declare the causes which impel them to the change.

We hold these truths to be sacred and undeniable; that all men are created equal and independant, that from that equal creation they derive rights inherent and inalienable, among which are the preservation of life, and liberty, and the pursuit of happiness; that to secure these ends, governments are instituted among men, deriving their just powers from the consent of the governed; that whenever any form of government shall become destructive of these ends, it is the right of the people to alter or to abolish it, and to institute new government, laying it's foundation on such principles and organising it's powers in such form, as to them shall seem most likely to effect their safety and happiness. prudence indeed will dictate that governments long established should not be changed for light and transient causes: and accordingly all experience hath shewn that mankind are more disposed to suffer while evils are sufferable, than to right themselves by abolishing the forms to which they are accustomed. but when a long train of abuses and usurpations, begun at a distinguished period, and pursuing invariably the same object, evinces a design to subject them to arbitrary power, it is their right, it is their duty, to throw off such government and to provide new guards for their future security. such has been the patient sufferance of these colonies; and such is now the necessity which constrains them to expunge their former systems of government. the history of his present majesty, is a history of unremitting injuries and usurpations, among which no one fact stands single or solitary to contradict the uniform tenor of the rest, all of which have in direct object the establishment of an absolute tyranny over these states. to prove this, let facts be submitted to a candid world, for the truth of which we pledge a faith yet unsullied by falsehood.

he has refused his assent to laws the most wholesome and necessary for the public good:

he has forbidden his governors to pass laws of immediate and pressing importance, unless suspended in their operation till his assent should be obtained; and when so suspended, he has neglected utterly to attend to them.

he has refused to pass other laws for the accomodation of large districts of people unless those people would relinquish the right of representation, a right inestimable to them, formidable to tyrants alone:

he has dissolved Representative houses repeatedly and continually, for opposing with manly firmness his invasions on the rights of the people:

he has refused for a long space of time to cause others to be elected, whereby the legislative powers, incapable of annihilation, have returned to the people at large for their exercise, the state remaining in the mean time exposed to all the dangers of invasion from without, and convulsions within:

he has endeavored to prevent the population of these states; for that purpose obstructing the laws for naturalization of foreigners; refusing to pass others to encourage their migrations hither; and raising the conditions of new appropriations of lands:

he has suffered the administration of justice totally

to cease in some of these colonies, refusing his assent to laws for establishing judiciary powers:

he has made our judges dependant on his will alone, for the tenure of their offices, and amount of their salaries:

he has erected a multitude of new offices by a self-assumed power, and sent hither swarms of officers to harrass our people and eat out their substance:

he has kept among us in times of peace standing armies and ships of war:

he has affected to render the military, independant of and superior to the civil power:

he has combined with others to subject us to a jurisdiction foreign to our constitutions and unacknoleged by our laws; giving his assent to their pretended acts of legislation, for quartering large bodies of armed troops among us;

for protecting them by a mock-trial from punishment for any murders they should commit on the inhabitants of these states;

for cutting off our trade with all parts of the world;

for imposing taxes on us without our consent;

for depriving us of the benefits of trial by jury;

for transporting us beyond seas to be tried for pretended offences:

for taking away our charters, and altering fundamentally the forms of our governments;

for suspending our own legislatures and declaring themselves invested with power to legislate for us in all cases whatsoever:

he has abdicated government here, withdrawing his governors, and declaring us out of his allegiance and protection:

he has plundered our seas, ravaged our coasts,

burnt our towns and destroyed the lives of our people:

he is at this time transporting large armies of foreign mercenaries to compleat the works of death, desolation and tyranny, already begun with circumstances of cruelty and perfidy unworthy the head of a civilized nation:

he has endeavored to bring on the inhabitants of our frontiers the merciless Indian savages, whose known rule of warfare is an undistinguished destruction of all ages, sexes, and conditions of existence:

he has incited treasonable insurrections in our fellow-subjects, with the allurements of forfeiture and confiscation of our property:

he has waged cruel war against human nature itself, violating it's most sacred rights of life and liberty in the persons of a distant people who never offended him, captivating and carrying them into slavery in another hemisphere, or to incur miserable death in their transportation thither. this piratical warfare, the opprobrium of infidel powers, is the warfare of the CHRISTIAN king of Great Britain. determined to keep open a market where MEN should be bought and sold, he has prostituted his negative for suppressing every legislative attempt to prohibit or to restrain this execrable commerce: and that this assemblage of horrors might want no fact of distinguished die, he is now exciting those very people to rise in arms among us, and to purchase that liberty of which he has deprived them, and murdering the people upon whom he also obtruded them; thus paying off former crimes committed against the liberties of one people, with crimes which he urges them to commit against the lives of another.

in every stage of these oppressions we have petitioned for redress in the most humble terms; our repeated petitions have been answered by repeated injury. a prince whose character is thus marked by every act which may define a tyrant, is

Slavery_____

unfit to be the ruler of a people who mean to be free. future ages will scarce believe that the hardiness of one man, adventured within the short compass of 12 years only, on so many acts of tyranny without a mask, over a people fostered and fixed in principles of liberty.

Nor have we been wanting in attentions to our British brethren. we have warned them from time to time of attempts by their legislature to extend a jurisdiction over these our states. we have reminded them of the circumstances of our emigration and settlement here, no one of which could warrant so strange a pretension: that these were effected at the expence of our own blood and treasure, unassisted by the wealth or the strength of Great Britain: that in constituting indeed our several forms of government, we had adopted one common king, thereby laying a foundation for perpetual league and amity with them: but that submission to their parliament was no part of our constitution, nor ever in idea, if history may be credited: and we appealed to their native justice and magnanimity, as well as to the ties of our common kindred to disavow these usurpations which were likely to interrupt our correspondence and connection. they too have been deaf to the voice of justice and of consanguinity, and when occasions have been given them, by the regular course of their laws, of removing from their councils the disturbers of our harmony, they have by their free election re-established them in power. at this very time too they are permitting their chief magistrate to send over not only soldiers of our common blood, but Scotch and foreign mercenaries to invade and deluge us in blood. these facts have given the last stab to agonizing affection, and manly spirit bids us to renounce for ever these unfeeling brethren. we must endeavor to forget our former love for them, and to hold them as we hold the rest of mankind, enemies in war, in peace friends. we might have been a free and great people together; but a communication of grandeur and of freedom it seems is below their dignity. be it so, since they will have it: the road to glory and happiness is open to us too; we will climb it in a separate state, and acquiesce in the necessity which pronounces our everlasting Adieu!

We therefore the representatives of the United States of America in General Congress assembled do, in the name and by authority of the good people of these states, reject and renounce all allegiance and subjection to the kings of Great Britain and all others who may hereafter claim by, through, or under them; we utterly dissolve and break off all political connection which may have heretofore subsisted between us and the people or parliament of Great Britain; and finally we do assert and declare these a colonies to be free and independant states, and that as free and independant states they shall hereafter have power to levy war, conclude peace, contract alliances, establish commerce, and to do all other acts and things which independent states may of right do. And for the support of this declaration we mutually pledge to each other our lives, our fortunes, and our sacred honour.

The questions that follow may be used for further discussion of the reading selection or as topics for essay writing.

1. Discuss the similarities and differences between the finished Declaration and this work in progress.

2. Discuss Jefferson's views on slavery. Why do you think it was edited out of the final document? Could the Northern and Southern States have reached an agreement on breaking away from Great Britain?

3. _____
_____
_____
_____
_____
_____

4. _____
_____
_____
_____
_____
_____
_____

5. _____
_____
_____
_____
_____
_____

Applying Reading Skills
(Neatly <u>PRINT</u> all answers using ink <u>not</u> pencil)

Title of the Reading Selection: _____

1. **What is the author's overall main idea, (central point, or thesis)?**

   _____

   _____

2. **There are two kinds of supporting details--major and minor. Major details are the primary points that support the main idea and minor details expand major details. List <u>three</u> details and explain how they support the author's primary point?**

Details used	Explanation of how they support the thesis
1.	

Details used	Explanation of how they support the thesis
2.	

Details used	Explanation of how they support the thesis
3.	

3. **The five major patterns of organization are the list of items pattern, the time order pattern, the example pattern, the comparison and/or contrast pattern, and the cause/effect pattern. What is the <u>main</u> pattern of organization used in this article? <u>Explain</u> why it is the major pattern. What other patterns are used? Give some examples.**

Main pattern: _____

Explain how the main pattern was used: _____

_____

Other pattern(s) used: _____

Explain how the additional pattern(s) were used:

_____

_____

130

4. If applicable: Give <u>two</u> examples that were used in the writing. <u>Explain</u> how they affected your understanding of the reading selection.

The example(s) given	How example(s) contributed to your understanding
1.	1.
2.	2.

5. If applicable: what is being compared and/or contrasted?

Show <u>two</u> comparisons between items A and B:

A	B

Show <u>two</u> contrasts between items A and B:

A	B

6. Show <u>two</u> cause/effect relationships:

Cause	Effect
1.	
2.	

7. List <u>three</u> facts and <u>three</u> opinions from the article. <u>Explain why</u> it is either a fact or an opinion.

	Explanation:
A.) fact:	A.)
B.) fact:	B.)
C.) fact:	C.)

	Explanation:
A.) opinion	A.)
B.) opinion:	B.)
C.) opinion:	C.)

8. What is the author's purpose in this article? Is it to inform, persuade, or entertain? <u>Tell me how you arrived at that conclusion.</u>

_____

_____

_____

9. What is the author's tone? <u>Explain your answer.</u>

_____

_____

_____

10. Discovering the ideas in writing that are <u>not stated directly</u> is called making inferences, or drawing conclusions. What inferences did you draw from the article you read? <u>Explain</u>.

_____

_____

_____

11. Authors often use connotative language. Return to the reading selection and circle (in red or green) all connotative words. List 10 of those words here and explain how those words might affect the reader.

_____

_____

_____

_____

_____

How the connotative words above might affect the reader:

_____

_____

_____

_____

_____

_____

_____

12. A good argument makes a point and then provides persuasive and logical evidence to back it up. However, a bad argument uses fallacies to support itself such as changing the subject, hasty generalization, circular reasoning, personal attack, straw man, false cause, false comparison, or either-or. Explain how the author supports his/her argument. <u>Does he/she use relevant and adequate support, or do fallacies exist? Explain.</u>

_____
_____
_____
_____
_____
_____
_____
_____
_____
_____
_____
_____
_____
_____
_____
_____
_____
_____

13. The seven most common propaganda techniques are bandwagon, testimonial, transfer, plain folks, name calling, glittering generalities, and card staking. <u>Which techniques are used in this reading selection? Explain.</u>

_____
_____
_____
_____
_____
_____
_____
_____
_____
_____
_____
_____
_____
_____
_____

The Communist Manifesto
(1848)

Karl Marx

A specter is haunting Europe--the specter of Communism. All the Powers of old Europe have entered into a holy alliance to exorcise this specter; Pope and Czar, Metternich and Guizot, French Radicals and German police-spies.

2   Where is the party in opposition that has not been decried as communistic by its opponents in power? Where the Opposition that has not hurled back the branding reproach of Communism against the more advanced opposition parties, as well as against its reactionary adversaries?

3   Two things result from this fact.

4   I. Communism is already acknowledged by all European Powers to be itself a Power.

5   II. It is high time that Communists should openly, in the face of the whole world, publish their views, their aims, their tendencies, and meet this nursery tale of the specter of Communism with a Manifesto of the party itself.

6   To this end, Communists of various nationalities have assembled in London and sketched the following Manifesto, to be published in the English, French, German, Italian, Flemish and Danish languages.

Bourgeois and Proletarians

7   The history of all hitherto existing society is the history of class struggles.

8   Freeman and slave, patrician and plebeian, lord and serf, guild- master and journeyman, in a word, oppressor and oppressed, stood in constant opposition to one another, carried on uninterrupted, now hidden, now open fight, a fight that each time ended, either in a revolutionary re-constitution of society at large, or in the common ruin of the contending classes.

9   In the earlier epochs of history we find almost everywhere a complicated arrangement of society into various orders, a manifold gradation of social rank. In ancient Rome we have patricians, knights, plebeians, slaves; in the Middle Ages, feudal lords, vassals, guild-masters, journeymen, apprentices, serfs; in almost all of these classes, again, subordinate gradations.

10   The modern bourgeois society that has sprouted from the

ruins of feudal society, has not done away with class antagonisms. It has but established new classes, new conditions of oppression, new forms of struggle in place of the old ones.

11   Our epoch, the epoch of the bourgeoisie, possesses, however, this distinctive feature; it has simplified the class antagonisms. Society as a whole is more and more splitting up into two great hostile camps, into two great classes directly facing each other; Bourgeoisie and Proletariat.

12   From the serfs of the Middle Ages sprang the chartered burghers of the earliest towns. From these burgesses the first elements of the bourgeoisie were developed.

The Discovery of America

13   The discovery of America, the rounding of the Cape, opened up fresh ground for the rising bourgeoisie. The East Indian and Chinese markets, the colonization of America, trade with the colonies, the increase in the means of exchange and in commodities generally, gave to commerce, to navigation, to industry, an impulse never before known, and thereby, to the revolutionary element in the tottering feudal society, a rapid development.

14   The feudal system of industry, under which industrial production was monopolized by closed guilds, now no longer sufficed for the growing wants of the new market. The manufacturing system took its place. The guild-masters were pushed on one side by the manufacturing middle-class: division of labor between the different corporate guilds vanished in the face of division of labor in each single workshop.

15   Meantime the markets kept ever growing, the demand ever rising. Even manufacture no longer sufficed. Thereupon, steam and machinery revolutionized industrial production. The place of manufacture was taken by the giant, Modern Industry, the place of the industrial middle-class, by industrial millionaires, the leaders of whole industrial armies, the modern bourgeois.

16   Modern industry has established the world market, for which the discovery of America paved the way. This market has given an immense development to commerce, to navigation, to communication by land. This development has, in its turn, reacted on the extension of industry; and in proportion as industry, commerce, navigation, railways extended, in the same proportion the bourgeoisie developed, increased its capital, and pushed into the background every class handed down from the Middle Ages.

Marx's Attack on the Bourgeoisie

17 – 19 abridged (may be read on the CD accompanying this text)

20   The bourgeoisie, wherever it has got the upper hand, has put an end to all feudal, patriarchal, idyllic relations. It has pitilessly torn asunder the motley feudal ties that bound man to his "natural superiors," and has left no other nexus between man and man than naked self-interest, than callous "cash payment." It has drowned the most heavenly ecstasies of religious fervor, of chivalrous enthusiasm, of Philistine sentimentalism, in the icy water of egotistical calculation. It has resolved personal worth into exchange value, and in place of the numberless indefeasible chartered freedoms, has set up that single, unconscionable freedom--Free Trade. In one word, for exploitation, veiled by religious and political illusions, it has substituted naked, shameless, direct, brutal exploitation.

21   The bourgeoisie has stripped of its halo every occupation hitherto honored and looked up to with reverent awe. It has converted the physician, the lawyer, the priest, the poet, the man of science, into its paid wage laborers.

22   The bourgeoisie has torn away from the family its sentimental veil, and has reduced the family relation to a mere money relation.

23   The bourgeoisie has disclosed how it came to pass that the brutal display of vigor in the Middle Ages, which reactionists so much admire, found its fitting complement in the most slothful indolence. It has been the first to show what man's activity can bring about. It has accomplished wonders far surpassing Egyptian pyramids, Roman aqueducts and Gothic cathedrals; it has conducted expeditions that put in the shade all former Exoduses of nations and crusades.

24   The bourgeoisie cannot exist without constantly revolutionizing the instruments of production, and thereby the relations of production, and with them the whole relations of society. Conservation of the old modes of production in unaltered form was, on the contrary, the first condition of existence for all earlier industrial classes. Constant revolutionizing of production, uninterrupted disturbance of all social conditions, everlasting uncertainty and agitation distinguish the bourgeois epoch from all earlier ones. All fixed, fast frozen relations, with their train of ancient and venerable prejudices and opinions, are swept away, all new formed ones become antiquated before they can ossify.

All that is solid melts into the air, all that is holy is profaned, and man is at last compelled to face with sober senses, his real conditions of life, and his relations with his kind.

25   The need of a constantly expanding market for its products chases the bourgeoisie over the whole surface of the globe. It must nestle everywhere, settle everywhere, establish connections everywhere.

26   The bourgeoisie has through its exploitation of the world-market given a cosmopolitan character to production and consumption in every country. To the great chagrin of reactionists, it has drawn from under the feet of industry the national ground on which it stood. All old-established national industries have been destroyed or are daily being destroyed. They are dislodged by new industries, whose introduction becomes a life and death question for all civilized nations, by industries that no longer work up indigenous raw material, but raw material drawn from the remotest zones; industries whose products are consumed, not only at home, but in every quarter of the globe. In place of the old wants, satisfied by the productions of the country, we find new wants, requiring for their satisfaction the products of distant lands and climes. In place of the old local and national seclusion and self-sufficiency, we have intercourse in every direction, universal interdependence of nations. And as in material, so also in intellectual production. The intellectual creations of individual nations become common property. National onesidedness and narrowmindedness become more and more impossible, and from the numerous national and local literatures there arises a world-literature.

27   abridged (may be read on the CD accompanying this text)

28   The bourgeoisie has subjected the country to the rule of the towns. It has created enormous cities, has greatly increased the urban population as compared with the rural and has thus rescued a considerable part of the population from the idiocy of rural life. Just as it has made the country dependent on the towns, so it has made barbarian and semi-barbarian countries dependent on civilized ones, nations of peasants on nations of bourgeois, the East on the West.

29   The bourgeoisie keeps more and more doing away with the scattered state of the population, of the means of production, and of property. It has agglomerated population, centralized means of production, and has concentrated property in a few hands. The necessary consequence of this was political centralization. Independent, or but loosely connected provinces, with separate

138

interests, laws, governments, and systems of taxation, became lumped together in one nation, with one government, one code of laws, one national class interest, one frontier and one customs tariff.

30   The bourgeoisie, during its rule of scarce one hundred years, has created more massive and more colossal productive forces than have all preceding generations together. Subjection of Nature's forces to man, machinery, application of chemistry to industry and agriculture, steam-navigation, railways, electric telegraphs, clearing of whole continents for cultivation, canalization of rivers, whole populations conjured out of the ground--what earlier century had even a presentiment that such productive forces slumbered in the lap of social labor?

31 – 33 abridged (may be read on the CD accompanying this text)

34   The weapons with which the bourgeoisie felled feudalism to the ground are now turned against the bourgeoisie itself.

35   But not only has the bourgeoisie forged the weapons that bring death to itself; it has also called into existence the men who are to wield those weapons--the modern working class--the proletarians.

The Proletariat

36   In proportion as the bourgeoisie, i.e., capital, is developed, in the same proportion is the proletariat, the modern working class, developed, a class of laborers who live only so long as they find work, and who find work only so long as their labor increases capital. These laborers, who must sell themselves piecemeal, are a commodity, like every other article of commerce, and are consequently exposed to all the vicissitudes of competition, to all the fluctuations of the market.

37   Owing to the extensive use of machinery and to division of labor, the work of the proletarians has lost all individual character, and, consequently, all charm for the workman. He becomes an appendage of the machine, and it is only the most simple, most monotonous and most easily acquired knack that is required of him. Hence, the cost of production of a workman is restricted almost entirely to the means of subsistence that he requires for his maintenance, and for the propagation of his race. But the price of a commodity, and also of labor, is equal to its cost of production. In proportion, therefore, as the repulsiveness of the work increases the wage decreases. Nay more, in proportion as the use of machinery and division of labor

increases, in the same proportion the burden of toil increases, whether by prolongation of the working hours, by increase of the work enacted in a given time, or by increased speed of the machinery, etc.

38   Modern industry has converted the little workshop of the patriarchal master into the great factory of the industrial capitalist. Masses of laborers, crowded into factories, are organized like soldiers. As privates of the industrial army they are placed under the command of a perfect hierarchy of officers and sergeants. Not only are they the slaves of the bourgeois class and of the bourgeois state, they are daily and hourly enslaved by the machine, by the over-looker, and, above all, by the individual bourgeois manufacturer himself. The more openly this despotism proclaims gain to be its end and aim, the more petty, the more hateful and the more embittering it is.

39   The less the skill and exertion or strength implied in manual labor, in other words, the more modem industry becomes developed, the more is the labor of men superseded by that of women. Differences of age and sex have no longer any distinctive social validity for the working class. All are instruments of labor, more or less expensive to use, according to their age and sex.

40   No sooner is the exploitation of the laborer by the manufacturer, so far at an end, that he receives his wages in cash, than he is set upon by the other portions of the bourgeoisie, the landlord, the shopkeeper, the pawnbroker, etc.

41   The lower strata of the middle class - the small tradespeople, shopkeepers and retired tradesmen generally, the handicraftsmen and peasants--all these sink gradually into the proletariat, partly because their diminutive capital does not suffice for the scale on which Modern Industry is carried on, and is swamped in the competition with the large capitalists, partly because their specialized skill is rendered worthless by new methods of production. Thus the proletariat is recruited from all classes of the population.

42   The proletariat goes through various stages of development. With its birth begins its struggle with the bourgeoisie. At first the contest is carried on by individual laborers, then by the workpeople of a factory, then by the operatives of one trade, in one locality, against the individual bourgeois who directly exploits them. They direct their attacks not against the bourgeois conditions of production, but against the instruments of production themselves; they destroy imported wares that compete with their labor, they smash to pieces

machinery, they set factories ablaze, they seek to restore by force the vanished status of the workman of the Middle Ages.

NOTE: Sections 43 through 52 have been deleted from the text but may be read in the Adobe e-book format on the CD Rom included with the text.

53   In the conditions of the proletariat, those of the old society at large are already virtually swamped. The proletarian is without property; his relation to his wife and children has no longer anything in common with the bourgeois family relations; modern industrial labor, modem subjection to capital, the same in England as in France, in America as in Germany, has stripped him of every trace of national character. Law, morality, religion, are to him so many bourgeois prejudices, behind which lurk in ambush just as many bourgeois interests.

54   All the preceding classes that got the upper hand sought to fortify their already acquired status by subjecting society at large to their conditions of appropriation. The proletarians cannot become masters of the productive forces of society, except by abolishing their own previous mode of appropriation, and thereby also every other previous mode of appropriation. They have nothing of their own to secure and to fortify; their mission is to destroy all previous securities for and insurances of individual property.

55   All previous historical movements were movements of minorities, or in the interest of minorities. The proletarian movement is the self-conscious, independent movement of the immense majority. The proletariat, the lowest stratum of our present society, cannot stir, cannot raise itself up without the whole superincumbent strata of official society being sprung into the air.

56   Though not in substance, yet in form, the struggle of the proletariat with the bourgeoisie is at first a national struggle. The proletariat of each country must, of course, first of all settle matters with its own bourgeoisie.

57   In depicting the most general phases of the development of the proletariat, we traced the more or less veiled civil war, raging within existing society, up to the point where that war breaks out into open revolution, and where the violent overthrow of the bourgeoisie, lays the foundations for the sway of the proletariat.

58   Hitherto every form of society has been based, as we have already seen, on the antagonism of oppressing and oppressed

classes. But in order to oppress a class, certain conditions must be assured to it under which it can, at least, continue its slavish existence. The serf, in the period of serfdom, raised himself to membership in the commune, just as the petty bourgeois, under the yoke of feudal absolutism, managed to develop into a bourgeois. The modem laborer, on the contrary, instead of rising with the progress of industry, sinks deeper and deeper below the conditions of existence of his own class. He becomes a pauper, and pauperism develops more rapidly than population and wealth. And here it becomes evident that the bourgeoisie is unfit any longer to be the ruling class in society, and to impose its conditions of existence upon society as an over-riding law. It is unfit to rule, because it is incompetent to assure an existence to its slave within his slavery, because it cannot help letting him sink into such a state that it has to feed him, instead of being fed by him. Society can no longer live under this bourgeoisie; in other words, its existence is no longer compatible with society.

59   The essential condition for the existence, and for the sway of the bourgeois class, is the formation and augmentation of capital; the condition for capital is wage labor. Wage labor rests exclusively on competition between the laborers. The advance of industry, whose involuntary promoter is the bourgeoisie, replaces the isolation of the laborers, due to competition, by their involuntary combination, due to association. The development of Modern Industry, therefore, cuts from under its feet the very foundation on which the bourgeoisie produces and appropriates products. What the bourgeoisie therefore produces, above all, are its own grave diggers. Its fall and the victory of the proletariat are equally inevitable.

Proletarians and Communists

60   In what relation do the Communists stand to the proletarians as a whole?
61   The Communists do not form a separate party opposed to other working class parties.
62   They have no interests separate and apart from those of the proletariat as a whole.
63   They do not set up any sectarian principles of their own, by which to shape and mold the proletarian movement.
64   The Communists are distinguished from the other working class parties by this only: 1. In the national struggles of the proletarians of the different countries, they point out and bring to

the front the common interests of the entire proletariat, independently of all nationality. 2. In the various stages of development which the struggle of the working class against the bourgeoisie has to pass through, they always and everywhere represent the interests of the movement as a whole.

65   The Communists, therefore, are on the one hand practically the most advanced and resolute section of the working class parties of every country, that section which pushes forward all others; on the other hand, theoretically, they have over the great mass of the proletariat the advantage of clearly understanding the line of march, the conditions, and the ultimate general results of the proletarian movement.

66   The immediate aim of the Communists is the same as that of all the other proletarian parties: formation of the proletariat into a class, overthrow of the bourgeois of supremacy, conquest of political power by the proletariat.

Abolition of Private Property

67   The theoretical conclusions of the Communists are in no way based on ideas or principles that have been invented or discovered by this or that would-be universal reformer.

68   They merely express, in general terms, actual relations springing from an existing class struggle, from a historical movement going on under our very eyes. The abolition of existing property relations is not at all a distinctive feature of Communism.

69   All property relations in the past have continually been subject to historical change consequent upon the change in historical conditions.

70   The French Revolution, for example, abolished feudal property in favor of bourgeois property.

71   The distinguishing feature of Communism is not the abolition of property generally, but the abolition of bourgeois property. But modern bourgeois private property is the final and most complete expression of the system of producing and appropriating products, that is based on class antagonism, on the exploitation of the many by the few.

72   In this sense, the theory of the Communists may be summed up in the single sentence: Abolition of private property.

73   We Communists have been reproached with the desire of abolishing the right of personally acquiring property as the fruit of a man's own labor, which property is alleged to be the

groundwork of all personal freedom, activity and independence.

74   Hard won, self-acquired, self-earned property! Do you mean the property of the petty artisan and of the small peasant, a form of property that preceded the bourgeois form? There is no need to abolish that; the development of industry has to a great extent already destroyed it, and is still destroying it daily.

75   Or do you mean modern bourgeois private property?

76   But does wage labor create any property for the laborer? Not a bit. It creates capital, i.e., that kind of property which exploits wage labor, and which cannot increase except upon condition of getting a new supply of wage labor for fresh exploitation. Property, in its present form, is based on the antagonism of capital and wage labor. Let us examine both sides of this antagonism.

77   To be a capitalist is to have not only a purely personal, but a social status in production. Capital is a collective product, and only by the united action of many members, nay, in the last resort, only by the united action of all members of society, can it be set in motion.

78   Capital is therefore not a personal, it is a social power.

79   When, therefore, capital is converted into common property, into the property of all members of society, personal property is not thereby transformed into social property. It is only the social character of the property that is changed. It loses its class character.

Marx's Antagonism Towards Wage Labor & Free Trade

80   Let us now take wage labor.

81   The average price of wage labor is the minimum wage, i.e., that quantum of the means of subsistence which is absolutely requisite to keep the laborer in bare existence as a laborer. What, therefore, the wage laborer appropriates by means of his labor, merely suffices to prolong and reproduce a bare existence. We by no means intend to abolish this personal appropriation of the products of labor, an appropriation that is made for the maintenance and reproduction of human life, and that leaves no surplus wherewith to command the labor of others. All that we want to do away with is the miserable character of this appropriation, under which the laborer lives merely to increase capital and is allowed to live only in so far as the interests of the ruling class require it.

82   In bourgeois society, living labor is but a means to increase

144

accumulated labor. In Communist society accumulated labor is but a means to widen, to enrich, to promote the existence of the laborer.

83   In bourgeois society, therefore, the past dominates the present; in Communist society the present dominates the past. In bourgeois society, capital is independent and has individuality, while the living person is dependent and has no individuality.

84   And the abolition of this state of things is called by the bourgeois abolition of individuality and freedom! And rightly so. The abolition of bourgeois individuality, bourgeois independence and bourgeois freedom is undoubtedly aimed at.

85   By freedom is meant, under the present bourgeois conditions of production, free trade, free selling and buying.

86   But if selling and buying disappears, free selling and buying disappears also. This talk about free selling and buying, and all the other "brave words" of our bourgeoisie about freedom in general have a meaning, if any, only in contrast with restricted selling and buying, with the fettered traders of the Middle Ages, but have no meaning when opposed to the Communistic abolition of buying and selling, of the bourgeois conditions of production, and of the bourgeoisie itself.

87   You are horrified at our intending to do away with private property. But in your existing society private property is already done away with for nine-tenths of the population; its existence for the few is solely due to its lion-existence in the hands of those nine-tenths. You reproach us, therefore, with intending to do away with a form of property, the necessary condition for whose existence is the nonexistence of any property for the immense majority of society.

88   In one word, you reproach us with intending to do away with your property. Precisely so: that is just what we intend.

89   From the moment when labor can no longer be converted into capital, money, or rent, into a social power capable of being monopolized, i.e., from the moment when individual property can no longer be transformed into bourgeois property, into capital, from that moment, you say, individuality vanishes.

90   You must, therefore, confess that by "individual" you mean no other person than the bourgeois, than the middle-class owner of property. This person must, indeed, be swept out of the way and made impossible.

91   Communism deprives no man of the power to appropriate the products of society: all that it does is to deprive him of the power to subjugate the labor of others by means of such

appropriation.

92   It has been objected that upon the abolition of private property all work will cease and universal laziness will overtake us.

93   According to this, bourgeois society ought long ago to have gone to the dogs through sheer idleness; for those of its members who work acquire nothing, and those who acquire anything do not work. The whole of this objection is but another expression of the tautology: that there can no longer be any wage labor when there is no longer any capital.

94   All objections urged against the Communistic mode of producing and appropriating material products have, in the same way, been urged against the Communistic modes of producing and appropriating intellectual products. Just as, to the bourgeois, the disappearance of class property is the disappearance of production itself, so the disappearance of class culture is to him identical with the disappearance of all culture.

95   That culture, the loss of which he laments, is, for the enormous majority, a mere training to act as a machine.

96   But don't wrangle with us so long as you apply, to our intended abolition of bourgeois property, the standard of your bourgeois notions of freedom, culture, law, etc. Your very ideas are but the out-growth of the conditions of your bourgeois production and bourgeois property, just as your jurisprudence is but the will of your class made into a law for all, a will whose essential character and direction are determined by the economical conditions of existence of your class.

97   The selfish misconception that induces you to transform into eternal laws of nature and of reason the social forms springing from your present mode of production and form of property--historical relations that rise and disappear in the progress of production--this misconception you share with every ruling class that has preceded you. What you see clearly in the case of ancient property, what you admit in the case of feudal property, you are of course for-bidden to admit in the case of your own bourgeois form of property.

Abolition of the Family

98   Abolition of the family! Even the most radical flare up at this infamous proposal of the Communists.

99   On what foundation is the present family, the bourgeois family, based? On capital, on private gain. In its completely

developed form this family exists only among the bourgeoisie. But this state of things finds its complement in the practical absence of the family among the proletarians, and in public prostitution.

100   The bourgeois family will vanish as a matter of course when its complement vanishes, and both will vanish with the vanishing of capital.

101   Do you charge us with wanting to stop the exploitation of children by their parents? To this crime we plead guilty.

102   But, you will say, we destroy the most hallowed of relations when we replace home education by social.

103   And your education! Is not that also social, and determined by the social conditions under which you educate; by the intervention, direct or indirect, of society by means of schools, etc.? The Communists have not invented the intervention of society in education; they do but seek to alter the character of that intervention, and to rescue education from the influence of the ruling class.

104   The bourgeois clap-trap about the family and education, about the hallowed correlation of parent and child, become all the more disgusting, the more, by the action of Modern Industry, all family ties among the proletarians are torn asunder and their children transformed into simple articles of commerce and instruments of labor.

A "Community of Woman" (Prostitution)

105   But you Communists would introduce community of women, screams the whole bourgeoisie chorus.

106   The bourgeois sees in his wife a mere instrument of production. He hears that the instruments of production are to be exploited in common, and, naturally, can come to no other conclusion, than that the lot of being common to all will likewise fall to the women.

107   He has not even a suspicion that the real point aimed at is to do away with the status of women as mere instruments of production.

108   For the rest, nothing is more ridiculous than the virtuous indignation of our bourgeois at the community of women which, they pretend, is to be openly and officially established by the Communists. The Communists have no need to introduce community of women, it has existed almost from time immemorial.

109   Our bourgeois, not content with having the wives and daughters of their proletarians at their disposal, not to speak of common prostitutes, take the greatest pleasure in seducing each others' wives.

110   Bourgeois marriage is in reality a system of wives in common, and thus, at the most, what the Communists might possibly be reproached with, is that they desire to introduce, in substitution for a hypocritically concealed, an openly legalized community of women. For the rest, it is self-evident that the abolition of the present system of production must bring with it the abolition of the community of women springing from that system, i.e., of prostitution both public and private.

Abolition of Countries and Nationalities

111   The Communists are further reproached with desiring to abolish countries and nationalities.

112   The working men have no country. We cannot take from them what they don't possess. Since the proletariat must first of all acquire political supremacy, must rise to be the leading class of the nation, must constitute itself the nation, it is, so far, itself national, though not in the bourgeois sense of the word.

113   National differences and antagonisms between peoples are daily more and more vanishing, owing to the development of the bourgeoisie, to freedom of commerce, to the world-market, to uniformity in the mode of production and in the conditions of life corresponding thereto.

114   The supremacy of the proletariat will cause them to vanish still faster. United action, of the leading civilized countries at least, is one of the first conditions for the emancipation of the proletariat.

115   In proportion as the exploitation of one individual by another is put an end to, the exploitation of one nation by another will also be put an end to. In proportion as the antagonism between classes within the nation vanishes, the hostility of one nation to another will come to an end.

Communism vs. Religion, Philosophy, Idealism & Abolition of "Eternal Truths"

116   The charges against Communism made from a religious, a philosophical, and generally, from an ideological standpoint, are not deserving of serious examination.

117   Does it require deep intuition to comprehend that man's ideas, views and conceptions, in one word, man's consciousness, changes with every change in the conditions of his material existence, in his social relations and in his social life?

118   What else does the history of ideas prove than that intellectual production changes in character in proportion as material production is changed? The ruling ideas of each age have ever been the ideas of its ruling class.

119   When people speak of ideas that revolutionize society they do but express the fact that within the old society the elements of a new one have been created, and that the dissolution of the old ideas keeps even pace with the dissolution of the old conditions of existence.

120   When the ancient world was in its last throes the ancient religions were overcome by Christianity. When Christian ideas succumbed in the 18th century to rationalist ideas, feudal society fought its deathbattle with the then revolutionary bourgeoisie. The ideas of religious liberty and freedom of conscience merely gave expression to the sway of free competition within the domain of knowledge.

121   "Undoubtedly," it will be said, "religious, moral, philosophical and judicial ideas have been modified in the course of historical development. But religion, morality, philosophy, political science, and law, constantly survived this change.

122   "There are, besides, eternal truths such as Freedom, Justice, etc., that are common to all states of society. But Communism abolishes eternal truths, it abolishes all religion and all morality, instead of constituting them on a new basis; it therefore acts in contradiction to all past historical experience."

123   What does this accusation reduce itself to? The history of all past society has consisted in the development of class antagonisms, antagonisms that assumed different forms at different epochs.

124   But whatever form they may have taken, one fact is common to all past ages, viz., the exploitation of one part of society by the other. No wonder, then, that the social consciousness of past ages, despite all the multiplicity and variety it displays, moves within certain common forms, or general ideas, which cannot completely vanish except with the total disappearance of class antagonisms.

125   The Communist revolution is the most radical rupture with traditional property relations; no wonder that its development involves the most radical rupture with traditional ideas.

149

126   But let us have done with the bourgeois objections to Communism.

127   We have seen above that the first step in the revolution by the working class is to raise the proletariat to the position of ruling class, to win the battle of democracy.

128   The proletariat will use its political supremacy to wrest, by degrees, all capital from the bourgeoisie, to centralize all instruments of production in the hands of the State, i.e., of the proletariat organized as a ruling class; and to increase the total productive forces as rapidly as possible.

129   Of course, in the beginning, this cannot be effected except by means of despotic inroads on the rights of property, and on the conditions of bourgeois productions; by means of measures, therefore, which appear economically insufficient and untenable, but

which in the course of the movement outstrip themselves, necessitate further inroads upon the old social order, and are unavoidable as a means of entirely revolutionizing the mode of production.

130   These measures will of course be different in different countries.

131   Nevertheless in the most advanced countries the following will be pretty generally applicable:

Marx's Plan For All Nations

1. Abolition of property in land and application of all rents of land to public purposes.
2. A heavy progressive or graduated income tax.
3. Abolition of all right of inheritance.
4. Confiscation of the property of all emigrants and rebels.
5. Centralization of credit in the hands of the State, by means of   a national bank with State capital and an exclusive monopoly.
6. Centralization of the means of communication and transport in the hands of the State.
7. Extension of factories and instruments of production owned by the State; the bringing into cultivation of waste lands, and the improvement of the soil generally in accordance with a common plan.
8. Equal liability of all to labor. Establishment of industrial armies, especially for agriculture.
9. Combination of agriculture with manufacturing industries; gradual abolition of the distinction between town and

country by a more equable distribution of the population over the country.

10. Free education for all children in public schools. Abolition of children's factory labor in its present form. Combination of education with industrial production, etc., etc.

132   When, in the course of development, class distinctions have disappeared, and all production has been concentrated in the hands of a vast association of the whole nation, the public power will lose its political character. Political power, properly so called, is merely the organized power of one class for oppressing another. If the proletariat during its contest with the bourgeoisie is compelled, by the force of circumstances, to organize itself as a class, if, by means of a revolution, it makes itself the ruling class, and, as such, sweeps away by force the old conditions of production, then it will, along with these conditions, have swept away the conditions for the existence of class antagonism, and of classes generally, and will thereby have abolished its own supremacy as a class.

133   In place of the old bourgeois society, with its classes and class antagonisms, we shall have an association in which the free development of each is the condition for the free development of all….

Relationship of the Communists to the Existing Parties of Opposition

134   [The preceding section] has made clear the relations of the Communists to the existing working class parties, such as the Chartists in England and the Agrarian Reforms in America.

135   The Communists fight for the attainment of the immediate aims, for the enforcement of the momentary interests of the working class; but in the movement of the present they also represent and take care of the future of that movement. In France the Communists ally themselves with the Social-Democrats against the conservative and radical bourgeoisie, reserving, however, the right to take up a critical position in regard to phrases and illusions traditionally handed down from the great Revolution.

136   In Switzerland they support the Radicals, without losing sight of the fact that this party consists of antagonistic elements, partly of Democratic Socialists, in the French sense, partly of

[handwritten margin note: Sounds good but its not attainable as shown by history since the time when he wrote this. Proletariats became dictators, who served with dictators would die in the effort to serve.]

151

radical bourgeois.

137   In Poland they support the party that insists on an agrarian revolution, as the prime condition for national emancipation, that party which fomented the insurrection of Cracow in 1846.

138   In Germany they fight with the bourgeoisie whenever it acts in a revolutionary way, against the absolute monarchy, the feudal squirearchy, and the petty bourgeoisie.

139   But they never cease for a single instant to instill into the working class the clearest possible recognition of the hostile antagonism between bourgeoisie and proletariat, in order that the German workers may straightway use, as so many weapons against the bourgeoisie, the social and political conditions that the bourgeoisie must necessarily introduce along with its supremacy, and in order that, after the fall of the reactionary classes in Germany, the fight against the bourgeoisie itself may immediately begin.

140   The Communists turn their attention chiefly to Germany, because that country is on the eve of a bourgeois revolution, that is bound to be carried out under more advanced conditions of European civilization, and with a more developed proletariat, than that of England was in the seventeenth and of France in the eighteenth century, and because the bourgeois revolution in Germany will be but the prelude to an immediately following proletarian revolution.

141   In short, the Communists everywhere support every revolutionary movement against the existing social and political order of things.

142   In all these movements they bring to the front, as the leading question in each, the property question, no matter what its degree of development at the time.

143   Finally, they labor everywhere for the union and agreement of the democratic parties of all countries.

144   The Communists disdain to conceal their views and aims. They openly declare that their ends can be attained only by the forcible overthrow of all existing social conditions. Let the ruling classes tremble at a Communistic revolution. The proletarians have nothing to lose but their chains. They have a world to win.

145   Working men of all countries, unite!

Constantly instill rebellion.

The questions that follow may be used for further discussion of the reading selection or as topics for essay writing.

1. Do some more research on the life of Karl Marx. Use several sources and discuss your findings.

2. Marx starts his manifesto by mocking those who would fear Communism yet later he contradicts himself and claims that the ultimate goal of Communism is World domination and control. Why do you think he does that?

3. Some people say Marx was a genius while others claim that he was a madman. What is your opinion? Defend your opinion with solid examples.

4. The phrase "the Good, the Bad, and the Ugly" has been used to describe the characters of Jefferson, Machiavelli, and Marx. Do you agree or disagree? Explain and defend your answer.

5. Is Marx's writing clear and concise, or muddled and rambling? Explain and defend your answer.

6. Reread Marx's ten point plan for the control of the nations of the world. How much of that plan has been implemented in the United States? Study each of the ten points and discuss the usefulness or detriment to the United States of each of these items. Are there alternatives?

7. _____
   _____
   _____
   _____
   _____
   _____
   _____

8. _____
   _____
   _____
   _____
   _____

Applying Reading Skills
(Neatly <u>PRINT</u> all answers using ink <u>not</u> pencil)

Title of the Reading Selection: ___*The Communist Manifesto.*___

1. What is the author's overall main idea, (central point, or thesis)?

   ___*Paragraph 5*_____

   _____

2. There are two kinds of supporting details--major and minor. Major details are the primary points that support the main idea and minor details expand major details. List <u>three</u> details and explain how they support the author's primary point?

Details used	Explanation of how they support the thesis
1. *no support*	

Details used	Explanation of how they support the thesis
2.	

Details used	Explanation of how they support the thesis
3.	

3. The five major patterns of organization are the list of items pattern, the time order pattern, the example pattern, the comparison and/or contrast pattern, and the cause/effect pattern. What is the <u>main</u> pattern of organization used in this article? <u>Explain</u> why it is the major pattern. What other patterns are used? Give some examples.

Main pattern: ___*List of Items*_____

Explain how the main pattern was used:

_____

Other pattern(s) used: _____

Explain how the additional pattern(s) were used:

_____

_____

154

4. **If applicable: Give two examples that were used in the writing. Explain how they affected your understanding of the reading selection.**

The example(s) given	How example(s) contributed to your understanding
1. No example	1.
2.	2.

5. **If applicable: what is being compared and/or contrasted?**

Show two comparisons between items A and B:

A	B
Bourgeoisie	Evil people
Proletariates	enslave
Communism	Other compared to a specter
Current class struggles to	Previous class struggles

Show two contrasts between items A and B:

A	B
Bourgeoisie	Proletariots
religion	Communism = no religion
Naturally superior people rich	Bourgeoisie & proletariots poor

6. **Show two cause/effect relationships:**

Cause	Effect
1. Bourgeoisie	Blamed for world's problem
2. Discovery of America	Catalyst for modern industry

7. **List three facts and three opinions from the article. Explain why it is either a fact or an opinion.**

	Explanation:
A.) fact: Bourgeoisie	A.) Middle & upper class
B.) fact: Industrialization	B.) lessen skills needed
C.) fact:	C.)

	Explanation:
A.) opinion _family doesn't matter_	A.)
B.) opinion: _religion is bad_	B.)
C.) opinion: _prostitute "sell" redistribute the wealth_	C.)

8. **What is the author's purpose in this article? Is it to inform, persuade, or entertain?** <u>Tell me how you arrived at that conclusion.</u>

Persuade

9. **What is the author's tone?** <u>Explain your answer.</u>

angry, contemptuous, hateful, bitter, mean, aggressive biased,

10. **Discovering the ideas in writing that are <u>not stated directly</u> is called making inferences, or drawing conclusions. What inferences did you draw from the article you read?** <u>Explain</u>.

Hes, confused, delusional, envious, sinister

11. **Authors often use connotative language. Return to the reading selection and circle (in red or green) all connotative words. List 10 of those words here and explain how those words might affect the reader.**

prejudice, abolish, ablaze, barbarian, egotistical

How the connotative words above might affect the reader:

12. **A good argument makes a point and then provides persuasive and logical evidence to back it up. However, a bad argument uses fallacies to support itself such as changing the subject, hasty generalization, circular reasoning, personal attack, straw man, false cause, false comparison, or either-or. Explain how the author supports his/her argument.** <u>Does he/she use relevant and adequate support, or do fallacies exist?</u> **Explain.**

Change the subject, circular reasoning, hasty generalization

13. **The seven most common propaganda techniques are bandwagon, testimonial, transfer, plain folks, name calling, glittering generalities, and card staking.** <u>Which techniques are used in this reading selection?</u> **Explain.**

Bandwagon, testimonial & transfer, name calling, glittering generalities

Theme 3
Civil Rights

Theme 3 takes us from the narrative of what slavery was like from the pen of a nearly self-educated slave to the dream of a Black Southern preacher a hundred years later.

What evil causes one human being to enslave another? What is the effect on the slaveholder who practices this evil? What type of man or woman gathers the courage to speak out about slavery? Why do "good" people so often remain silent in the face of injustice? What would you do in a similar circumstance?

This section is a journey from enslavement - to possibility - to promise - to freedom - to acceptance - to tolerance - and eventually (maybe?) to true brotherhood and sisterhood.

FREDERICK DOUGLASS
From **Narrative of the Life of Frederick Douglass, an American Slave**

My Kind Mistress

My new mistress proved to be all she appeared when I first met her at the door, —a woman of the kindest heart and finest feelings. She had never had a slave under her control previously to myself, and prior to her marriage she had been dependent upon her own industry for a living. She was by trade a weaver; and by constant application to her business, she had been in a good degree preserved from the blighting and dehumanizing effects of slavery. I was utterly astonished at her goodness. I scarcely knew how to behave towards her. She was entirely unlike any other white woman I had ever seen. I could not approach her as I was accustomed to approach other white ladies. My early instruction was all out of place. The crouching servility, usually so acceptable a quality in a slave, did not answer when manifested toward her. Her favor was not gained by it; she seemed to be disturbed by it. She did not deem it impudent or unmannerly for a slave to look her in the face. The meanest slave was put fully at ease in her presence, and none left without feeling better for having seen her. Her face was made of heavenly smiles, and her voice of tranquil music.

2   But, alas! This kind heart had but a short time to remain such. The fatal poison of irresponsible power was already in her hands, and soon commenced its infernal work. That cheerful eye, under the influence of slavery, soon became red with rage; that voice, made all of sweet accord, changed to one of harsh and horrid discord; and that angelic face gave place to that of a demon.

Unlawful to Teach a Slave to Read & Write

3   Very soon after I went to live with Mr. And Mrs. Auld, she very kindly commenced to teach me the A, B, C. After I had learned this, she assisted me in learning to spell words of three or four letters. Just at this point of my progress, Mr. Auld found out what was going on, and at once forbade Mrs. Auld to instruct me further telling her, among other things, that it was unlawful, as well as unsafe, to teach a slave to read. To use his own words, further, he said, "If you give a nigger an inch, he will take an ell. A nigger should know nothing but to obey his master— to do as he is told to do. Learning would *spoil* the best nigger in the world.   Now," said he, "if you teach that nigger (speaking of myself) how to read, there would he no keeping him. It would forever unfit him to be a slave. He would at once become unmanageable, and of no value to his master. As to himself, it could do him no good, but a great deal of harm. It would make him discontented and unhappy." These words sank deep into my heart, stirred up sentiments within that lay slumbering, and called into existence an entirely new train of thought. It was a new and special revelation, explaining dark and mysterious things, with which my youthful understanding had struggled, but struggled in vain. I now understood what had been to me a most perplexing difficulty—to wit, the white man's power to enslave the black man. It was a grand achievement, and I prized it highly. From that moment, I understood the pathway from slavery to freedom. It was just what I wanted, and I got it at a time when I the least expected it. Whilst I was saddened by the thought of losing the aid of my kind mistress, I was gladdened by the invaluable instruction which, by the merest accident, I had gained from my master. Though conscious of the difficulty of learning without a teacher, I set out with high hope, and a fixed purpose, at whatever cost of trouble, to learn how to read. The very decided manner with which he spoke, and strove to impress his wife with the evil consequences of giving me instruction, served to convince me that he was deeply sensible of

the truths he was uttering. It gave me the best assurance that I might rely with the utmost confidence on the results which, he said, would flow from teaching me to read. What he most dreaded, that I most desired. What he most loved, that I most hated. That which to him was a great evil, to be carefully shunned, was to me a great good, to be diligently sought; and the argument which he so warmly urged, against my learning to read, only served to inspire me with a desire and determination to learn. In learning to read, I owe almost as much to the bitter opposition of my master, as to the kindly aid of my mistress. I acknowledge the benefit of both.

City Slaves Vs Plantation Slaves

4   I had resided but a short time in Baltimore before I observed a marked difference, in the treatment of slaves, from that which I had witnessed in the country. A city slave is almost a freeman, compared with a slave on the plantation. He is much better fed and clothed, and enjoys privileges altogether unknown to the slave on the plantation. There is a vestige of decency, a sense of shame that does much to curb and check those outbreaks of atrocious cruelty so commonly enacted upon the plantation. He is a desperate slaveholder, who will shock the humanity of his nonslaveholding neighbors with the cries of his lacerated slave. Few are willing to incur the odium attaching to the reputation of being a cruel master; and above all things, they would not be known as not giving a slave enough to eat. Every city slaveholder is anxious to have it known of him, that he feeds his slaves well; and it is due to them to say, that most of them do give their slaves enough to eat. There are, however, some painful exceptions to this rule. Directly opposite to us, on Philpot Street, lived Mr. Thomas Hamilton. He owned two slaves. Their names were Henrietta and Mary. Henrietta was about twenty-two years of age, Mary was about fourteen; and of all the mangled and emaciated creatures I ever looked upon, these two were the most so. His heart must be harder than stone that could look upon these unmoved. The head, neck, and shoulders of Mary were

literally cut to pieces. I have frequently felt her head, and found it nearly covered with festering sores, caused by the lash of her cruel mistress. I do not know that her master ever whipped her, but I have been an eye-witness to the cruelty of Mrs. Hamilton. I used to be in Mr. Hamilton's house nearly every day. Mrs. Hamilton used to sit in a large chair in the middle of the room, with a heavy cowskin always by her side, and scarce an hour passed during the day but was marked by the blood of one of these slaves. The girls seldom passed her without her saying, "Move faster, you *black gip!*" at the same time giving them a blow with the cowskin over the head or shoulders, often drawing the blood. She would then say, "Take that, you *black gip!*" — continuing, "If you don't move faster, I'll move you!" Added to the cruel lashings to which these slaves were subjected, they were kept nearly half-starved. They seldom knew what it was to eat a full meal. I have seen Mary contending with the pigs for the offal thrown into the street. So much was Mary kicked and cut to pieces, that she was oftener called "*pecked*" than by her name.

From an Angel to a Demon

5   I lived in Master Hugh's family about seven years. During this time, I succeeded in learning to read and write. In accomplishing this, I was compelled to resort to various stratagems. I had no regular teacher. My mistress, who had kindly commenced to instruct me, had, in compliance with the advice and direction of her husband, not only ceased to instruct, but had set her face against my being instructed by any one else. It is due, however, to my mistress to say of her, that she did not adopt this course of treatment immediately. She at first lacked the depravity indispensable to shutting me up in mental darkness. It was at least necessary for her to have some training in the exercise of irresponsible power, to make her equal to the task of treating me as though I were a brute.

6   My mistress was, as I have said, a kind and tender-hearted woman; and in the simplicity of her soul she commenced, when I first went to live with her, to treat me as she supposed one human being ought to treat another. In entering upon the duties of a slaveholder,

she did not seem to perceive that I sustained to her the relation of a mere chattel, and that for her to treat me as a human being was not only wrong, but dangerously so. Slavery proved as injurious to her as it did to me. When I went there, she was a pious, warm, and tender-hearted woman. There was no sorrow or suffering for which she had not a tear. She had bread for the hungry, clothes for the naked, and comfort for every mourner that came within her reach. Slavery soon proved its ability to divest her of these heavenly qualities. Under its influence, the tender heart became stone, and the lamblike disposition gave way to one of tiger-like fierceness. The first step in her downward course was in her ceasing to instruct me. She now commenced to practice her husband's precepts. She finally became even more violent in her opposition than her husband himself. She was not satisfied with simply doing as well as he had commanded; she seemed anxious to do better. Nothing seemed to make her more angry than to see me with a newspaper. She seemed to think that here lay the danger. I have had her rush at me with a face made all up of fury, and snatch from me a newspaper, in a manner that fully revealed her apprehension. She was an apt woman; and a little experience soon demonstrated, to her satisfaction, that education and slavery were incompatible with each other.

7   From this time I was most narrowly watched. If I was in a separate room any considerable length of time, I was sure to be suspected of having a book, and was at once called to give an account of myself. All this, however, was too late. The first step bad been taken. Mistress, in teaching me the alphabet, had given me the *inch*, and no precaution could prevent me from taking the *ell*.

My Helpers

8   The plan which I adopted, and the one by which I was most successful, was that of making friends of all the little white boys whom I met in the street. As many of these as I could, I converted into teachers. With their kindly aid, obtained at different times and in different places, I finally succeeded in learning to read. When I was sent to errands, I always took my book with me,

and by going one part of my errand quickly, I found time to get a lesson before my return. I used also to carry bread with me, enough of which was always in the house, and to which I was always welcome; for I was much better off in this regard than many of the poor white children in our neighborhood. This bread I used to bestow upon the hungry little urchins, who, in return, would give me that more valuable bread of knowledge. I am strongly tempted to give the names of two or three of those little boys, as a testimonial of the gratitude and affection I bear them; but prudence forbids; —not that it would injure me, but it might embarrass them; for it is almost an unpardonable offence to teach slaves to read in this Christian country. It is enough to say of the dear little fellows, that they lived on Philpot Street, very near Durgin and Bailey's ship-yard. I used to talk this matter of slavery over with them. I would sometimes say to them, I wished I could be as free as they would be when they got to be men. "You will be free as soon as you are twenty-one, but *I am a slave for life*! Have not I as good a right to be free as you have?" These words used to trouble them; they would express for me the liveliest sympathy, and console me with the hope that something would occur by which I might be free.

The Columbian Orator & Emancipation

9   I was now about twelve years old, and the thought of being *a slave for life* began to bear heavily upon my heart. Just about this time, I got hold of a hook entitled "The Columbian Orator." Every opportunity I got, I used to read this book. Among much of other interesting matter, I found in it a dialogue between a master and his slave. The slave was represented as having run away from his master three times. The dialogue represented the conversation which took place between them, when the slave was retaken the third time. In this dialogue, the whole argument in behalf of slavery was brought forward by the master, all of which was disposed of by the slave. The slave was made to say some very smart as well as impressive things in reply to his master—things which had the desired though unexpected effect; for the conversation

resulted in the voluntary emancipation of the slave on the part of the master.

Ignorance is Bliss?

10   In the same book, I met with one of Sheridan's mighty speeches on and in behalf of Catholic emancipation. These were choice documents to me. I read them over and over again with unabated interest. They gave tongue to interesting thoughts of my own soul, which had frequently flashed through my mind, and died away for want of utterance. The moral which I gained from the dialogue was the power of truth over the conscience of even a slaveholder. What I got from Sheridan was a bold denunciation of slavery, and a powerful vindication of human rights. The reading of these documents enabled me to utter my thoughts, and to meet the arguments brought forward to sustain slavery; but while they relieved me of one difficulty, they brought on another even more painful than the one of which I was relieved. The more I read, the more I was led to abhor and detest my enslavers. I could regard them in no other light than a band of successful robbers, who had left their homes, and gone to Africa, and stolen us from our homes, and in a strange land reduced us to slavery. I loathed them as being the meanest as well as the most wicked of men. As I read and contemplated the subject, behold! That very discontentment which Master Hugh had predicted would follow my learning to read had already come, to torment and sting my soul to unutterable anguish. As I writhed under it, I would at times feel that learning to read had been a curse rather than a blessing. It had given me a view of my wretched condition, without the remedy. It opened my eyes to the horrible pit, but to no ladder upon which to get out. In moments of agony, I envied my fellow-slaves for their stupidity. I have often wished myself a beast. I preferred the condition of the meanest reptile to my own. Any thing, no matter what, to get rid of thinking! It was this everlasting thinking of my condition that tormented me. There was no getting rid of it. It was pressed upon me by every object within sight or hearing, animate or inanimate. The silver trump of freedom had roused my soul to eternal

wakefulness. Freedom now appeared, to disappear no more forever. It was heard in every sound, and seen in every thing. It was ever present to torment me with a sense of my wretched condition. I saw nothing without seeing it, I heard nothing without hearing it, and felt nothing without feeling it. It looked from every star, it smiled in every calm, breathed in every wind, and moved in every storm.

11   I often found myself regretting my own existence, and wishing myself dead; and but for the hope of being free, I have no doubt but that I should have killed myself, or done something for which I should have been killed. While in this state of mind, I was eager to hear any one speak of slavery. I was a ready listener. Every little while, I could hear something about the abolitionists. It was some time before I found what the word meant. It was always used in such connections as to make it an interesting word to me. If a slave ran away and succeeded in getting clear, or if a slave killed his master, set fire to a ham, or did any thing very wrong in the mind of a slaveholder, it was spoken of as the fruit of *abolition*. Hearing the word in this connection very often, I set about learning what it meant. The dictionary afforded me little or no help. I found it was "the act of abolishing"; but then I did not know what was to be abolished. Here I was perplexed. I did not dare to ask any one about its meaning, for I was satisfied that it was something they wanted me to know very little about. After a patient waiting, I got one of our city papers, containing an account of the number of petitions from the north, praying for the abolition of slavery in the District of Columbia, and of the slave trade between the States. From this time I understood the words **abolition** and **abolitionist**, and always drew near when that word was spoken, expecting to hear something of importance to myself and fellow-slaves. The light broke in upon me by degrees. I went one day down on the wharf of Mr. Waters; and seeing two Irishmen unloading a scow of stone, I went, unasked, and helped them. When we had finished, one of them came to me and asked me if I were a slave. I told him I was. He asked, "Are ye a slave for life?" I told him that I was. The good Irishman seemed to be deeply affected by the statement. He said

to the other that it was a pity so fine a little fellow as myself should be a slave for life. He said it was a shame to hold me. They both advised me to run away to the north; that I should find friends there, and that I should be free. I pretended not to be interested in what they said, and treated them as if I did not understand them; for I feared they might be treacherous. White men have been known to encourage slaves to escape, and then, to get the reward, catch them and return them to their masters. I was afraid that these seemingly good men might use me so; but I nevertheless remembered their advice, and from that time I resolved to run away. I looked forward to a time at which it would be safe for me to escape. I was too young to think of doing so immediately; besides, I wished to learn how to write, as I might have occasion to write my own pass. I consoled myself with the hope that I should one day find a good chance. Meanwhile, I would learn to write.

Learning to Write

12   The idea as to how might learn to write was suggested to me by being in Durgin and Bailey's ship-yard, and frequently seeing the ship carpenters, after hewing, and getting a piece of timber ready for use, write on the timber the name of that part of the ship for which it was intended. When a piece of timber was intended for the larboard side, it would be marked thus— "L." When a piece was for the starboard side, it would be marked thus— "S." A piece for the larboard side forward, would be marked thus— "L.F." When a piece was for starboard side forward, it would be marked thus—"S.F." For larboard aft, it would he marked thus-"L.A." For starboard aft, it would be marked thus—".S.A." I soon learned the names of these letters, and for what they were intended when placed upon a piece of timber in the ship-yard. I immediately commenced copying them, and in a short time was able to make the four letters named. After that, when I met with any boy who I knew could write, I would tell him I could write as well as he. The next word would be, "I don't believe you. Let me see you try it." I would then make the letters which I had been so fortunate as to learn, and ask him to beat that. In this

way I got a good many lessons in writing, which it is quite possible I should never have gotten in any other way. During this time, my copy-book was the board fence, brick wall, and pavement; my pen and ink was a lump of chalk. With these, I learned mainly how to write. I then commenced and continued copying the Italics in Webster's Spelling Book, until I could make them all without looking on the book. By this time, my little Master Thomas had gone to school, and learned how to write, and had written over a number of copy-books. These had been brought home, and shown to some of our near neighbors, and then laid aside. My mistress used to go to class meeting at the Wilk Street meeting-house every Monday afternoon, and leave me to take care of the house. When left thus, I used to spend the time in writing in the spaces left in Master Thomas's copy-book, copying what he had written. I continued to do this until I could write a hand very similar to that of Master Thomas. Thus, after a long, tedious effort for years, I finally succeeded in learning how to write.

The Valuation and Division

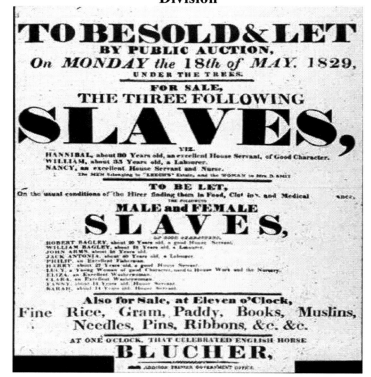

13   In a very short time after I went to live at Baltimore, my old master's youngest son Richard died; and in about three years and six months after his death, my old master, Captain Anthony, died, leaving only his son, Andrew, and daughter, Lucretia, to share his estate. He died while on a visit to see his daughter at Hillsborough.   Cut off thus unexpectedly, he left no will as to the disposal of his property. It was therefore necessary to have a valuation of the property, that it might be equally' divided between Mrs. Lucretia and Master Andrew.   I was immediately sent for, to be valued with the other property. Here again my feelings rose up in detestation of slavery.   I had now a new conception of my degraded condition.   Prior to this, bad become, if not insensible to my lot, at least partly so.   I left Baltimore with a young heart overborne with sadness, and a soul full of apprehension.   I took passage with Captain Rowe, in the schooner Wild Cat, and, after a sail of about twenty-four hours, I found myself near the place of my birth.   I had now been absent from it almost, if not quite, five years.   I, however, remembered the place very well. I was only about five years old when I left it, to go and live with my old master on Colonel Lloyd's plantation; so that I was now between ten and eleven years old.

14   We were all ranked together at the valuation. Men and women, old and young, married and single, were ranked with horses, sheep, and swine. There were horses and men, cattle and women, pigs and children, all holding the same rank in the scale of being, and were all subjected to the same narrow examination. Silvery-headed age and sprightly youth, maids and matrons, had to undergo the same indelicate inspection. At this moment, I saw more clearly than ever the brutalizing effects of slavery upon both slave and slaveholder.

15   After the valuation, then came the division. I have no language to express the high excitement and deep anxiety which were felt among us poor slaves during this time. Our fate for life was now to be decided. We had no more voice in that decision than the brutes among whom we were ranked. A single word from the white men was enough— against all our wishes, prayers, and entreaties— to sunder forever the dearest

friends, dearest kindred, and strongest ties known to human beings. In addition to the pain of separation, there was the horrid dread of falling into the hands of Master Andrew. He was known to us all as being a most cruel wretch,— a common drunkard, who had, by his reckless mismanagement and profligate dissipation, already wasted a large portion of his father's property. We all felt that we might as well be sold at once to the Georgia traders, as to pass into his hands; for we knew that that would be our inevitable condition,— a condition held by us all in the utmost horror and dread.

16 I suffered more anxiety than most of my fellow-slaves. I had known what it was to be kindly treated; they had known nothing of the kind. They had seen little or nothing of the world. They were in very deed men and women of sorrow, and acquainted with grief. Their backs had been made familiar with the bloody lash, so that they had become callous; mine was yet tender; for while at Baltimore I got few whippings, and few slaves could boast of a kinder master and mistress than myself; and the thought of passing out of their hands into those of Master Andrew— a man who, but a few days before, to give me a sample of his bloody disposition, took my little brother by the throat, threw him on the ground, and with the heel of his boot stamped upon his head till the blood gushed from his nose and ears— was well calculated to make me anxious as to my fate. After he had committed this savage outrage upon my brother, he turned to me, and said that was the way he meant to serve me one of these days— meaning, I suppose, when I came into his possession.

Grandmother

17 Thanks to a kind Providence, I fell to the portion of Mrs. Lucretia, and was sent immediately back to Baltimore, to live again in the family of Master Hugh. Their joy at my return equalled their sorrow at my departure. It was a glad day to me. I had escaped a worse fate than lion's jaws. I was absent from Baltimore, for the purpose of valuation and division, just about one month, and it seemed to have been six.

18 Very soon after my return to Baltimore, my

172

mistress, Lucretia, died, leaving her husband and child, Amanda; and in a very short time after her death, Master Andrew died. Now all the property of my old master, slaves included, was in the hands of strangers— strangers who had had nothing to do with accumulating it. Not a slave was left free. All remained slaves, from the youngest to the oldest. If any one thing in my experience, more than another, served to deepen my conviction of the infernal character of slavery, and to fill me with unutterable loathing of slaveholders, it was their base in-gratitude to my poor old grandmother. She had served my old master faithfully from youth to old age. She had been the source of all his wealth; she had peopled his plantation with slaves; she had become a great grandmother in his service. She had rocked him in in-fancy, attended him in childhood, served him through life, and at his death wiped from his icy brow the cold death-sweat, and closed his eyes forever. She was nevertheless left a slave— a slave for life— a slave in the hands of strangers; and in their hands she saw her children, her grandchildren, and her great-grandchildren, divided, like so many sheep, without being gratified with the small privilege of a single word, as to their or her own destiny. And, to cap the climax of their base ingratitude and fiendish barbarity, my grandmother, who was now very old, having outlived my old master and all his children, having seen the beginning and end of all of them, and her present owners finding she was of but little value, her frame already racked with the pains of old age, and complete helplessness fast stealing over her once active limbs, they took her to the woods, built her a little hut, put up a little mud-chimney, and then made her welcome to the privilege of supporting herself there in the perfect loneliness; thus virtually turning her out to die! If my poor old grand-mother now lives, she lives to suffer in utter loneliness; she lives to remember and mourn over the loss of children, the loss of grand-

173

children, and the loss of great-grandchildren. They are, in the language of the slave's poet, Whittier,—

> *Gone, gone, sold and gone*
> *To the rice swamp dank and lone,*
> *Where the slave-whip ceaseless*
> *swings,*
> *Where the noisome insect stings,*
> *Where the fever-demon strews*
> *Poison with the failing dews,*
> *Where the sickly sunbeams glare*
> *Through the hot and misty air:—*
> *Gone, gone, sold and gone*
> *To the rice swamp dank and tone,*
> *From Virginia hills and waters—*
> *Woe is me, my stolen daughters.*

19   The hearth is desolate. The children, the unconscious children, who once sang and danced in her presence, are gone. She gropes her way, in the darkness of age, for a drink of water. Instead of the voices of her children, she hears by day the moans of the dove, and by night the screams of the hideous owl. All is gloom. The grave is at the door. And now, when weighed down by the pains and aches of old age, when the head inclines to the feet, when the beginning and ending of human existence meet, and helpless infancy and painful old age combine together— at this time, this most needful time, the time for the exercise of that tenderness and affection which children only can exercise towards a declining parent— my poor old grandmother, the devoted mother of twelve children, is left all alone, in yonder little hut, before a few dim embers. She stands— she sits— she staggers— she falls— she groans— she dies— and there are none of her children or grandchildren present, to wipe from her wrinkled brow the cold sweat of death, or to place beneath the sod her fallen remains. Will not a righteous God visit for these things?

20   In about two years after the death of Mrs. Lucretia, Master Thomas married his second wife. Her name was Rowena Hamilton. She was the eldest daughter of Mr. William Hamilton. Master now lived in St. Michael's.

Not long after his marriage, a misunderstanding took place between himself and Master Hugh; and as a means of punishing his brother, he took me from him to live with himself at St. Michael's. Here I underwent another most painful separation. It, however, was not so severe as the one I dreaded at the division of property; for, during this interval, a great change had taken place in Master Hugh and his once kind and affectionate wife. The influence of brandy upon him, and of slavery upon her, had effected a disastrous change in the characters of both; so that, as far as they were concerned, I thought I had little to lose by the change. But it was not to them that I was attached. It was to those little Baltimore boys that I felt the strongest attachment. I had received many good lessons from them, and was still receiving them, and the thought of leaving them was painful indeed. I was leaving, too, without the hope of ever being allowed to return. Master Thomas had said he would

never let me return again. The barrier betwixt himself and brother he considered impassable.

21   I then had to regret that I did not at least make the attempt to carry out my resolution to run away; for the chances of success are tenfold greater from the city than from the country.

22   I sailed from Baltimore for St. Michael's in the sloop Amanda, Captain Edward Dodson.   On my passage, I paid particular attention to the direction which the steamboats took to go to Philadelphia.   I found, instead of going down, on reaching North Point they went up the bay, in a north-easterly direction. I deemed this knowledge of the utmost importance. My determination to run away was again revived.   I resolved to wait only so long as the offering of a favorable opportunity.   When that came, I was determined to be off.

The questions that follow may be used for further discussion of the reading selection or as topics for essay writing.

1. Douglass portrays Mrs. Auld first as an angel and then as a demon. Notice the connotations that each of those words have. Can you think of any other words that could appropriately replace those words and still be as effective?

2. What effect did slavery have on Mrs. Auld? Do you think that similar effects occurred to other slave holders? Do you think that those who were born as slave holders ever knew any other type of personality or lifestyle? Were the slaveholders enslaved mentally perhaps without even realizing it?

3. Douglass discovered that ignorance is enslavement and that an education could mean freedom. Research some more about the life of Frederick Douglass and explain how this realization manifested in his own life and accomplishments.

4. What effect does slavery have on a society? Discuss several societies that had slavery as contrasted to those that didn't have slavery.

5. The Irish men at the docks were indentured servants – enslaved for a set period of time - perhaps to gain transportation to America. Besides Black slavery, what other types of slavery have existed?

6. _____
   _____
   _____
   _____
   _____
   _____

7. _____
   _____
   _____
   _____
   _____

Applying Reading Skills
(Neatly **PRINT** all answers using ink **not** pencil)

Title of the Reading Selection: _____

1. **What is the author's overall main idea, (central point, or thesis)?**

    Life of a slave and evil treatment of slaves in America
    and his struggle in learning how to read and write.

2. **There are two kinds of supporting details--major and minor. Major details are the primary points that support the main idea and minor details expand major details. List three details and explain how they support the author's primary point?**

Details used	Explanation of how they support the thesis
1. _Unlawful to teach read and write._	

Details used	Explanation of how they support the thesis
2. _City slaves and plantation slaves_	

Details used	Explanation of how they support the thesis
3. _Two girls were whipped and beaten._	

3. **The five major patterns of organization are the list of items pattern, the time order pattern, the example pattern, the comparison and/or contrast pattern, and the cause/effect pattern. What is the <u>main</u> pattern of organization used in this article? <u>Explain</u> why it is the major pattern. What other patterns are used? Give some examples.**

Main pattern: _Time Order_

Explain how the main pattern was used:
_____

Other pattern(s) used: _Cause /effect / examples_

Explain how the additional pattern(s) were used:
_____
_____

177

4. **If applicable: Give <u>two</u> examples that were used in the writing. <u>Explain</u> how they affected your understanding of the reading selection.**

The example(s) given	How example(s) contributed to your understanding
1. Regrets his own existence	1.
2. Mr. Auld's anger and statement	2.

5. **If applicable: what is being compared and/or contrasted?**

Show <u>two</u> comparisons between items A and B:

A	B
slave Men, women, kids	animals
heart	stone
Bread food	Bread of knowledge.

Show <u>two</u> contrasts between items A and B:

A	B
Ignorance	Bliss
Worst fate	lion jaws

6. **Show <u>two</u> cause/effect relationships:**

Cause	Effect
1. like an angel	like devil
City slave	Plantation slaves
2. blacks	white
lamb -like	tiger -like -

7. **List <u>three</u> facts and <u>three</u> opinions from the article. <u>Explain why</u> it is either a fact or an opinion.**

	Explanation:
A.) fact: he's slave	A.)
B.) fact: learned to read and write mostly on his own	B.)
C.) fact: Grandma is the woods	C.)

	Explanation:
A.) opinion _I am slave for life_	A.)
B.) opinion: _Learning would spoil a slave_	B.)
C.) opinion: _City slave almost a free man_	C.)

8. **What is the author's purpose in this article? Is it to inform, persuade, or entertain? <u>Tell me how you arrived at that conclusion.</u>**

persuade, enslaving a human beings is inhumane and unlawful.

9. **What is the author's tone? <u>Explain your answer.</u>**

Angry, sad, determined.

10. **Discovering the ideas in writing that are <u>not stated directly</u> is called making inferences, or drawing conclusions. What inferences did you draw from the article you read? <u>Explain.</u>**

Probably going to get his freedom. He learns read & write well.   He becomes successful.

11. **Authors often use connotative language. Return to the reading selection and circle (in red or green) all connotative words. List 10 of those words here and explain how those words might affect the reader.**

Treacherous, nigger, curse, slaveholder, brutalizing, angel, demon, loath, wicked, abolition, mourn, supremacy, hideous.

How the connotative words above might affect the reader:

Testimonial - his own testimony, heavenly, angelic.

12. A good argument makes a point and then provides persuasive and logical evidence to back it up. However, a bad argument uses fallacies to support itself such as changing the subject, hasty generalization, circular reasoning, personal attack, straw man, false cause, false comparison, or either-or. Explain how the author supports his/her argument. <u>Does he/she use relevant and adequate support, or do fallacies exist?</u> <u>Explain.</u>

13. The seven most common propaganda techniques are bandwagon, testimonial, transfer, plain folks, name calling, glittering generalities, and card staking. <u>Which techniques are used in this reading selection? Explain.</u>

Civil Disobedience
(1849)
HENRY DAVID THOREAU

This edition is slightly abridged from the original document-editor.

Government

I heartily accept the motto—"That government is best which governs least," and I should like to see it acted up to more rapidly and systematically. Carried out, it finally amounts to this, which also I believe— "That government is best which governs not at all"; and when men are prepared for it, that will be the kind of government which they will have. Government is at best but an expedient; but most governments are usually, and all governments are sometimes, inexpedient. The objections which have been brought against a standing army, and they are many and weighty, and deserve to prevail, may also at last be brought against a standing government. The standing army is only an arm of the standing government. The government itself, which is only the mode which the people have chosen to execute their will, is equally liable to be abused and perverted before the people can act through it. Witness the present Mexican war, the work of comparatively a few individuals using the standing government as their tool; for in the outset the people would not have consented to this measure.

2   This American government—what is it but a tradition, a recent one, endeavoring to transmit itself unimpaired to posterity but each instant losing some of its integrity? It has not the vitality and force of a single living man; for a single man can bend it to his will. It is a sort of wooden gun to the people themselves. But it is not the less necessary for this; for the people must have some complicated machinery or other, and hear its din, to satisfy that idea of government which they have. Governments show thus how successfully men can be imposed on, even impose on themselves, for their own advantage. It is excellent, we must all allow. Yet this government never of itself furthered any enterprise but by the alacrity with which it got out of its way. It does

not keep the country free. It does not settle the West. It does not educate. The character inherent in the American people has done all that has been accomplished; and it would have done somewhat more if the government had not sometimes got in its way. For government is an expedient by which men would fain succeed in letting one another alone; and, as has been said, when it is most expedient the governed are most let alone by it. Trade and commerce, if they were not made of India-rubber, would never manage to bounce over the obstacles which legislators are continually putting in their way; and, if one were to judge these men wholly by the effects of their actions and not partly by their intentions, they would deserve to be classed and punished with those mischievous persons who put obstructions on the railroads.

3   But to speak practically and as a citizen, unlike those who call themselves no-government men, I ask for, not at once no government, but *at once* a better government. Let every man make known what kind of government would command his respect, and that will be one step toward obtaining it.

4   After all, the practical reason why, when the power is once in the hands of the people, a majority are permitted, and for a long period continue, to rule is not because they are most likely to be in the right, nor because this seems fairest to the minority but because they are physically the strongest. But a government in which the majority rule in all cases cannot be based on justice, even as far as men understand it. Can there not be a government in which majorities do not virtually decide right and wrong but conscience?—in which majorities decide only those questions to which the rule of expediency is applicable? Must the citizen ever for a moment, or in the least degree, resign his conscience to the legislator? Why has every man a conscience then? I think that we should be men first and subjects afterward. It is not desirable to cultivate a respect for the law, so much as for the right. The only obligation which I have a right to assume is to do at any time what I think right. It is truly enough said that a corporation has no conscience; but a corporation of conscientious men is a corporation *with* a conscience. Law never made men a

whit more just; and, by means of their respect for it, even the well disposed are daily made the agents of injustice. A common and natural result of an undue respect for law is that you may see a file of soldiers, colonel, captain, corporal, privates, powder-monkeys, and all, marching in admirable order over hill and dale to the wars, against their wills, ay, against their common sense and consciences, which makes it very steep marching indeed and produces a palpitation of the heart. They have no doubt that it is a damnable business in which they are concerned; they are all peaceably inclined. Now, what are they? Men at all? or small movable forts and magazines at the service of some unscrupulous man in power? Visit the Navy Yard, and behold a marine, such a man as an American government can make, or such as it can make a man with its black arts—a mere shadow and reminiscence of humanity, a man laid out alive and standing, and already, as one may say, buried under arms with funeral accompaniments, though it may be—

Not a drum was heard, not a funeral note,
As his corpse to the rampart we hurried;
Not a soldier discharged his farewell shot
O'er the grave where our hero we

Serving the State

5   The mass of men serve the state thus, not as men mainly, but as machines, with their bodies. They are the standing army, and the militia, jailers, constables, posse comitatus, &c. In most cases there is no free exercise whatever of the judgment or of the moral sense; but they put themselves on a level with wood and earth and stones; and wooden men can perhaps be manufactured that will serve the purpose as well. Such command no more respect than men of straw or a lump of dirt. They have the same sort of worth only as horses and dogs. Yet such as these even are commonly esteemed good citizens. Others--as most legislators, politicians, lawyers, ministers, and office-holders— serve the state chiefly with their heads; and, as they rarely make any moral distinctions, they are as likely to serve the Devil,

without *intending* it, as God. A very few, as heroes, patriots, martyrs, reformers in the great sense, and *men,* serve the state with their consciences also and so necessarily resist it for the most part; and they are commonly treated as enemies by it. A wise man will only be useful as a man and will not submit to be "clay" and "stop a hole to keep the wind away."

6   He who gives himself entirely to his fellow-men appears to them useless and selfish; but he who gives himself partially to them is pronounced a benefactor and philanthropist.

7   How does it become a man to behave toward this American government today? I answer, that he cannot without disgrace be associated with it. I cannot for an instant recognize that political organization as my government which is the slave's government also.

8   All men recognize the right of revolution; that is, the right to refuse allegiance to, and to resist the government when its tyranny or its inefficiency are great and unendurable. But almost all say that such is not the case now. But such was the case, they think, in the Revolution of '75. If one were to tell me that this was a bad government because it taxed certain foreign commodities brought to its ports, it is most probable that I should not make an ado about it, for I can do without them. All machines have their friction; and possibly this does enough good to counterbalance the evil. At any rate, it is a great evil to make a stir about it. But when the friction comes to have its machine, and oppression and robbery are organized, I say let us not have such a machine any longer. In other words, when a sixth of the population of a nation which has undertaken to be the refuge of liberty are slaves, and a whole country is unjustly overrun and conquered by a foreign army and subjected to military law, I think that it is not too soon for honest men to rebel and revolutionize. What makes this duty the more urgent is the fact that the country so overrun is not our own, but ours is the invading army.

185

Moral Questions & Expediency

9   Paley, a common authority with many on moral questions, in his chapter on the "Duty of Submission to Civil Government," resolves all civil obligation into expediency; and he proceeds to say, "that so long as the interest of the whole society requires it, that is, so long as the established government cannot be resisted or charged without public inconveniency, it is the will of God that the established government be obeyed, and no longer.... This principle being admitted, the justice of every particular case of resistance is reduced to a computation of the quantity of the danger and grievance on the one side, and of the probability and expense of redressing it on the other." Of this, he says, every man shall judge for himself. But Paley appears never to have contemplated those cases to which the rule of expediency does not apply, in which a people, as well as an individual, must do justice, cost what it may. If I have unjustly wrested a plank from a drowning man, I must restore it to him though I drown myself. This, according to Paley, would be inconvenient. But he that would save his life, in such a case, shall lose it. This people must cease to hold slaves and to make war on Mexico, though it cost them their existence as a people.

10 In their practice, nations agree with Paley; but does anyone think that Massachusetts does exactly what is right at the present crisis?

11 Practically speaking, the opponents to a reform in Massachusetts are not a hundred thousand politicians at the South but a hundred thousand merchants and farmers here, who are more interested in commerce and agriculture than they are in humanity, and are not prepared to do justice to the slave and to Mexico, cost what it may. I quarrel not with far-off foes but with those who, near at home, cooperate with, and do the bidding of, those far away, and without whom the latter would be harmless. We are accustomed to say that the mass of men are unprepared; but improvement is slow because the few are not materially wiser or better than the many. It is not so important that many should be as good as you as that there be some absolute goodness

somewhere; for that will leaven the whole lump. There are thousands who are in opinion opposed to slavery and to the war who yet in effect do nothing to put an end to them; who, esteeming themselves children of Washington and Franklin, sit down with their hands in their pockets and say that they know not what to do, and do nothing; who even postpone the question of freedom to the question of free trade, and quietly read the prices-current along with the latest advices from Mexico after dinner and, it may be, fall asleep over them both. What is the price-current of an honest man and patriot today? They hesitate and they regret and sometimes they petition; but they do nothing in earnest and with effect They will wait, well disposed, for others to remedy the evil, that they may no longer have it to regret. At most, they give only a cheap vote, and a feeble countenance and God-speed, to the right, as it goes by them. There are nine hundred and ninety-nine patrons of virtue to one virtuous man. But it is easier to deal with the real possessor of a thing than with the temporary guardian of it.

Voting

12 All voting is a sort of gaming, like checkers or backgammon, with a slight moral tinge to it, a playing with right and wrong, with moral questions; and betting naturally accompanies it. The character of the voters is not staked. I cast my vote, perchance, as I think right; but I am not vitally concerned that that right should prevail. I am willing to leave it to the majority. Its obligation, therefore, never exceeds that of expediency. Even voting *for the right* is *doing* nothing for it. It is only expressing to men feebly your desire that it should prevail. A wise man will not leave the right to the mercy of chance, nor wish it to prevail through the power of the majority. There is but little virtue in the action of masses of men. When the majority shall at length vote for the abolition of slavery, it will be because they are indifferent to slavery, or because there is but little slavery left to be abolished by their vote. *They* will then be the only slaves. Only *his* vote can hasten the abolition of slavery who asserts his own freedom by his

187

vote.

13   I hear of a convention to be held at Baltimore, or elsewhere, for the selection of a candidate for the Presidency, made up chiefly of editors, and men who are politicians by profession; but I think, what is it to any independent, intelligent, and respectable man what decision they may come to? Shall we not have the advantage of his wisdom and honesty nevertheless? Can we not count upon some independent votes? Are there not many individuals in the country who do not attend conventions? But no: I find that the responsible man, so called, has immediately drifted from his position, and despairs of his country when his country has more reason to despair of him. He forthwith adopts one of the candidates thus selected as the only *available* one, thus proving that he is himself *available* for any purposes of the demagogue. His vote is of no more worth than that of any unprincipled foreigner or hireling native who may have been bought. O for a man who is a *man* and, as my neighbor says has a bone in his back which you cannot pass your hand through! Our statistics are at fault: the population has been returned too large. How many *men* are there to a square thousand miles in this country? Hardly one. Does not America offer any inducement for men to settle here? The American has dwindled into an Odd Fellow--one who may be known by the development of his organ of gregariousness and a manifest lack of intellect and cheerful self-reliance; whose first and chief concern, on coming into the world, is to see that the Almshouses are in good repair; and, before yet he has lawfully donned the virile garb, to collect a fund for the support of the widows and orphans that may be; who, in short, ventures to live only by the aid of the Mutual Insurance Company, which has promised to bury him decently.

Wrong Actions

14   It is not a man's duty, as a matter of course, to devote himself to the eradication of any, even the most enormous wrong; he may still properly have other concerns to engage him; but it is his duty, at least, to wash his hands of it and, if he gives it no thought

longer, not to give it practically his support. If I devote myself to other pursuits and contemplations, I must first see, at least, that I do not pursue them sitting upon another man's shoulders. I must get off him first, that he may pursue his contemplations too. See what gross inconsistency is tolerated. I have heard some of my townsmen say, "I should like to have them order me out to help put down an insurrection of the slaves, or to march to Mexico—see if I would go"; and yet these very men have each directly by their allegiance and so indirectly, at least, by their money, furnished a substitute. The soldier is applauded who refuses to serve in an unjust war by those who do not refuse to sustain the unjust government which makes the war; is applauded by those whose own act and authority he disregards and sets at naught; as if the State were penitent to that degree that it hired one to scourge it while it sinned, but not to that degree that it left off sinning for a moment. Thus, under the name of Order and Civil Government, we are all made at last to pay homage to and support our own meanness. After the first blush of sin comes its indifference; and from immoral it becomes, as it were, unmoral, and not quite unnecessary to that life which we have made.

15   The broadest and most prevalent error requires the most disinterested virtue to sustain it. The slight reproach to which the virtue of patriotism is commonly liable, the noble are most likely to incur. Those who, while they disapprove of the character and measures of a government, yield to it their allegiance and support, are undoubtedly its most conscientious supporters, and so frequently the most serious obstacles to reform. Some are petitioning the State to dissolve the Union, to disregard the requisitions of the President. Why do they not dissolve it themselves--the union between themselves and the State— and refuse to pay their quota into its treasury? Do not they stand in the same relation to the State that the State does to the Union? And have not the same reasons prevented the State from resisting the Union which have prevented them from resisting the State?

16   How can a man be satisfied to entertain an opinion merely, and enjoy it? Is there any enjoyment in it if his

opinion is that he is aggrieved? If you are cheated out of a single dollar by your neighbor, you do not rest satisfied with knowing that you are cheated, or with saying that you are cheated, or even with petitioning him to pay you your due; but you take effectual steps at once to obtain the full amount and see that you are never cheated again. Action from principle, the perception and the performance of right, changes things and relations; it is essentially revolutionary and does not consist wholly with anything which was. It not only divides states and churches, it divides families; ay, it divides the *individual,* separating the diabolical in him from the divine.

Just and Unjust Laws

17   Unjust laws exist: shall we be content to obey them, or shall we endeavor to amend them and obey them until we have succeeded, or shall we transgress them at once? Men generally, under such a government as this, think that they ought to wait until they have persuaded the majority to alter them. They think that if they should resist the remedy would be worse than the evil. It makes it worse. Why is it not more apt to anticipate and provide for reform? Why does it not cherish its wise minority? Why does it cry and resist before it is hurt? Why does it not encourage its citizens to be on the alert to point out its faults and *do* better than it would have them? Why does it always crucify Christ and excommunicate Copernicus and Luther and pronounce Washington and Franklin rebels?

18   One would think that a deliberate and practical denial of its authority was the only offence never contemplated by government; else why has it not assigned its definite, its suitable and proportionate penalty? If a man who has no property refuses but once to earn nine shillings for the State, he is put in prison for a period unlimited by any law that I know, and determined only by the discretion of those who placed him there; but if he should steal ninety times nine shillings from the State, he is soon permitted to go at large again.

19   If the injustice is part of the necessary friction of the

machine of government, let it go, let it go: perchance it will wear smooth— certainly the machine will wear out. If the injustice has a spring or a pulley or a rope or a crank exclusively for itself, then perhaps you may consider whether the remedy will not be worse than the evil; but if it is of such a nature that it requires you to be the agent of injustice to another, then I say break the law. Let your life be a counter friction to stop the machine. What I have to do is to see, at any rate, that I do not lend myself to the wrong which I condemn.

20   As for adopting the ways which the State has provided for remedying the evil, I know not of such ways. They take too much time, and a man's life will be gone. I have other affairs to attend to. I came into this world, not chiefly to make this a good place to live in, but to live in it, be it good or bad. A man has not everything to do, but something; and because he cannot do *everything*, it is not necessary that he should do *something* wrong. It is not my business to be petitioning the Governor or the Legislature any more than it is theirs to petition me; and if they should not hear my petition what should I do then? But in this case the State has provided no way; its very Constitution is the evil. This may seem to be harsh and stubborn and unconciliatory; but it is to treat with the utmost kindness and consideration the only spirit that can appreciate or deserves it. So is all change for the better, like birth and death, which convulse the body.

21   I do not hesitate to say that those who call themselves Abolitionists should at once effectually withdraw their support, both in person and property, from the government of Massachusetts, and not wait till they constitute a majority of one before they suffer the right to prevail through them. I think that it is enough if they have God on their side, without waiting for that other one. Moreover, any man more right than his neighbors constitutes a majority of one already.

22   I meet this American government or its representative, the State government, directly and face to face once a year— no more— in the person of its tax-gatherer; this is the only mode in which a man situated as I am necessarily meets it; and it then says distinctly, Recognize me; and the simplest, the most effectual and,

in the present posture of affairs, the indispensablest mode of treating with it on this head, of expressing your little satisfaction with and love for it, is to deny it then. My civil neighbor, the tax-gatherer, is the very man I have to deal with— for it is, after all, with men and not with parchment that I quarrel— and he has voluntarily chosen to be an agent of the government. How shall he ever know well what he is and does as an officer of the government, or as a man, until he is obliged to consider whether he shall treat me, his neighbor, for whom he has respect, as a neighbor and well-disposed man, or as a maniac and disturber of the peace, and see if he can get over this obstruction to his neighborliness without a ruder and more impetuous thought or speech corresponding with his action. I know this well, that if one thousand, if one hundred, if ten men whom I could name— if ten *honest* men only— ay, if *one* HONEST man in this State of Massachusetts, *ceasing to hold slaves,* were actually to withdraw from this co-partnership and be locked up in the county jail therefor, it would be the abolition of slavery in America. For it matters not how small the beginning may seem to be: what is once well done is done forever. But we love better to talk about it: that we say is our mission. Reform keeps many scores of newspapers in its service but not one man. If my esteemed neighbor, the State's ambassador, who will devote his days to the settlement of the question of human rights in the Council Chamber, instead of being threatened with the prisons of Carolina, were to sit down the prisoner of Massachusetts, that State which is so anxious to foist the sin of slavery upon her sister— though at present she can discover only an act of inhospitality to be the ground of a quarrel with her— the Legislature would not wholly waive the subject the following winter.

23   Under a government which imprisons any unjustly, the true   place for a just man is also a prison. The proper place today, the only place which Massachusetts has provided for her freer and less desponding spirits is in her prisons, to be put out and locked out of the State by her own act, as they have already put themselves out by their principles. It is there that the fugitive slave and the Mexican prisoner on parole and the Indian come to

192

plead the wrongs of his race should find them; on that separate but more free and honorable ground where the State places those who are not *with* her but *against* her— the only house in a slave State in which a free man can abide with honor. If any think that their influence would be lost there, and their voices no longer afflict the ear of the State, that they would not be as an enemy within its walls, they do not know by how much truth is stronger than error, nor how much more eloquently and effectively he can combat injustice who has experienced a little in his own person. Cast your whole vote, not a strip of paper merely, but your whole influence. A minority is powerless while it conforms to the majority; it is not even a minority then; but it is irresistible when it clogs by its whole weight. If the alternative is to keep all just men in prison or give up war and slavery, the State will not hesitate which to choose. If a thousand men were not to pay their tax-bills this year, that would not be a violent bloody measure, as it would be to pay them, and enable the State to commit violence and shed innocent blood. This is, in fact, the definition of a peaceable revolution, if any such is possible. If the tax-gatherer or any other public officer asks me, as one has done, "But what shall I do?" my answer is, "If you really wish to do anything, resign your office." When the subject has refused allegiance and the officer has resigned his office, then the revolution is accomplished. But even suppose blood should flow. Is there not a sort of blood shed when the conscience is wounded? Through this wound a man's real manhood and immortality flow out, and he bleeds to an everlasting death. I see this blood flowing now.

24   I have contemplated the imprisonment of the offender rather than the seizure of his goods— though both will serve the same purpose— because they who assert the purest right, and consequently are most dangerous to a corrupt State, commonly have not spent much time in accumulating property. To such the State renders comparatively small service, and a slight tax is wont to appear exorbitant, particularly if they are obliged to earn it by special labor with their hands. If there were one who lived wholly without the use of money, the State itself would hesitate to demand it of

him. But the rich man— not to make any invidious comparison— is always sold to the institution which makes him rich. Absolutely speaking, the more money, the less virtue; for money comes between a man and his objects and obtains them for him; and it was certainly no great virtue to obtain it. It puts to rest many questions which he would otherwise be taxed to answer; while the only new question which it puts is the hard but superfluous one, how to spend it. Thus his moral ground is taken from under his feet. The opportunities of living are diminished in proportion as what are called the "means" are increased. The best thing a man can do for his culture when he is rich is to endeavor to carry out those schemes which he entertained when he was poor. Christ answered the Herodians according to their condition. "Show me the tribute-money," said he— and one took a penny out of his pocket— if you use money which has the image of Caesar on it, and which he has made current and valuable, that is, if *you are men of the State* and gladly enjoy the advantages of Caesar's government, then pay him back some of his own when he demands it; "Render therefore to Caesar that which is Caesar's, and to God those things which are God's"— leaving them no wiser than before as to which was which; for they did not wish to know.

Taxes

25   When I converse with the freest of my neighbors, I perceive that whatever they may say about the magnitude and seriousness of the question, and their regard for the public tranquillity, the long and the short of the matter is that they cannot spare the protection of the existing government, and they dread the consequences to their property and families of disobedience to it. For my own part, I should not like to think that I ever rely on the protection of the State. But if I deny the authority of the State when it presents its tax-bill, it will soon take and waste all my property and so harass me and my children without end. This is hard. This makes it impossible for a man to live honestly, and at the same time comfortably, in outward respects. It will not be worth the while to accumulate property; that

would be sure to go again. You must hire or squat some-where and raise but a small crop and eat that soon. You must live within yourself and depend upon yourself always tucked up and ready for a start, and not have many affairs. A man may grow rich in Turkey even, if he will be in all respects a good subject of the Turkish government. Confucius' said: "If a state is governed by the principles of reason, poverty and misery are subjects of shame; if a state is not governed by the principles of reason, riches and honors are the subjects of shame." No; until I want the protection of Massachusetts to be extended to me in some distant Southern port, where my liberty is endangered, or until I am bent solely on building up an estate at home by peaceful enterprise, I can afford to refuse allegiance to Massachusetts and her right to my property and life. It costs me less in every sense to incur the penalty of disobedience to the State than it would to obey. I should feel as if I were worth less in that case.

26   Some years ago the State met me in behalf of the Church and commanded me to pay a certain sum toward the support of a clergyman whose preaching my father attended, but never I myself. "Pay," it said, "or be locked up in the jail." I declined to pay. But, unfortu-nately, another man saw fit to pay it. I did not see why the schoolmaster should be taxed to support the priest, and not the priest the schoolmaster; for I was not the State's schoolmaster, but I supported myself by voluntary subscription. I did not see why the lyceum should not present its tax-bill and have the State to back its demand, as well as the Church. However, at the request of the selectmen, I condescended to make some such statement as this in writing:—"Know all men by these presents, that I, Henry Thoreau, do not wish to be regarded as a member of any incorporated society which I have not joined." This I gave to the town clerk; and he has it. The State, having thus learned that I did not wish to be regarded as a member of that church, has never made a like demand on me since; though it said that it must adhere to its original presumption that time. If I had known how to name them, I should then have signed off in detail from all the societies which I never signed on to; but I did not know where to find a

complete list.

27 I have paid no poll-tax for six years. I was put into a jail once on this account, for one night; and, as I stood considering the walls of solid stone, two or three feet thick, the door of wood and iron, a foot thick, and the iron grating which strained the light, I could not help being struck with the foolishness of that institution which treated me as if I were mere flesh and blood and bones, to be locked up. I wondered that it should have concluded at length that this was the best use it could put me to and had never thought to avail itself of my services in some way. I saw that if there was a wall of stone between me and my townsmen, there was a still more difficult one to climb or break through before they could get to be as free as I was. I did not for a moment feel confined, and the walls seemed a great waste of stone and mortar. I felt as if I alone of all my townsmen had paid my tax. They plainly did not know how to treat me but behaved like persons who are underbred. In every threat and in every compliment there was a blunder; for they thought that my chief desire was to stand the other side of that stone wall. I could not but smile to see how industriously they locked the door on my meditations, which followed them out again without let or hindrance, and *they* were really all that was dangerous. As they could not reach me, they had resolved to punish my body; just as boys, if they cannot come at some person against whom they have a spite, will abuse his dog. I saw that the State was half-witted, that it was timid as a lone woman with her silver spoons, and that it did not know its friends from its foes, and I lost all my remaining respect for it and pitied it.

Physical Force & a Night in Jail

28 Thus the State never intentionally confronts a man's sense, intellectual or moral, but only his body, his senses. It is not armed with superior wit or honesty but with superior physical strength. I was not born to be forced. I will breathe after my own fashion. Let us see who is the strongest. What force has a multitude? They only can force me who obey a higher law than I. They force me to become like themselves. I do not hear of

men being *forced* to live this way or that by masses of men. What sort of life were that to live? When I meet a government which says to me, "Your money or your life," why should I be in haste to give it my money? It may be in a great strait and not know what to do: I cannot help that. It must help itself; do as I do. It is not worth the while to snivel about it. I am not responsible for the successful working of the machinery of society. I am not the son of the engineer. I perceive that, when an acorn and a chestnut fall side by side, the one does not remain inert to make way for the other, but both obey their own laws and spring and grow and flourish as best they can till one, perchance, overshadows and destroys the other. If a plant cannot live according to its nature, it dies; and so a man.

29   The night in prison was novel and interesting enough. The prisoners in their shirt-sleeves were enjoying a chat and the evening air in the doorway when I entered. But the jailer said, "Come, boys, it is time to lock up"; and so they dispersed, and I heard the sound of their steps returning into the hollow apartments. My room-mate was introduced to me by the jailer as "a first-rate fellow and a clever man." When the door was locked, he showed me where to hang my hat and how he managed matters there. The rooms were whitewashed once a month; and this one, at least, was the whitest, most simply furnished, and probably the neatest apartment in the town. He naturally wanted to know where I came from and what brought me there; and when I had told him, I asked him in my turn how he came there, presuming him to be an honest man, of course; and, as the world goes, I believe he was. "Why," said he, "they accuse me of burning a barn; but I never did it." As near as I could discover, he had probably gone to bed in a barn when drunk and smoked his pipe there; and so a barn burnt. He had the reputation of being a clever man, had been there some three months waiting for his trial to come on, and would have to wait as much longer; but he was quite domesticated and contented, since he got his board for nothing and thought that he was well treated.

30 He occupied one window, and I the other; and I saw that if one stayed there long, his principal business

would be to look out the window. I had soon read all the tracts that were left there and examined where former prisoners had broken out and where a grate had been sawed off and heard the history of the various occupants of that room; for I found that even here there was a history and a gossip which never circulated beyond the walls of the jail. Probably this is the only house in the town where verses are composed, which afterward printed in a circular form but not published. I was shown quite a long list of verses which were composed by some young men who had been detected in an attempt to escape, who avenged themselves by signing them.

31   I pumped my fellow-prisoner as dry as I could, for fear I should never see him again; but at length he showed me which was my bed and left me to blow out the lamp.

32   It was like travelling into a far country, such as I had never expected to behold, to lie there for one night. It seemed to me that I never had heard the town-clock strike before, nor the evening sounds of the village; for we slept with the windows open, which were inside the grating. It was to see my native village in the light of the Middle Ages, and our Concord was turned into a Rhine stream, and visions of knights and castles passed before me. They were the voices of old burghers that I heard in the streets. I was an involuntary spectator and auditor of whatever was done and said in the kitchen of the adjacent village-inn— a wholly new and rare experience to me. It was a closer view of my native town. I was fairly inside of it. I never had seen its institutions before. This is one of its peculiar institutions; for it is a shire town. I began to comprehend what its inhabitants were about.

33   In the morning our breakfasts were put through the hole in the door, in small oblong-square tin pans, made to fit, and holding a pint of chocolate, with brown bread and an iron spoon. When they called for the vessels again, I was green enough to return what bread I had left; but my comrade seized it and said that I should lay that up for lunch or dinner. Soon after he was let out to work at haying in a neighboring field, whither he went every day, and would not be back till noon; so he bade

me good-day, saying that he doubted if he should see me again.

34   When I came out of prison— for someone interfered and paid that tax— I did not perceive that great changes had taken place on the common, such as he observed who went in a youth and emerged a tottering and gray-headed man; and yet a change had to my eyes come over the scene— the town and State and country— greater than any that mere time could effect. I saw yet more distinctly the State in which I lived. I saw to what extent the people among whom I lived could be trusted as good neighbors and friends; that their friendship was for summer weather only; that they did not greatly propose to do right; that they were a distinct race from me by their prejudices and superstitions, as the Chinamen and Malays are; that, in their sacrifices to humanity, they ran no risks, not even to their property; that, after all, they were not so noble but they treated the thief as he had treated them and hoped, by a certain outward observance and a few prayers, and by walking in a particular straight though useless path from time to time, to save their souls. This may be to judge my neighbors harshly; for I believe that many of them are not aware that they have such an institution as the jail in their village.

35   It was formerly the custom in our village, when a poor debtor came out of jail, for his acquaintances to salute him, looking through their fingers, which were crossed to represent the grating of a jail window, "How do ye do?" My neighbors did not thus salute me but first looked at me and then at one another as if I had returned from a long journey. I was put into jail as I was going to the shoemaker's to get a shoe which was mended. When I was let out the next morning I proceeded to finish my errand, and having put on my mended shoe, joined a huckleberry party who were impatient to put themselves under my conduct; and in half an hour— for the horse was soon tackled— was in the midst of a huckleberry field on one of our highest hills two miles off, and then the State was nowhere to be seen.

36   This is the whole history of "My Prisons."

199

More on Taxes

37   I have never declined paying the highway tax, because I am as desirous of being a good neighbor as I am of being a bad subject; and as for supporting schools I am doing my part to educate my fellow countrymen now. It is for no particular item in the tax-bill that I refuse to pay it. I simply wish to refuse allegiance to the State, to withdraw and stand aloof from it effectually. I do not care to trace the course of my dollar, if I could, till it buys a man or a musket to shoot one with— the dollar is innocent— but I am concerned to trace the effects of my allegiance. In fact, I quietly declare war with the State, after my fashion, though I will still make what use and get what advantage of her I can, as is usual in such cases.

38   If others pay the tax which is demanded of me from a sympathy with the State, they do but what they have already done in their own case, or rather they abet injustice to a greater extent than the State requires. If they pay the tax from a mistaken interest in the individual taxed, to save his property, or prevent his going to jail, it is because they have not considered wisely how far they let their private feelings interfere with the public good.

39   This, then, is my position at present. But one cannot be too much on his guard in such a case, lest his action be biased by obstinacy or an undue regard for the opinions of men. Let him see that he does only what belongs to himself and to the hour.

40   I think sometimes, Why, this people mean well; they are only ignorant; they would do better if they knew how; why give your neighbors this pain to treat you as they are not inclined to? But I think again, this is no reason why I should do as they do or permit others to suffer much greater pain of a different kind. Again, I sometimes say to myself, When many millions of men, without heat, without ill will, without personal feeling of any kind, demand of you a few shillings only, without the possibility, such is their constitution, of retracting or altering their present demand, and without the possibility, on your side, of appeal to any other

millions, why expose yourself to this overwhelming brute force? You do not resist cold and hunger, the winds and the waves, thus obstinately; you quietly submit to a thousand similar necessities. You do not put your head into the fire. But just in proportion as I regard this as not wholly a brute force but partly a human force, and consider that I have relations to those millions as to so many millions of men, and not of mere brute or inanimate things, I see that appeal is possible, first and instantaneously, from them to the Maker of them, and secondly, from them to themselves. But if I put my head deliberately into the fire, there is no appeal to fire or to the Maker of fire, and I have only myself to blame. If I could convince myself that I have any right to be satisfied with men as they are, and to treat them accordingly, and not according, in some respects, to my requisitions and expectations of what they and I ought to be, then, like a good Mussulman and fatalist, I should endeavor to be satisfied with things as they are and say it is the will of God. And, above all, there is this difference between resisting this and a purely brute or natural force, that I can resist this with some effect; but I cannot expect, like Orpheus, to change the nature of the rocks and trees and beasts.

41   I do not wish to quarrel with any man or nation. I do not wish to split hairs, to make fine distinctions, or set myself up as better than my neighbors. I seek rather, I may say, even an excuse for conforming to the laws of the land. I am but too ready to conform to them. Indeed, I have reason to suspect myself on this head; and each year, as the tax-gatherer comes round, I find myself disposed to review the acts and position of the general and State governments, and the spirit of the people, to discover a pretext for conformity.

We must affect our country as our parents;
And if at any time we alienate
Our love or industry from doing it honor,
We must respect effects and teach the soul
Matter of conscience and religion,
And not desire of rule or benefit.

Thoughts on Perfecting this American Government

I believe that the State will soon be able to take all my work of this sort out of my hands, and then I shall be no better a patriot than my fellow-countrymen. Seen from a lower point of view, the Constitution, with all its faults, is very good; the law and the courts are very respectable; even this State and this American government are, in many respects, very admirable and rare things, to be thankful for, such as a great many have described them; but seen from a point of view a little higher, they are what I have described them; seen from a higher still, and the highest, who shall say what they are, or that they are worth looking at or thinking of at all?

42   However, the government does not concern me much, and I shall bestow the fewest possible thoughts on it. It is not many moments that I live under a government, even in this world. If a man is thought-free, fancy-free, imagination-free, that which *is not* never for a long time appearing *to be* to him, unwise rulers or reformers cannot fatally interrupt him.

43   I know that most men think differently from myself; but those whose lives are by profession devoted to the study of these or kindred subjects content me as little as any. Statesmen and legislators, standing so completely within the institution, never distinctly and nakedly behold it. They speak of moving society but have no resting-place without it. They may be men of a certain experience and discrimination and have no doubt invented ingenious and even useful systems, for which we sincerely thank them; but all their wit and usefulness lie within certain not very wide limits. They are wont to forget that the world is not governed by policy and expediency. Webster never goes behind government and so cannot speak with authority about it. His words are wisdom to those legislators who contemplate no essential reform in the existing government; but for thinkers, and those who legislate for all time, he never once glances at the subject. I know of those whose serene and wise speculations on this theme would soon reveal the limits of his mind's range and hospitality. Yet, compared with the cheap professions of most reformers, and the still cheaper wisdom and eloquence of

politicians in general, his are almost the only sensible and valuable words, and we thank Heaven for him. Comparatively, he is always strong, original, and, above all, practical. Still his quality is not wisdom but prudence. The lawyer's truth is not Truth but consistency, or a consistent expediency. Truth is always in harmony with herself and is not concerned chiefly to reveal the justice that may consist with wrongdoing. He well deserves to be called, as he has been called, the Defender of the Constitution. There are really no blows to be given by him but defensive ones. He is not a leader but a follower. His leaders are the men of '87. "I have never made an effort," he says, "and never propose to make an effort; I have never countenanced an effort, and never mean to countenance an effort, to disturb the arrangement as originally made, by which the various States came into the Union." Still thinking of the sanction which the Constitution gives to slavery, he says, "Because it was a part of the original compact— let it stand." Notwithstanding his special acuteness and ability, he is unable to take a fact out of its merely political relations and behold it as it lies absolutely to be disposed of by the intellect—what, for instance, it behooves a man to do here in America today with regard to slavery but ventures, or is driven, to make some such desperate answer as the following, while professing to speak absolutely, and as a private man— from which what new and singular code of social duties might be inferred? "The manner," says he, "in which the governments of those States where slavery exists are to regulate it, is for their own consideration, under their responsibility to their constituents, to the general laws of propriety, humanity, and justice, and to God. Associations formed elsewhere, springing from a feeling of humanity, or any other cause, have nothing whatever to do with it. They have never received any encouragement from me, and they never will."

44 They who know of no purer sources of truth, who have traced up its stream no higher, stand, and wisely stand, by the Bible and the Constitution, and drink at it there with reverence and humility; but they who behold where it comes trickling into this lake or that pool gird up their loins once more and continue their pilgrimage

toward its fountain-head.

45   No man with a genius for legislation has appeared in America. They are rare in the history of the world. There are orators, politicians, and eloquent men by the thousand; but the speaker has not yet opened his mouth to speak who is capable of settling the much-vexed questions of the day. We love eloquence for its own sake and not for any truth which it may utter or any heroism it may inspire. Our legislators have not yet learned the comparative value of free-trade and of freedom, of union, and of rectitude, to a nation. They have no genius or talent for comparatively humble questions of taxation and finance, commerce and manufacturers and agriculture. If we were left solely to the wordy wit of legislators in Congress for our guidance, uncorrected by the seasonable experience and the effectual complaints of the people, America would not long retain her rank among the nations. For eighteen hundred years, though perchance I have no right to say it, the New Testament has been written; yet where is the legislator who has wisdom and practical talent enough to avail himself of the light which it sheds on the science of legislation?

46   The authority of government, even such as I am willing to submit to— for I will cheerfully obey those who know and can do better than I, and in many things even those who neither know nor can do so well— is still an impure one: to be strictly just, it must have the sanction and consent of the governed. It can have no pure right over my person and property but what I concede to it. The progress from an absolute to a limited monarchy, from a limited monarchy to a democracy, is a progress toward a true respect for the individual. Even the Chinese philosopher was wise enough to regard the individual as the basis of the empire. Is a democracy such as we know it the last improvement possible in government? Is it not possible to take a step further towards recognizing and organizing the rights of man? There will never be a really free and enlightened State until the State comes to recognize the individual as a higher and independent power, from which all its own power and authority are derived, and treats him accordingly. I please myself with imagining a State at

last which can afford to be just to all men and to treat the individual with respect as a neighbor; which even would not think it inconsistent with its own repose if a few were to live aloof from it, not meddling with it, nor embraced by it, who fulfilled all the duties of neighbors and fellow-men. A State which bore this kind of fruit and suffered it to drop off as fast as it ripened would prepare the way for a still more perfect and glorious State, which also I have imagined but not yet anywhere seen.

The questions that follow may be used for further discussion of the reading selection or as topics for essay writing.

1. Thoreau states that he accepts the motto, "That government is best which governs least." What did he mean by that statement, and how would that apply to our current society.

2. Discuss Thoreau's views on slavery.

3. Discuss Thoreau's views on taxes.

4. Discuss Thoreau's views on right and wrong.

5. What does Thoreau mean when he writes, "They who know of no purer sources of truth, who have traced up its stream no higher, stand, and wisely stand, by the Bible and the Constitution, and drink at it there with reverence and humility; but they who behold where it comes trickling into this lake or that pool gird up their loins once more and continue their pilgrimage toward its fountainhead"?

6. Choose a favorite passage from *Civil Disobedience* and discuss why you choose it.

7. _____
_____
_____
_____
_____
_____

8. _____
_____
_____
_____
_____

Applying Reading Skills
(Neatly **PRINT** all answers using ink <u>not</u> pencil)

Title of the Reading Selection: _____

1. **What is the author's overall main idea, (central point, or thesis)?**

_____

_____

2. **There are two kinds of supporting details--major and minor. Major details are the primary points that support the main idea and minor details expand major details. List <u>three</u> details and explain how they support the author's primary point?**

Details used	Explanation of how they support the thesis
1.	

Details used	Explanation of how they support the thesis
2.	

Details used	Explanation of how they support the thesis
3.	

3. **The five major patterns of organization are the list of items pattern, the time order pattern, the example pattern, the comparison and/or contrast pattern, and the cause/effect pattern. What is the <u>main</u> pattern of organization used in this article? <u>Explain</u> why it is the major pattern. What other patterns are used? Give some examples.**

Main pattern: _____

Explain how the main pattern was used:

_____

Other pattern(s) used: _____

Explain how the additional pattern(s) were used:

_____

_____

207

4. If applicable: Give <u>two</u> examples that were used in the writing. <u>Explain</u> how they affected your understanding of the reading selection.

The example(s) given	How example(s) contributed to your understanding
1.	1.
2.	2.

5. If applicable: what is being compared and/or contrasted?

Show <u>two</u> comparisons between items A and B:

A	B

Show <u>two</u> contrasts between items A and B:

A	B

6. Show <u>two</u> cause/effect relationships:

Cause	Effect
1.	
2.	

7. List <u>three</u> facts and <u>three</u> opinions from the article. <u>Explain why</u> it is either a fact or an opinion.

	Explanation:
A.) fact:	A.)
B.) fact:	B.)
C.) fact:	C.)

	Explanation:
A.) opinion	A.)
B.) opinion:	B.)
C.) opinion:	C.)

8. What is the author's purpose in this article? Is it to inform, persuade, or entertain? <u>Tell me how you arrived at that conclusion.</u>

_____
_____
_____

9. What is the author's tone? <u>Explain your answer.</u>

_____
_____
_____

10. Discovering the ideas in writing that are <u>not stated directly</u> is called making inferences, or drawing conclusions. What inferences did you draw from the article you read? <u>Explain.</u>

_____
_____
_____

11. Authors often use connotative language. Return to the reading selection and circle (in red or green) all connotative words. List 10 of those words here and explain how those words might affect the reader.

_____
_____
_____
_____
_____

How the connotative words above might affect the reader:

_____
_____
_____
_____
_____
_____
_____
_____

12. **A good argument makes a point and then provides persuasive and logical evidence to back it up. However, a bad argument uses fallacies to support itself such as changing the subject, hasty generalization, circular reasoning, personal attack, straw man, false cause, false comparison, or either-or. Explain how the author supports his/her argument. <u>Does he/she use relevant and adequate support, or do fallacies exist? Explain.</u>**

13. **The seven most common propaganda techniques are bandwagon, testimonial, transfer, plain folks, name calling, glittering generalities, and card staking. <u>Which techniques are used in this reading selection? Explain.</u>**

A CALL FOR UNITY

By The Undersigned Persons

April 12, 1963

We the undersigned clergymen are among those who, in January, issued "An Appeal for Law and Order and Common Sense," in dealing with racial problems in Alabama. We expressed understanding that honest convictions in racial matters could properly be pursued in the courts, but urged that decisions of those courts should in the meantime be peacefully obeyed.

2   Since that time there had been some evidence of increased forebearance and a willingness to face facts. Responsible citizens have undertaken to work on various problems which cause racial friction and unrest. In Birmingham, recent public events have given indication that we all have opportunity for a new constructive and realistic approach to racial problems.

3 However, we are now confronted by a series of demonstrations by some of our Negro citizens, directed and led in part by outsiders. We recognize the natural impatience of people who feel that their hopes are slow in being realized. But we are convinced that these demonstrations are unwise and untimely.

4   We agree rather with certain local Negro leadership which has called for honest and open negotiation of racial issues in our area. And we believe this kind of facing of issues can best be accomplished by citizens of our own metropolitan area, white and Negro, meeting with their knowledge and experience of the local situation. All of us need to face that responsibility and find proper channels for its accomplishment.

5   Just as we formerly pointed out that "hatred and violence have no sanction in our religious and political traditions," we also point out that such actions as incite to hatred and violence, however technically peaceful those actions may be, have not contributed to the resolution of our local problems. We do not believe that these days of new hope are days when extreme measures are justified in Birmingham.

6   We commend the community as a whole, and the local news media and law enforcement officials in particular, on the calm manner in which these demonstrations have been handled. We urge the public to continue to show restraint should the demonstrations continue, and the law enforcement officials to remain calm and continue to protect our city from violence.

7   We further strongly urge our own Negro community to withdraw support from these demonstrations, and to unite locally in working peacefully for a better Birmingham. When rights are consistently denied, a cause should be pressed in the courts and in negotiations among local leaders, and not in the streets. We appeal to both our white and Negro citizenry to observe the principles of law and order and common sense.

8   C.C.J. Carpenter, D.D., L.L.D., Bishop of Alabama, Joseph A. Durick, D.D., Auxiliary Bishop, Diocese of Mobile-Birmingham; Rabbi Milton L. Grafman, Temple Emanu-EI, Birmingham, Alabana; Bishop Paul Hardin, Bishop of the Alabama-West Florida Conference of the Methodist Church; Bishop Nolan B. Harmon, Bishop of the North Alabama Conference of the Methodist Church; George M. Murray, D.D., LL.D., Bishop Coadjutor, Episcopal Diocese of Alabama; Edward V. Ramage, Moderator, Synod of the Alabama Presbyterian Church in the United States; Earl Stallings, Pastor, First Baptist Church, Birmingham, Alabama.

The questions that follow may be used for further discussion of the reading selection or as topics for essay writing.

1. Many of the Statements put forth in *A Call to Unity* sound reasonable at first. Using the three column list below, do the following: In the first column, list each of the arguments put forth. Next, in the second column, write whether you agree or disagree with each point. Third, read King's reply. Finally, using the same list, in the third column write which points you agree or disagree with. Have any of your answers changed. Explain why.

Point Made:	Initial Response:	Second Response:
1. Pursue in court	Not trusting the courts	Courts were biased.
2. cooperation by public	Nice to cooperate	Police often brutal Rights denied.
3. local manner	Let the local decide	Not a local matter He was invited
4. Dont demonstrate untimely and unwise have patience	what is untimely	Had waited since beginning of country for their rights
5. Commending law enforcement & need...	Almost laughable	Abuse from law enforcement.
6. demonstration have no place	U.S. constitutional right to protest and peaceful assembly	US constitution right to protest and peaceful
7. Responsible citizen	Good to be responsible	"responsible" is a value word. They were irresponble
8. Hatred & violence have no place	Hatred and violence not good	They were not the ones hating and doing violence.

Letter from Birmingham Jail

MARTIN LUTHER KING, JR.

April 16, 1963

MY DEAR FELLOW CLERGYMEN:

While confined here in the Birmingham city jail, I came across your recent statement calling my present activities "unwise and untimely." Seldom do I pause to answer criticism of my work and ideas. If I sought to answer all the criticisms that cross my desk, my secretaries would have little time for anything other than such correspondence in the course of the day, and I would have no time for constructive work. But since I feel that you are men of genuine good will and that your criticisms are sincerely set forth, I want to try to answer your statement in what I hope will be patient and reasonable terms.

Why I Am Here

2   I think I should indicate why I am here in Birmingham, since you have been influenced by the view which argues against "outsiders coming in." I have the honor of serving as president of the Southern Christian Leadership Conference, an organization operating in every southern state, with headquarters in Atlanta, Georgia. We have some eighty-five affiliated organizations across the South, and one of them is the Alabama Christian Movement for Human Rights. Frequently we share staff, educational, and financial resources with our affiliates. Several months ago the affiliate here in Birmingham asked us to be on call to engage in a nonviolent direct-action program if such were deemed necessary. We readily consented, and when the hour came we lived up to our promise. So I, along with several members of my staff, am here because I was invited here. I am here

because I have organizational ties here.

3   But more basically, I am in Birmingham because injustice is here. Just as the prophets of the eighth century B.C. left their villages and carried their "thus saith the Lord" far beyond the boundaries of their home towns, and just as the Apostle Paul left his village of Tarsus and carried the gospel of Jesus Christ to the far corners of the Greco-Roman world, so am I compelled to carry the gospel of freedom beyond my own home town. Like Paul, I must constantly respond to the Macedonian call for aid.

4   Moreover, I am cognizant of the interrelatedness of all communities and states. I cannot sit idly by in Atlanta and not be concerned about what happens in Birmingham. Injustice anywhere is a threat to justice everywhere. We are caught in an inescapable network of mutuality, tied in a single garment of destiny. Whatever affects one directly, affects all indirectly. Never again can we afford to live with the narrow, provincial, "outside agitator" idea. Anyone who lives inside the United States can never be considered an outsider anywhere within its bounds.

5   You deplore the demonstrations taking place in Birmingham. But your statement, I am sorry to say, fails to express a similar concern for the conditions that brought about the demonstrations. I am sure that none of you would want to rest content with the superficial kind of social analysis that deals merely with effects and does not grapple with underlying causes. It is unfortunate that demonstrations are taking place in Birmingham, but it is even more unfortunate that the city's white power structure left the Negro community with no alternative.

Nonviolence

6   In any nonviolent campaign there are four basic steps: collection of the facts to determine whether injustices exist; negotiation; self-purification; and direct action. We have gone through all these steps in Birmingham. There can be no gainsaying the fact that racial injustice engulfs this community. Birmingham is probably the most thoroughly segregated city in the

United States. Its ugly record of brutality is widely known. Negroes have experienced grossly unjust treatment in the courts. There have been more unsolved bombings of Negro homes and churches in Birmingham than in any other city in the nation. These are the hard brutal facts of the case. On the basis of these conditions, Negro leaders sought to negotiate with the city fathers. But the latter consistently refused to engage in good-faith negotiation.

7   Then, last September, came the opportunity to talk with leaders of Birmingham's economic community. In the course of the negotiations, certain promises were made by the merchants— for example, to remove the stores' humiliating racial signs. On the basis of these promises, the Reverend Fred Shuttlesworth and the leaders of the Alabama Christian Movement for Human Rights agreed to a moratorium on all demonstrations. As the weeks and months went by, we realized that we were the victims of a broken promise. A few signs, briefly removed, returned; the others remained.

8   As in so many past experiences, our hopes had been blasted, and the shadow of deep disappointment settled upon us. We had no alternative except to prepare for direct action, whereby we would present our very bodies as a means of laying our case before the conscience of the local and the national community. Mindful of the difficulties involved, we decided to undertake a process of self-purification. We began a series of workshops on nonviolence, and we repeatedly asked ourselves: "Are you able to accept blows without retaliating?" "Are you able to endure the ordeal of jail?" We decided to schedule our direct-action program for the Easter season, realizing that except for Christmas, this is the main shopping period of the year. Knowing that a strong economic-withdrawal program would be the by-product of direct action, we felt that this would be the best time to bring pressure to bear on the merchants for the needed change.

9   Then it occurred to us that Birmingham's mayoral election was coming up in March, and we speedily decided to postpone action until after election day. When we discovered that the Commissioner of Public Safety, Eugene "Bull" Connor, had piled up enough

votes to be in the run-off, we decided again to postpone action until the day after the run-off so that the demonstrations could not be used to cloud the issues. Like many others, we waited to see Mr. Connor defeated, and to this end we endured postponement after postponement. Having aided in this community need, we felt that our direct-action program could be delayed no longer.

10   You may well ask, "Why direct action? Why sit-ins, marches, and so forth? Isn't negotiation a better path?" You are quite right in calling for negotiation. Indeed, this is the very purpose of direct action. Nonviolent direct action seeks to create such a crisis and foster such a tension that a community which has constantly refused to negotiate is forced to confront the issue. It seeks so to dramatize the issue that it can no longer be ignored. My citing the creation of tension as part of the work of the nonviolent resister may sound rather shocking. But I must confess that I am not afraid of the word "tension." I have earnestly opposed violent tension, but there is a type of constructive, nonviolent tension which is necessary for growth. Just as Socrates felt that it was necessary to create a tension in the mind so that individuals could rise from the bondage of myths and half truths to the unfettered realm of creative analysis and objective appraisal, so must we see the need for nonviolent gadflies to create the kind of tension in society that will help men rise from the dark depths of prejudice and racism to the majestic heights of understanding and brotherhood.

11   The purpose of our direct-action program is to create a situation so crisis-packed that it will inevitably open the door to negotiation. I therefore concur with you in your call for negotiation. Too long has our beloved Southland been bogged down in a tragic effort to live in monologue rather than dialogue.

Untimely?

12   One of the basic points in your statement is that the action that I and my associates have taken in Birmingham is untimely. Some have asked: "Why didn't you give the new city administration time to

act?" The only answer that I can give to this query is that the new Birmingham administration must be prodded about as much as the outgoing one, before it will act. We are sadly mistaken if we feel that the election of Albert Boutwell as mayor will bring the millennium to Birmingham. While Mr. Boutwell is a much more gentle person than Mr. Connor, they are both segregationists, dedicated to maintenance of the status quo. I have hoped that Mr. Boutwell will be reasonable enough to see the futility of massive resistance to desegregation. But he will not see this without pressure from devotees of civil rights. My friends, I must say to you that we have not made a single gain in civil rights without determined legal and nonviolent pressure. Lamentably, it is an historical fact that privileged groups seldom give up their privileges voluntarily. Individuals may see the moral light and voluntarily give up their unjust posture; but, as Reinhold Niebuhr has reminded us, groups tend to be more immoral than individuals.

13   We know through painful experience that freedom is never voluntarily given by the oppressor; it must be demanded by the oppressed. Frankly, I have yet to engage in a direct-action campaign that was "well timed" in the view of those who have not suffered unduly from the disease of segregation. For years now I have heard the word "Wait!" It rings in the ear of every Negro with piercing familiarity. This "Wait" has almost always meant "Never." We must come to see, with one of our distinguished jurists, that "justice too long delayed is justice denied."

14   We have waited for more than 340 years for our constitutional and God-given rights. The nations of Asia and Africa are moving with jet like speed toward gaining political independence, but we still creep at horse-and-buggy pace toward gaining a cup of coffee at a lunch counter. Perhaps it is easy for those who have never felt the stinging darts of segregation to say, "Wait." But when you have seen vicious mobs lynch your mothers and fathers at will and drown your sisters and brothers at whim; when you have seen hate-filled policemen curse, kick, and even kill your black brothers and sisters; when you see the vast majority of

your twenty million Negro brothers smothering in an airtight cage of poverty in the midst of an affluent society; when you suddenly find your tongue twisted and your speech stammering as you seek to explain to your six-year-old daughter why she can't go to the public amusement park that has just been advertised on television, and see tears welling up in her eyes when she is told that Fun Town is closed to colored children, and see ominous clouds of inferiority beginning to form in her little mental sky, and see her beginning to distort her personality by developing an unconscious bitterness toward white people; when you have to concoct an answer for a five-year-old son who is asking, "Daddy, why do white people treat colored people so mean?"; when you take a cross-country drive and find it necessary to sleep night after night in the uncomfortable corners of your automobile because no motel will accept you; when you are humiliated day in and day out by nagging signs reading "white" and "colored"; when your first name becomes "nigger," your middle name becomes "boy" (however old you are) and your last name becomes "John," and your wife and mother are never given the respected title "Mrs."; when you are harried by day and haunted by night by the fact that you are a Negro, living constantly at tiptoe stance, never quite knowing what to expect next, and are plagued with inner fears and outer resentments; when you are forever fighting a degenerating sense of "nobodiness"— then you will understand why we find it difficult to wait. There comes a time when the cup of endurance runs over, and men are no longer willing to be plunged into the abyss of despair. I hope, sirs, you can understand our legitimate and unavoidable impatience.

Just and Unjust Laws

15   You express a great deal of anxiety over our willingness to break laws. This is certainly a legitimate concern. Since we so diligently urge people to obey the Supreme Court's decision of 1954 outlawing segregation in the public schools, at first glance it may seem rather paradoxical for us consciously to break

laws. One may well ask: "How can you advocate breaking some laws and obeying others?" The answer lies in the fact that there are two types of laws: just and unjust. I would be the first to advocate obeying just laws. One has not only a legal but a moral responsibility to obey just laws. Conversely, one has a moral responsibility to disobey unjust laws. I would agree with St. Augustine[8] that "an unjust law is no law at all."

16   Now, what is the difference between the two? How does one determine whether a law is just or unjust? A just law is a manmade code that squares with the moral law or the law of God. An unjust law is a code that is out of harmony with the moral law. To put it in the terms of St. Thomas Aquinas: An unjust law is a human law that is not rooted in eternal law and natural law. Any law that uplifts human personality is just. Any law that degrades human personality is unjust. All segregation statutes are unjust because segregation distorts the soul and damages the personality. It gives the segregator a false sense of superiority and the segregated a false sense of inferiority. Segregation, to use the terminology of the Jewish philosopher Martin Buber, substitutes an "I-it" relationship for an "I-thou" relationship and ends up relegating persons to the status of things. Hence segregation is not only politically, economically, and sociologically unsound, it is morally wrong and sinful. Paul Tillich has said that sin is separation. Is not segregation an existential expression of man's tragic separation, his awful estrangement, his terrible sinfulness? Thus it is that I can urge men to obey the 1954 decision of the Supreme Court, for it is morally right; and I can urge them to disobey segregation ordinances, for they are morally wrong.

17 Let us consider a more concrete example of just and unjust
Laws. An unjust law is a code that a numerical or power majority group compels a minority group to obey but does not make binding on itself. This is *difference* made legal. By the same token, a just law is a code that a majority compels a minority to follow and that it is willing to follow itself. This is *sameness* made

legal.

18   Let me give another explanation. A law is unjust if it is inflicted on a minority that, as a result of being denied the right to vote, had no part in enacting or devising the law. Who can say that the legislature of Alabama which set up that state's segregation laws was democratically elected? Throughout Alabama all sorts of devious methods are used to prevent Negroes from becoming registered voters, and there are some counties in which, even though Negroes constitute a majority of the population, not a single Negro is registered. Can any law enacted under such circumstances be considered democratically structured?

19   Sometimes a law is just on its face and unjust in its application. For instance, I have been arrested on a charge of parading without a permit. Now, there is nothing wrong in having an ordinance which requires a permit for a parade. But such an ordinance becomes unjust when it is used to maintain segregation and to deny citizens the First Amendment privilege of peaceful assembly and protest.

20   I hope you are able to see the distinction I am trying to point out. In no sense do I advocate evading or defying the law, as would the rabid segregationist. That would lead to anarchy. One who breaks an unjust law must do so openly, lovingly, and with a willingness to accept the penalty. I submit that an individual who breaks a law that conscience tells him is unjust, and who willingly accepts the penalty of imprisonment in order to arouse the conscience of the community over its injustice, is in reality expressing the highest respect for law.

21   Of course, there is nothing new about this kind of civil disobedience. It was evidenced subliminally in the refusal of Shadrach, Meshach, and Abednego to obey the laws of Nebuchadnezzar, on the ground that a higher moral law was at stake. It was practiced superbly by the early Christians, who were willing to face hungry lions and the excruciating pain of chopping blocks rather than submit to certain unjust laws of the Roman Empire. To a degree, academic freedom is a reality today because Socrates practiced civil disobedience. In our own nation, the Boston Tea Party

represented a massive act of civil disobedience.

22 We should never forget that everything Adolph Hitler did in Germany was "legal" and everything the Hungarian freedom fighters did in Hungary was "illegal." It was "illegal" to aid and comfort a Jew in Hitler's Germany. Even so, I am sure that, had I lived in Germany at the time, I would have aided and comforted my Jewish brothers If today I lived in a Communist country where certain principles dear to the Christian faith are suppressed, I would openly advocate disobeying that country's antireligious laws.

Great Disappointment

23 I must make two honest confessions to you, my Christian and Jewish brothers. First, I must confess that over the past few years I have been gravely disappointed with the white moderate. I have almost reached the regrettable conclusion that the Negro's great stumbling block in his stride toward freedom is not the White Citizen's Counciler or the Ku Klux Klanner, but the white moderate, who is more devoted to "order" than to justice; who prefers a negative peace which is the absence of tension to a positive peace which is the presence of justice; who constantly says, "I agree with you in the goal you seek, but I cannot agree with your methods of direct action"; who paternalistically believes he can set the timetable for another man's freedom; who lives by a mythical concept of time and who constantly advises the Negro to wait for a "more convenient season." Shallow understanding from people of good will is more frustrating than absolute misunderstanding from people of ill will. Lukewarm acceptance is much more bewildering than outright rejection.

24 I had hoped that the white moderate would understand that law and order exist for the purpose of establishing justice and that when they fail in this purpose they become the dangerously structured dams that block the flow of social progress. I had hoped that the white moderate would understand that the present tension in the South is a necessary phase of the transition from an obnoxious negative peace, in which

the Negro passively accepted his unjust plight, to a substantive and positive peace, in which all men will respect the dignity and worth of human personality. Actually, we who engage in nonviolent direct action are not the creators of tension. We merely bring to the surface the hidden tension that is already alive. We bring it out in the open, where it can be seen and dealt with. Like a boil that can never be cured so long as it is covered up but must be opened with all its ugliness to the natural medicines of air and light, injustice must be exposed, with all the tension its exposure creates, to the light of human conscience and the air of national opinion, before it can be cured.

Cause or Effect?

25   In your statement you assert that our actions, even though peaceful, must be condemned because they precipitate violence. But is this a logical assertion? Isn't this like condemning a robbed man because his possession of money precipitated the evil act of robbery? Isn't this like condemning Socrates because his unswerving commitment to truth and his philosophical inquiries precipitated the act by the misguided populace in which they made him drink hemlock? Isn't this like condemning Jesus because his unique God consciousness and never-ceasing devotion to God's will precipitated the evil act of crucifixion? We must come to see that, as the federal courts have consistently affirmed, it is wrong to urge an individual to cease his efforts to gain his basic constitutional fights because the quest may precipitate violence. Society must protect the robbed and punish the robber.
26   I had also hoped that the white moderate would reject the myth concerning time in relation to the struggle for freedom. I have just received a letter from a white brother in Texas. He writes: "All Christians know that the colored people will receive equal rights eventually, but it is possible that you are in too great a religious hurry. It has taken Christianity almost two thousand years to accomplish what it has. The teachings of Christ take time to come to earth." Such an attitude stems from a tragic misconception of time,

226

from the strangely irrational notion that there is something in the very flow of time that will inevitably cure all ills. Actually, time itself is neutral; it can be used either destructively or constructively. More and more I feel that the people of ill will have used time much more effectively than have the people of good will. We will have to repent in this generation not merely for the hateful words and actions of the bad people, but for the appalling silence of the good people. Human progress never rolls in on wheels of inevitability; it comes through the tireless efforts of men willing to be co-workers with God, and without this hard work, time itself becomes an ally of the forces of social stagnation. We must use time creatively, in the knowledge that the time is always ripe to do right. Now is the time to make real the promise of democracy and transform our pending national elegy into a creative psalm of brotherhood. Now is the time to lift our national policy from the quicksand of racial injustice to the solid rock of human dignity.

Extreme Actions?

27   You speak of our activity in Birmingham as extreme. At first I was rather disappointed that fellow clergymen would see my nonviolent efforts as those of an extremist. I began thinking about the fact that I stand in the middle of two opposing forces in the Negro community. One is a force of complacency, made up in part of Negroes who, as a result of long years of oppression, are so drained of self-respect and a sense of "somebodiness" that they have adjusted to segregation; and in part of a few middle-class Negroes who, because of a degree of academic and economic security and because in some ways they profit by segregation, have become insensitive to the problems of the masses. The other force is one of bitterness and hatred, and it comes perilously close to advocating violence. It is expressed in the various black nationalist groups that are springing up across the nation, the largest and best known being Elijah Muhammad's Muslim movement. Nourished by the Negro's frustration over the continued existence of racial discrimination, this movement is

made up of people who have lost faith in America, who have absolutely repudiated Christianity, and who have concluded that the white man is an incorrigible "devil."

28 I have tried to stand between these two forces, saying that we need emulate neither the "do-nothingism" of the complacent nor the hatred and despair of the black nationalist. For there is the more excellent way of love and nonviolent protest. I am grateful to God that, through the influence of the Negro church, the way of nonviolence became an integral part of our struggle.

29 If this philosophy had not emerged, by now many streets of the South would, I am convinced, be flowing with blood. And I am further convinced that if our white brothers dismiss as "rabble-rousers" and "outside agitators" those of us who employ nonviolent direct action, and if they refuse to support our nonviolent efforts, millions of Negroes will, out of frustration and despair, seek solace and security in black nationalist ideologies— a development that would inevitably lead to a frightening racial nightmare.

30   Oppressed people cannot remain oppressed forever. The yearning for freedom eventually manifests itself, and that is what has happened to the American Negro. Something within has reminded him of his birthright of freedom, and something without has reminded him that it can be gained. Consciously or unconsciously, he has been caught up by the Zeitgeist, and with his black brothers of Africa and his brown and yellow brothers of Asia, South America, and the Caribbean, the United States Negro is moving with a sense of great urgency toward the promised land of racial justice. If one recognizes this vital urge that has engulfed the Negro community, one should readily understand why public demonstrations are taking place. The Negro has many pent-up resentments and latent frustrations, and he must release them. So let him march; let him make prayer pilgrimages to the city hall; let him go on freedom rides— and try to understand why he must do so. If his repressed emotions are not released in nonviolent ways, they will seek expression through violence; this is not a threat but a fact of history. So I have not said to my people, "Get rid of

your discontent." Rather, I have tried to say that this normal and healthy discontent can be channeled into the creative outlet of nonviolent direct action. And now this approach is being termed extremist.

31 But though I was initially disappointed at being categorized as an extremist, as I continued to think about the matter I gradually gained a measure of satisfaction from the label. Was not Jesus an extremist for love: "Love your enemies, bless them that curse you, do good to them that hate you, and pray for them which despitefully use you, and persecute you." Was not Amos an extremist for justice: "Let justice roll down like waters and righteousness like an ever-flowing stream." Was not Paul an extremist for the Christian gospel: "I bear in my body the marks of the Lord Jesus." Was not Martin Luther an extremist: "Here I stand; I cannot do otherwise, so help me God." And John Bunyan: "I will stay in jail to the end of my days before I make a butchery of my conscience." And Abraham Lincoln: "This nation cannot survive half slave and half free." And Thomas Jefferson: "We hold these truths to be self-evident, that all men are created equal. . . ." So the question is not whether we will be extremists, but what kind of extremists we will be. Will we be extremists for hate or for love? Will we be extremists for the preservation of injustice or for the extension of justice? In that dramatic scene on Calvary's hill three men were crucified. We must never forget that all three were crucified for the same crime—the crime of extremism. Two were extremists for immorality, and thus fell below their environment. The other, Jesus Christ, was an extremist for love, truth, and goodness, and thereby rose above his environment. Perhaps the South, the nation, and the world are in dire need of creative extremists.

Our White Brothers and Sisters

32 I had hoped that the white moderate would see this need. Perhaps I was too optimistic; perhaps I expected too much. I suppose I should have realized that few members of the oppressor race can understand the deep groans and passionate yearnings of the oppressed race,

229

and still fewer have the vision to see that injustice must be rooted out by strong, persistent, and determined action. I am thankful, however, that some of our white brothers in the South have grasped the meaning of this social revolution and committed themselves to it. They are still all too few in quantity, but they are big in quality. Some— such as Ralph McGill, Lillian Smith, Harry Golden, James McBride Dabbs, Ann Braden, and Sarah Patton Boyle— have written about our struggle in eloquent and prophetic terms. Others have marched with us down nameless streets of the South. They have languished in filthy, roach-infested jails, suffering the abuse and brutality of policemen who view them as "dirty nigger-lovers." Unlike so many of their moderate brothers and sisters, they have recognized the urgency of the moment and sensed the need for powerful "action" antidotes to combat the disease of segregation.

Disappointment with the Church

33   Let me take note of my other major dis-appointment. I have been so greatly disappointed with the white church and its leadership. Of course, there are some notable exceptions. I am not unmindful of the fact that each of you has taken some significant stands on this issue. I commend you, Reverend Stallings for your Christian stand on this past Sunday, in welcoming Negroes to your worship service on a non-segregated basis. I commend the Catholic leaders of this state for integrating Spring Hill College several years ago.

34   But despite these notable exceptions, I must honestly reiterate that I have been disappointed with the church. I do not say this as one of those negative critics who can always find something wrong with the church. I say this as a minister of the gospel, who loves the church; who was nurtured in its bosom; who has been sustained by its spiritual blessings and who will remain true to it as long as the cord of life shall lengthen.

35   When I was suddenly catapulted into the leadership of the bus protest in Montgomery, Alabama, a few years ago, I felt we would be supported by the

white church. I felt that the white ministers, priests, and rabbis of the South would be among our strongest allies. Instead, some have been outright opponents, refusing to understand the freedom movement and misrepresenting its leaders; all too many others have been more cautious than courageous and have remained silent behind the anesthetizing security of stained-glass windows.

36   In spite of my shattered dreams, I came to Birmingham with the hope that the white religious leadership of this community would see the justice of our cause and, with deep moral concern, would serve as the channel through which our just grievances could reach the power structure. I had hoped that each of you would understand. But again I have been disappointed.

The Early Church & Christianity vs. Today

37   There was a time when the church was very powerful— in the time when the early Christians rejoiced at being deemed worthy to suffer for what they believed. In those days the church was not merely a thermometer that recorded the ideas and principles of popular opinion; it was a thermostat that transformed the mores of society. Whenever the early Christians entered a town, the people in power became disturbed and immediately sought to convict the Christians for being "disturbers of the peace" and "outside agitators." But the Christians pressed on, in the conviction that they were "a colony of heaven," called to obey God rather than man. Small in number, they were big in commitment. They were too God intoxicated to be "astronomically intimidated." By their effort and example they brought an end to such ancient evils as infanticide and gladiatorial contests.

38   Things are different now. So often the contemporary church is a weak, ineffectual voice with an uncertain sound. So often it is an arch defender of the status quo. Far from being disturbed by the presence of the church, the powerful structure of the average community is consoled by the church's silent— and often even vocal— sanction of things as they are.

39   But the judgment of God is upon the church as

never before. If today's church does not recapture the sacrificial spirit of the early church, it will lose its authenticity, forfeit the loyalty of millions, and be dismissed as an irrelevant social club with no meaning for the twentieth century. Every day I meet young people whose disappointment with the church has turned into outright disgust.

40   Perhaps I have once again been too optimistic. Is organized religion too inextricably bound to the status quo to save our nation and the world? Perhaps I must turn my faith to the inner spiritual church, the church within the church, as the true *ekklesia* and the hope of the world. But again I am thankful to God that some noble souls from the ranks of organized religion have broken loose from the paralyzing chains of conformity and joined us as active partners in the struggle for freedom. They have left their secure congregations and walked the streets of Albany, Georgia, with us. They have gone down the highways of the South on torturous rides for freedom. Yes, they have gone to jail with us. Some have been dismissed from their churches, have lost the support of their bishops and fellow ministers. But they have acted in the faith that right defeated is stronger than evil triumphant. Their witness has been the spiritual salt that has preserved the true meaning of the gospel in these troubled times. They have carved a tunnel of hope through the dark mountain of disappointment.

41   I hope the church as a whole will meet the challenge of this decisive hour. But even if the church does not come to the aid of justice, I have no despair about the future. I have no fear about the outcome of our struggle in Birmingham, even if our motives are at present misunderstood. We will reach the goal of freedom in Birmingham and all over the nation, because the goal of America is freedom. Abused and scorned though we may be, our destiny is tied up with America's destiny. Before the pilgrims landed at Plymouth, we were here. Before the pen of Jefferson etched the majestic words of the Declaration of Independence across the pages of history, we were here. For more than two centuries our forebears labored in this country without wages; they made cotton king;

232

they built the homes of their masters while suffering gross injustice and shameful humiliation— and yet out of a bottomless vitality they continued to thrive and develop. If the inexpressible cruelties of slavery could not stop us, the opposition we now face will surely fail. We will win our freedom because the sacred heritage of our nation and the eternal will of God are embodied in our echoing demands.

Keeping Order & Preventing Violence?

42   Before closing I feel impelled to mention one other point in your statement that has troubled me profoundly. You warmly commended the Birmingham police force for keeping "order" and "preventing violence." I doubt that you would have so warmly commended the police force if you had seen its dogs sinking their teeth into unarmed, nonviolent Negroes. I doubt that you would so quickly commend the policemen if you were to observe their ugly and inhumane treatment of Negroes here in the city jail; if you were to watch them push and curse old Negro women and young Negro girls; if you were to see them slap and kick old Negro men and young boys; if you were to observe them, as they did on two occasions, refuse to give us food because we wanted to sing our grace together. I cannot join you in your praise of the Birmingham police department.

43   It is true that the police have exercised a degree of discipline in handling the demonstrators. In this sense they have conducted themselves rather "nonviolently" in public. But for what purpose? To preserve the evil system of segregation. Over the past few years I have consistently preached that nonviolence demands that the means we use must be as pure as the ends we seek. I have tried to make clear that it is wrong to use immoral means to attain moral ends. But now I must affirm that it is just as wrong, or perhaps even more so, to use moral means to preserve immoral ends. Perhaps Mr. Connor and his policemen have been rather nonviolent in public, as was Chief Pritchett in Albany, Georgia, but they have used the moral means of nonviolence to maintain the immoral end of racial

233

injustice. As T. S. Eliot has said, "The last temptation is the greatest treason: To do the right deed for the wrong reason."

Real Heroes

44   I wish you had commended the Negro sit-inners and demonstrators of Birmingham for their sublime courage, their willingness to suffer, and their amazing discipline in the midst of great provocation. One day the South will recognize its real heroes. They will be the James Merediths, with the noble sense of purpose that enables them to face jeering and hostile mobs, and with the agonizing loneliness that characterizes the life of the pioneer. They will be old, oppressed, battered Negro women, symbolized in a seventy-two-year-old woman in Montgomery, Alabama, who rose up with a sense of dignity and with her people decided not to ride segregated buses, and who responded with ungrammatical profundity to one who inquired about her weariness: "My feets is tired, but my soul is at rest." They will be the young high school and college students, the young ministers of the gospel and a host of their elders, courageously and nonviolently sitting in at lunch counters and willingly going to jail for conscience' sake. One day the South will know that when these disinherited children of God sat down at lunch counters, they were in reality standing up for what is best in the American dream and for the most sacred values in our Judaeo-Christian heritage, thereby bringing our nation back to those great wells of democracy which were dug deep by the founding fathers in their formulation of the Constitution and the Declaration of Independence.

Sincerely

45   Never before have I written so long a letter. I'm afraid it is much too long to take your precious time. I can assure you that it would have been much shorter if I had been writing from a comfortable desk, but what else can one do when he is alone in a narrow jail cell, other than write long letters, think long thoughts, and

pray long prayers?

46 If I have said anything in this letter that overstates the truth and indicates an unreasonable impatience, I beg you to forgive me. If I have said anything that understates the truth and indicates my having a patience that allows me to settle for anything less than brotherhood, I beg God to forgive me.

47 I hope this letter finds you strong in the faith. I also hope that circumstances will soon make it possible for me to meet each of you, not as an

integrationist or a civil rights leader but as a fellow clergyman and a Christian brother. Let us all hope that the dark clouds of racial prejudice will soon pass away and the deep fog of misunderstanding will be lifted from our fear-drenched communities, and in some not too distant tomorrow the radiant stars of love and brotherhood will shine over our great nation with all their scintillating beauty.

Yours in the cause of
Peace and Brotherhood,

                    Martin Luther King, Jr.

The questions that follow may be used for further discussion of the reading selection or as topics for essay writing.

1. If you didn't do this question relating to *A Call to Unity*, you might want to try it now: Many of the Statements put forth in *A Call to Unity* sound reasonable at first. Using the three column list below, do the following: In the first column, list each of the arguments put forth. Next, in the second column, write whether you agree or disagree with each point. Third, read King's reply. Finally, using the same list, in the third column write which points you agree or disagree with. Have any of your answers changed. Explain why.

Point Made:	Initial Response:	Second Response:
1.		
2.		
3.		
4.		
5.		
6.		
7.		
8.		

2. What does the tone of this selection tell you about the person who wrote it?

3. Dr. Martin Luther King Jr. spent many days in jail. How was his experience different from that of Henry David Thoreau? Who would be better able to write about the jail resistance?

4. How did King respond to his attackers in the press? Do you think his response was effective?

5. What are king's views on the Black Muslim experience? Does it seem prophetic?

6. Many stood idly by as people were denied their Constitutional Rights. King was especially upset by the religious leaders' lack of involvement and desire to wait for another time (that might never come). Some would call them hypocrites. How did King address this issue?

7. How did King view his oppressors? Are there any similarities between his views of oppression and those of Socrates, Thoreau, or Douglass? Explain.

8. _____
_____
_____
_____
_____
_____

9. _____
_____
_____
_____
_____

Applying Reading Skills

(Neatly **PRINT** all answers using ink **not** pencil)

Title of the Reading Selection: _____

1. What is the author's overall main idea, (central point, or thesis)?

MLk Response to Call to Unity and justification for their actions in Birmingham.

2. There are two kinds of supporting details—major and minor. Major details are the primary points that support the main idea and minor details expand major details. List **three** details and explain how they support the author's primary point?

Details used	Explanation of how they support the thesis
1. Non-violence campaign with 4-steps: Collecting the facts negotiation, self purification, direct actions	

Details used	Explanation of how they support the thesis
2. Not a local issue just vs. unjust laws not ultimately.	

Details used	Explanation of how they support the thesis
3.	

3. The five major patterns of organization are the list of items pattern, the time order pattern, the example pattern, the comparison and/or contrast pattern, and the cause/effect pattern. What is the **main** pattern of organization used in this article? **Explain** why it is the major pattern. What other patterns are used? Give some examples.

Main pattern: _____Listing_____

Explain how the main pattern was used:

Other pattern(s) used: ___Compare & contrast, cause/effect._____

Explain how the additional pattern(s) were used:

_____

_____

238

4. If applicable: Give two examples that were used in the writing. Explain how they affected your understanding of the reading selection.

The example(s) given	How example(s) contributed to your understanding
1. 340 years of waiting	1.
2. jail for not having parade permit.	2.

5. If applicable: what is being compared and/or contrasted?

Show two comparisons between items A and B:

A	B

Show two contrasts between items A and B:

A	B

6. Show two cause/effect relationships:

Cause	Effect
1.	
2.	

7. List three facts and three opinions from the article. Explain why it is either a fact or an opinion.

	Explanation:
A.) fact:	A.)
B.) fact:	B.)
C.) fact:	C.)

Explanation:	
A.) opinion	A.)
B.) opinion:	B.)
C.) opinion:	C.)

8. What is the author's purpose in this article? Is it to inform, persuade, or entertain? <u>Tell me how you arrived at that conclusion.</u>

_____
_____
_____

9. What is the author's tone? <u>Explain your answer.</u>

_____
_____
_____

10. Discovering the ideas in writing that are <u>not stated directly</u> is called making inferences, or drawing conclusions. What inferences did you draw from the article you read? <u>Explain.</u>

_____
_____
_____

11. Authors often use connotative language. Return to the reading selection and circle (in red or green) all connotative words. List 10 of those words here and explain how those words might affect the reader.

_____
_____
_____
_____
_____

How the connotative words above might affect the reader:

_____
_____
_____
_____
_____
_____
_____
_____

12. **A good argument makes a point and then provides persuasive and logical evidence to back it up. However, a bad argument uses fallacies to support itself such as changing the subject, hasty generalization, circular reasoning, personal attack, straw man, false cause, false comparison, or either-or. Explain how the author supports his/her argument. <u>Does he/she use relevant and adequate support, or do fallacies exist?</u> <u>Explain</u>.**

13. **The seven most common propaganda techniques are bandwagon, testimonial, transfer, plain folks, name calling, glittering generalities, and card staking. <u>Which techniques are used in this reading selection? Explain.</u>**

I Have a Dream
(1963)
MARTIN LUTHER KING, JR.

I am happy to join with you today in what will go down in history as the greatest demonstration for freedom in the history of our nation.

2   Five score years ago, a great American, in whose symbolic shadow we stand today, signed the Emancipation Proclamation. This momentous decree came as a great beacon light of hope to millions of Negro slaves who bad been seared in the flames of withering injustice. It came as a joyous daybreak to end the long night of their captivity. But one hundred years later, the Negro still is not free. One hundred years later, the life of the Negro is still sadly crippled by the manacles of segregation and the chains of discrimination. One hundred years later, the Negro lives on a lonely island of poverty in the midst of a vast ocean of material prosperity. One hundred years later, the Negro is still anguished in the corners of American society and finds himself in exile in his own land. And so we have come here today to dramatize a shameful condition.

3   In a sense we have come to our nation's capital to cash a check. When the architects of our republic wrote the magnificent words of the Constitution and the Declaration of Independence, they were signing a promissory note to which every American was to fall heir. This note was the promise that all men-yes, black men as well as white men— would be guaranteed the inalienable rights of life, liberty, and the pursuit of happiness.

4   It is obvious today that America has defaulted on this promissory note insofar as her citizens of color are concerned. Instead of honoring this sacred obligation,

America has given the Negro people a bad check, a check which has come back marked "insufficient funds." But we refuse to believe that the bank of justice is bankrupt. We refuse to believe that there are insufficient funds in the great vaults of opportunity of this nation; and so we have come to cash this check, a check that will give us upon demand the riches of freedom and the security of justice.

5   We have also come to this hallowed spot to remind America of the fierce urgency of *now*. This is no time to engage in the luxury of cooling off or to take the tranquilizing drug of gradualism. *Now* is the time to make real the promises of democracy. *Now* is the time to rise from the dark and desolate valley of segregation to the sunlit path of racial justice. *Now* is the time to lift our nation from the quicksands of racial injustice to the solid rock of brotherhood. Now is the time to make justice a reality for all of God's children.

6   It would be fatal for the nation to overlook the urgency of the moment. This sweltering summer of the Negro's legitimate discontent will not pass until there is an invigorating autumn of freedom and equality. Nineteen sixty-three is not an end, but a beginning. And those who hope that the Negro needed to blow off steam and will now be content will have a rude awakening if the nation returns to business as usual. There will be neither rest nor tranquility in America until the Negro is granted his citizenship rights. The whirlwinds of revolt will continue to shake the foundations of our nation until the bright day of justice emerges.

7   But there is something that I must say to my people who stand on the warm threshold which leads into the palace of justice. In the process of gaining our rightful place, we must not be guilty of wrongful deeds. Let us not seek to satisfy our thirst for freedom by drinking from the cup of bitterness and hatred. We must forever conduct our struggle on the high plane of dignity and discipline. We must not allow our creative protest to degenerate into physical violence. Again and again we must rise to the majestic heights of meeting physical

Tone

Opinion

Opinion

Opinion

force with soul force. And the marvelous new militancy which has engulfed the Negro community must not lead us to a distrust of all white people; for many of our white brothers, as evidenced by their presence here today, have come to realize that their destiny is tied up with our destiny, and they have come to realize that their freedom is inextricably bound to our freedom.

8   We cannot walk alone. And as we walk we must make the pledge that we shall always march ahead. We cannot turn back. There are those who are asking the devotees of civil rights, "When will you be satisfied?" We can never be satisfied as long as the Negro is the victim of the unspeakable horrors of police brutality. We can never be satisfied as long as our bodies, heavy with the fatigue of travel, cannot gain lodging in the motels of the highways and the hotels of the cities. We cannot be satisfied as long as the Negro's basic mobility is from a smaller ghetto to a larger one. We can never be satisfied as long as our children are stripped of their selfhood and robbed of their dignity by signs stating "For Whites Only." We cannot be satisfied as long as the Negro in Mississippi cannot vote and a Negro in New York believes he has nothing for which to vote. No, no, we are not satisfied, and we will not be satisfied until justice rolls down like waters and righteousness like a mighty stream.

9   I am not unmindful that some of you have come here out of great trials and tribulations. Some of you have come fresh from narrow jail cells. Some of you have come from areas where your quest for freedom left you battered by the storms of persecution and staggered by the winds of police brutality. You have been the veterans of creative suffering. Continue to work with the faith that unearned suffering is redemptive.

10   Go back to Mississippi, and go back to Alabama. Go back to South to Carolina. Go back to Georgia. Go back to Louisiana. Go back to the slums and ghettos of our Northern cities, knowing that somehow this situation can and will be changed. Let us not wallow in the valley of despair.

Major and minor supporting details.

11   I say to you today, my friends, even though we face the difficulties of today and tomorrow, I still have a dream. It is a dream deeply rooted in the American dream. I have a dream that one day this nation will rise up and live out the true meaning of its creed: "We hold these truths to be self-evident, that all men are created equal." I have a dream that one day, on the red hills of Georgia; sons of former slaves and the sons of former slave owners will be able to sit down together at the table of brotherhood. I have a dream that one day even the state of Mississippi, a state sweltering with the heat of injustice, sweltering with the heat of oppression, will be transformed into an oasis of freedom and justice. I have a dream that my four little children will one day live in a nation where they will not be judged by the color of their skin, but by the content of their character.

12   I have a dream today. I have a dream that one day down in Alabama— with its vicious racists, with its governor's lips dripping with the words of interposition and nullification— one day right there in Alabama, little black boys and black girls will be able to join hands with little white boys and white girls as sisters and brothers.

13   I have a dream today. I have a dream that one day every valley shall be exalted and every hill and mountain shall be made low, the rough places will be made plain and the crooked places will be made straight, and the glory of the Lord shall be revealed, and all flesh shall see it together.

14   This is our hope. This is the faith that I go back to the South with. And with this faith we will be able to hew out of the mountain of despair a stone of hope. With this faith we will be able to transform the jangling discords of our nation into a beautiful symphony of brotherhood. With this faith we will be able to work together, to play together, to struggle together, to go to jail together, to stand up for freedom together, knowing that we will be free one day.

15   And this will be the day-this will be the day when all of God's children is will be able to sing with new meaning.

Main point

My country, 'tis of thee,
Sweet land of liberty,
Of thee I sing;
Land where my fathers died,
Land of tile Pilgrims' pride,
From every mountainside
Let freedom ring.

And if America is to be a great nation, this must become true.

16   And so let freedom ring from the prodigious hilltops of New Hampshire. Let freedom ring from the mighty mountains of New York. Let freedom ring from the heightening Alleghenies of Pennsylvania. Let freedom ring from the snow-capped Rockies of Colorado. Let freedom ring from the curvaceous slopes of California.

17   But not only that. Let freedom ring from Stone Mountain of Georgia. Let freedom ring from Lookout Mountain of Tennessee. Let freedom ring from every hill and molehill of Mississippi. "From every mountainside let freedom ring."

18   And when this happens— when we allow freedom to ring, when we let it ring from every village and every hamlet, from every state and every city— we will be able to speed up that day when all of God's children, black men and white men, Jews and Gentiles, Protestants and Catholics, will be able to join hands and sing in the words of the old Negro spiritual: "Free at last! Free at last! Thank God Almighty. We are free at last!"

April 4, 1968

The questions that follow may be used for further discussion of the reading selection or as topics for essay writing.

1. Discuss the many facets of King's "Dream". What parts of the "dream" have been accomplished, what parts are still evolving, and what parts are in a worse state than before.

2. Look up some of the places mentioned in his speech. What significance did each of those references to a particular place have on the speech and the hearers of the speech?

3. Notice how King paints many verbal pictures in his speech. Notice especially his portrayal of darkness to light, despair to hopefulness, and so forth. Discuss each instance of his use of extremes in painting his verbal pictures.

4. Dr. King stood on the steps of the Lincoln Memorial in Washington D.C. This is an example of a good use of the Transfer technique (discussed in the supplemental section of this book). Discuss the implications of this physical location, the content of the speech, and the possible effect on his audience.

5. _Dr. King mention urgency in his speech._ _Discuss about the impact he made by_ _emphasising freedom as an emergency and how_ _did it influence the readers_

6. _Dr king use comparison and contrast to_ _get his point across from the begining,_ _what are the other component he used_ _to build the rest of his speech._

Applying Reading Skills
(Neatly **PRINT** all answers using ink **not** pencil)

Title of the Reading Selection: ___I have a Dream___

1. **What is the author's overall main idea, (central point, or thesis)?**

   He wanted the nation of all race and color
   live in peace together knowing that all men is created equal.
   Main Point · He has a dream.

2. **There are two kinds of supporting details--major and minor. Major details are the primary points that support the main idea and minor details expand major details. List _three_ details and explain how they support the author's primary point?**

Details used	Explanation of how they support the thesis
1. "We will not be satisfied until justice roll down like water and righteousness like a mighty stream".	He seeks justice and equality through his rich literature that describes it all.

Details used	Explanation of how they support the thesis
2. "From every mountain side let freedom ring.	He states directly to his point which is freedom.

Details used	Explanation of how they support the thesis
3. "We hold these truths to be self-evident, that all men are created equal	again he's really pushing on about the equality of race and color.

3. **The five major patterns of organization are the list of items pattern, the time order pattern, the example pattern, the comparison and/or contrast pattern, and the cause/effect pattern. What is the _main_ pattern of organization used in this article? _Explain_ why it is the major pattern. What other patterns are used? Give some examples.**

   Main pattern: The list of Items

   Explain how the main pattern was used:
   He listed the main things about freedom and equality

   Other pattern(s) used: X Example pattern - Comparison and Contrast

   Explain how the additional pattern(s) were used:
   He uses example to support the main idea.

250

4. If applicable: Give two examples that were used in the writing. Explain how they affected your understanding of the reading selection.

The example(s) given	How example(s) contributed to your understanding
1. ... former slave sons and slave owners will join table together.	1. Just speaks about straight forward freedom.
2.	2.

5. If applicable: what is being compared and/or contrasted?

Show two comparisons between items A and B:

A	B
Declaration of Independence	U.S. Constitution.

Show two contrasts between items A and B:

A	B
Emancipation Proclamation	Slavery

6. Show two cause/effect relationships:

Cause	Effect
1. Battered supporters	Led to the freedom of discrimination.
2.	

7. List three facts and three opinions from the article. Explain why it is either a fact or an opinion.

	Explanation:
A.) fact: Declaration of Indepence signed	A.) A promise to every American to abide by.
B.) fact: Battered supporters	B.) He mention in his speech by police brutality.
C.) fact:	C.)

251

Explanation:

	Explanation:
A.) opinion *Let us not drink from the cup of bitterness & hatred*	A.) *King's opinion about earning a rightful place*
B.) opinion: *No be guilty of our wrongful deeds.*	B.)
C.) opinion:	C.)

8. **What is the author's purpose in this article? Is it to inform, persuade, or entertain? <u>Tell me how you arrived at that conclusion.</u>**

The author uses persuasion to accomplish his goals. He uses many examples to persuade the readers that all men are created equal and, injustice shall not exist.

9. **What is the author's tone? <u>Explain your answer</u>.**

Hopeful and a sense of urgency also at time He also showed some enrage.

10. **Discovering the ideas in writing that are <u>not stated directly</u> is called making inferences, or drawing conclusions. What inferences did you draw from the article you read? <u>Explain</u>.**

First time reading this article I kinda got a sense where he talk about injustice between races and I thought by just acquiring that info he would be talking about justice and freedom.

11. **Authors often use connotative language. Return to the reading selection and circle (in red or green) all connotative words. List 10 of those words here and explain how those words might affect the reader.**

Police brutality, racial injustice, urgency, slaves, segregation, march ahead, freedom, equality

How the connotative words above might affect the reader:

It help shaped the view of injustice that having been going on through the past and stir different emotion and image to the readers.

12. A good argument makes a point and then provides persuasive and logical evidence to back it up. However, a bad argument uses fallacies to support itself such as changing the subject, hasty generalization, circular reasoning, personal attack, straw man, false cause, false comparison, or either-or. Explain how the author supports his/her argument. **Does he/she use relevant and adequate support, or do fallacies exist? Explain.**

Yes, the author was straight to point about his writing and what he wanted to accomplish. He supports his arguments with facts from the U.S constitution and the mistreating of the race and color. He also mention that the declaration of Independence was a promisory that all men would be guaranteed inalienable rights.

13. The seven most common propaganda techniques are bandwagon, testimonial, transfer, plain folks, name calling, glittering generalities, and card staking. **Which techniques are used in this reading selection? Explain.**

I think the main technique used in this article was testimonial. The wrote thing that not only related to himself, but many of the readers as well. Also Transfer technique in the steps of Lincoln memorial.

Theme 4

Philosophies
That
Shape Our World

What is Reality? What is Truth? What is Right? How should we live our lives? How should we treat others? What should we teach and what should we learn? What is really important, and who really knows the answer to these questions?

This theme explores some of the writings that have influenced humanity for centuries and still exert their powerful influences today. The written word is powerful and it influences people to think, act, and live in a certain manner.

In being fair and sensitive to the many readers, each who may hold their own belief system in high esteem, let us remember that this only a very small sampling of the writings that compose each of these philosophies.

The terrorist attacks of 9/11/2001 on the Twin Towers in New York City trace their motivations back to what some refer to as a radical interpretation of the Koran. We need to realize that those men may have been influenced by their culture and religion – "and there but for 'fortune' go you or I."

I am not excusing their actions, but we must explore the reasons behind those actions if we are to prevent future catastrophes.

Also, as I write this, India (heavily influenced by Hinduism) stands face to face, with Pakistan (heavily influenced by Islam and the Koran) – and both countries are armed with Nuclear weapons! Israel (influenced by the Bible) is surrounded by Muslim nations (influenced by the Koran) and Nuclear weapons are stockpiled, or available, in nearly all of those countries. China (heavily influenced by Buddhism and now Atheism) has stockpiled Nuclear weapons and is ready to sell them to like minded countries.

We can see the importance of understanding and accepting, or possibly altering, one another's religions – the fate of the world - ironically - may depend on that!

The Allegory of the Cave

(From Plato's Republic)
PLATO
(428-347 B.C.)

And now, I said, let me show in a figure how far our nature is enlightened or unenlightened: Behold! Human beings living in an underground den, which has a mouth open towards the light and reaching all along the den; here they have been from their childhood, and have their legs and necks chained so that they cannot move, and can only see before them, being prevented by the chains from turning round their heads. Above and behind them a fire is blazing at a distance, and between the fire and the prisoners there is a raised way; and you will see, if you look, a low wall built along the way, like the screen which marionette players have in front of them, over which they show the puppets.

2   I see.

3   And do you see, I said, men passing along the wall carrying all sorts of vessels, and statues and figures of animals made of wood and stone and various materials, which appear over the wall? Some of them are talking, others silent.

4   You have shown me a strange image, and they are strange prisoners.

5   Like ourselves, I replied; and they see only their own shadows, or the shadows of one another, which the fire throws on the opposite wall of the cave?

6   True, he said; how could they see anything but the shadows if they were never allowed to move their heads?

7   And of the objects which are being carried in like manner they would only see the shadows?

8   Yes, he said.

9   And if they were able to converse with one another,

would they not suppose that they were naming what was actually before them?

10   Very true.

11   And suppose further that the prison had an echo which came from the other side, would they not be sure to fancy when one of the passers-by spoke that the voice which they heard came from the passing shadow?

12   No question, he replied.

13   To them, I said, the truth would be literally nothing but the shadows of the images.

14   That is certain.

15   And now look again, and see what will naturally follow if the prisoners are released and disabused of their error. At first, when any of them is liberated and compelled suddenly to stand up and turn his neck round and walk and look towards the light, he will suffer sharp pains; the glare will distress him, and he will be unable to see the realities of which in his former state he had seen the shadows; and then conceive some one saying to him, that what he saw before was an illusion, but that now, when he is approaching nearer to being and his eye is turned towards more real existence, he has a clearer vision— what will be his reply? And you may further imagine that his instructor is pointing to the objects as they pass and requiring him to name them,— will he not be perplexed? Will he not fancy that the shadows which he formerly saw are truer than the objects which are now shown to him?

16   Far truer.

17   And if he is compelled to look straight at the light, will he not have a pain in his eyes which will make him turn away to take refuge in the objects of vision which he can see, and which he will conceive to be in reality clearer than the things which are now being shown to him?

18   True, he said.

19   And suppose once more, that he is reluctantly dragged up a steep and rugged ascent, and held fast until he is forced into the presence of the sun himself, is he not likely to be pained and irritated? When he approaches the light his eyes will be dazzled, and he will not be able to see anything at all of what are now called realities.

20   Not all in a moment, he said.

21   He will require to grow accustomed to the sight of the upper world. And first he will see the shadows best, next the reflections of men and other objects in the water, and then the objects themselves; then he will gaze upon the light of the moon and the stars and the spangled heaven; and he will see the sky and the stars by night better than the sun or the light of the sun by day?

22   Certainly

23   Last of all he will be able to see the sun, and not mere reflections of him in the water, but he will see him in his own proper place, and not in another; and he will contemplate him as he is.

24   Certainly.

25   He will then proceed to argue that this is he who gives the season and the years, and is the guardian of all that is in the visible world, and in a certain way the cause of all things which he and his fellows have been accustomed to behold?

26   Clearly, he said, he would first see the sun and then reason about him.

27   And when he remembered his old habitation, and the wisdom of the den and his fellow prisoners, do you not suppose that he would felicitate himself on the change, and pity them?

28   Certainly, he would.

29   And if they were in the habit of conferring honors among themselves on those who were quickest to observe the passing shadows and to remark which of them went before, and which followed after, and which were together; and who were therefore best able to draw conclusions as to the future, do you think that he would care for such honors and glories, or envy the possessors of them? Would he not say with Homer,

   Better to be the poor servant of a poor master,
and to endure anything, rather than think as they do and live after their manner?

30   Yes, he said, I think that he would rather suffer anything than entertain these false notions and live in this miserable manner.

31   Imagine once more, I said, such an one coming suddenly out of the sun to be replaced in his old

situation; would he not be certain to have his eyes full of darkness?

32   To be sure, he said.

33   And if there were a contest, and he had to compete in measuring the shadows with the prisoners who had never moved out of the den, while his sight was still weak, and before his eyes had become steady (and the time which would be needed to acquire this new habit of sight might be very considerable), would he not be ridiculous? Men would say of him that up he went and down he came without his eyes; and that it was better not even to think of ascending; and if any one tried to loose another and lead him up to the light, let them only catch the offender, and they would put him to death.

34   No question, he said.

35   This entire allegory, I said, you may now append, dear Glaucon, to the previous argument; the prison house is the world of sight, the light of the fire is the sun, and you will not misapprehend me if you interpret the journey upwards to be the ascent of the soul into the intellectual world according to my poor belief, which, at your desire, I have expressed— whether rightly or wrongly God knows. But, whether true or false, my opinion is that in the world of knowledge the idea of good appears last of all, and is seen only with an effort; and, when seen, is also inferred to be the universal author of all things beautiful and right, parent of light and of the lord of light in this visible world, and the immediate source of reason and truth in the intellectual; and that this is the power upon which he who would act rationally either in public or private life must have his eye fixed.

36   I agree, he said, as far as I am able to understand you.

37   Moreover, I said, you must not wonder that those who attain to this beatific vision are unwilling to descend to human affairs; for their souls are ever hastening into the upper world where they desire to dwell; which desire of theirs is very natural, if our allegory may be trusted.

38   Yes, very natural.

39   And is there anything surprising in one who passes

from divine contemplations to the evil state of man, misbehaving himself in a ridiculous manner; if, while his eyes are blinking and before he has become accustomed to the surrounding darkness, he is compelled to fight in courts of law, or in other places, about the images or the shadows of images of justice, and is endeavoring to meet the conceptions of those who have never yet seen absolute justice?

40   Anything but surprising, he replied.

41   Anyone who has common sense will remember that the bewilderments of the eyes are of two kinds, and arise from two causes, either from coming out of the light or from going into the light, which is true of the mind's eye, quite as much as of the bodily eye; and he who remembers this when he sees anyone whose vision is perplexed and weak, will not be too ready to laugh; he will first ask whether that soul of man has come out of the brighter life, and is unable to see because unaccustomed to the dark, or having turned from darkness to the day is dazzled by excess of light. And he will count the one happy in his condition and state of being, and he will pity the the other; or, if he have a mind to laugh at the soul which comes from below into the light, there will be more reason in this than in the laugh which greets him who returns from above out of the light into the den.

42   That, he said, is a very just distinction.

43   But then, if I am right, certain professors of education must be wrong when they say that they can put a knowledge into the soul which was not before, like sight into blind eyes.

44   They undoubtedly say this, he replied.

45   Whereas, our argument shows that the power and capacity of learning exists in the soul already; and that just as the eye was unable to turn from darkness to light without the whole body, so too the instrument of knowledge can only by the movement of the whole soul be turned from the world of becoming into that of being, and learn by degrees to endure the sight of being, and of the brightest and best of being, or in other words, of the good.

46   Very true.

47   And must there not be some art which will effect

262

conversion in the easiest and quickest manner; not implanting the faculty of sight, for that exists already, but has been turned in the wrong direction, and is looking away from the truth?

48   Yes, he said, such an art may be presumed.

49   And whereas the other so-called virtues of the soul seem to be akin the bodily qualities, for even when they are not originally innate they can implanted later by habit and exercise, the virtue wisdom more than anything else contains a divine element which always remains, and by this conversion is rendered useful and profitable; or, on the other hand, hurtful and useless. Did you never observe the narrow intelligence flashing from the keen eye of a clever rogue— how eager he is, how clearly his paltry soul sees the way to his end; he is the reverse of blind, but his keen eyesight is forced into the service of evil, and he is mischievous in proportion to his cleverness?

50   Very true, he said.

51   But what if there had been a circumcision of such natures in the days of their youth; and they had been severed from those sensual pleasures, such as eating and drinking, which, like leaden weights, were attached to them at their birth, and which drag them down and turn the vision of their souls upon the things that are below— if, I say, they had been released from these impediments and turned in the opposite direction, the very same faculty in them would have seen the truth as keenly as they see what their eyes are turned to now.

52   Very likely.

53   Yes, I said; and there is another thing which is likely, or rather a necessary inference from what has preceded, that neither the uneducated and uniformed of the truth, nor yet those who never make an end of their education, will be able ministers of State; not the former, because they have no single aim of duty which is the rule of all their actions, private as well as public; nor the latter, because they will not act at all except upon compulsion, fancying that they are already dwelling apart in the islands of the blessed.

54   Very true, he replied.

55   Then, I said, the business of us who are the founders of the State will be to compel the best minds

to attain that knowledge which we have already shown to be the greatest of all— they must continue to ascend until they arrive at the good; but when they have ascended and seen enough we must not allow them to do as they do now.

56 What do you mean?

57 I mean that they remain in the upper world: but his must not be allowed; they must be made to descend again among the prisoners in the den, and partake of their labors and honors, whether they are worth having or not.

58 But is not this unjust? he said; ought we to give them a worse life, when they might have a better?

59 You have again forgotten, my friend, I said, the intention of the legislator, who did not aim at making any one class in the State happy above the rest; the happiness was to be in the whole State, and he held the citizens together by persuasion and necessity, making them benefactors of the State, and therefore benefactors of one another; to this end he created them, not to please themselves, but to be his instruments in binding up the State.

60 True, he said, I had forgotten.

61 Observe, Glaucon, that there will be no injustice in compelling our philosophers to have a care and providence of others; we shall explain to them that in other States, men of their class are not obliged to share in the toils of politics: and this is reasonable, for they grow up at their own sweet will, and the government would rather not have them. Being self-taught, they cannot be expected to show any gratitude for a culture which they have never received. But we have brought you into the world to be rulers of the hive, kings of yourselves and of the other citizens, and have educated you far better and more perfectly than they have been educated, and you are better able to share in the double duty. Wherefore each of you, when his turn comes, must go down to the general underground abode, and get the habit of seeing in the dark. When you have acquired the habit, you will see ten thousand times better than the inhabitants of the den, and you will know what the several images are, and what they represent, because you have seen the beautiful and just and good in their truth. And thus our State, which is

also yours, will be a reality, and not a dream only, and will be administered in a spirit unlike that of other States, in which men fight with one another about shadows only and are distracted in the struggle for power, which in their eyes is a great good. Whereas the truth is that the State in which the rulers are most reluctant to govern is always the best and most quietly governed, and the State in which they are most eager, the worst.

62   Quite true, he replied.

63   And will our pupils, when they hear this, refuse to take their turn at the toils of State, when they are allowed to spend the greater part of their time with one another in the heavenly light?

64   Impossible, he answered; for they are just men, and the commands which we impose upon them are just; there can be no doubt that every one of them will take office as a stern necessity, and not after the fashion of our present rulers of State.

65   Yes, my friend, I said; and there lies the point. You must contrive for your future rulers another and a better life than that of a ruler, and then you may have a well-ordered State; for only in the State which offers this, will they rule who are truly rich, not in silver and gold, but in virtue and wisdom, which are the true blessings of life. Whereas if they go to the administration of public affairs, poor and hungering after their own private advantage, thinking that hence they are to snatch the chief good, order there can never be; for they will be fighting about office, and the civil and domestic broils which thus arise will be the ruin of the rulers themselves and of the whole State.

66   Most true, he replied.

67   And the only life which looks down upon the life of political ambition is that of true philosophy.
Do you know of any other?

68   Indeed, I do not, he said.

The questions that follow may be used for further discussion of the reading selection or as topics for essay writing.

1. Discuss what Plato is saying about the true nature of most people's lives.

2. Discuss the *Allegory of the Cave* as it might relate to our modern society.

3. Who do the prisoners represent? Why won't they listen to one who returns from the upper world?

4. What does the light represent? What does darkness represent? What does the sun represent? What is Plato saying in reference to these three topics?

5. Compare and/or contrast Plato's views on knowledge to that of Thoreau's and Frederick Douglass' views.

6. _____
   _____
   _____
   _____
   _____
   _____

7. _____
   _____
   _____
   _____
   _____
   _____

Applying Reading Skills
(Neatly **PRINT** all answers using ink __not__ pencil)

Title of the Reading Selection: _____

1. **What is the author's overall main idea, (central point, or thesis)?**

Most people go through life not really knowing reality and Plato is trying to show that reality is beyond most people's perception.

2. **There are two kinds of supporting details--major and minor. Major details are the primary points that support the main idea and minor details expand major details. List __three__ details and explain how they support the author's primary point?**

Details used	Explanation of how they support the thesis
1. *Discussion on the people in the cave*	

Details used	Explanation of how they support the thesis
2. *Discussion on people who left the cave*	

Details used	Explanation of how they support the thesis
3. *Politics*	

3. **The five major patterns of organization are the list of items pattern, the time order pattern, the example pattern, the comparison and/or contrast pattern, and the cause/effect pattern. What is the __main__ pattern of organization used in this article? __Explain__ why it is the major pattern. What other patterns are used? Give some examples.**

Main pattern: *Compare & Contrast reality &* _____

Explain how the main pattern was used:

_____

Other pattern(s) used: *Cause & Effect* _____

Explain how the additional pattern(s) were used:

_____

_____

4. If applicable: Give two examples that were used in the writing. Explain how they affected your understanding of the reading selection.

	The example(s) given		How example(s) contributed to your understanding
1.	the Cave : the sun; light, truth God	1.	
2.	Darkness : evil, ignorance	2.	

5. If applicable: what is being compared and/or contrasted?

Show two comparisons between items A and B:

A	B
Light	God, Knowledge
darkness	Ignorance
guards	Authority symbols
Silver & God	Virtue & wisdom

Show two contrasts between items A and B:

A	B
Light	Darkess
God	evil
Just	unjust
ignorance	Knowledge

6. Show two cause/effect relationships:

	Cause	Effect
1.	sudden light	Blindness frustration
	sudden darkness	Blindness frustration
2.		

7. List three facts and three opinions from the article. Explain why it is either a fact or an opinion.

		Explanation:	
A.) fact:	prisoner released & eyes blinded at first	A.)	
B.) fact:	coming into darkness own produce temperol	B.)	
C.) fact:		C.)	

	Explanation:
A.) opinion *God is only God*	**A.)**
B.) opinion: *in the world of Knowledge, good appear last.*	**B.)**
C.) opinion:	**C.)**

8. **What is the author's purpose in this article? Is it to inform, persuade, or entertain? <u>Tell me how you arrived at that conclusion.</u>**

   Persuade

9. **What is the author's tone? <u>Explain your answer.</u>**

   Educated, calm, scholarly, knowledge

10. **Discovering the ideas in writing that are <u>not stated directly</u> is called making inferences, or drawing conclusions. What inferences did you draw from the article you read? <u>Explain.</u>**

    Plato is moral person he's done some deep thinking, he's more intelligent than most people.

11. **Authors often use connotative language. Return to the reading selection and circle (in red or green) all connotative words. List 10 of those words here and explain how those words might affect the reader.**

    blazing, fiery, cave, God, Glurtful.

How the connotative words above might affect the reader:

12. A good argument makes a point and then provides persuasive and logical evidence to back it up. However, a bad argument uses fallacies to support itself such as changing the subject, hasty generalization, circular reasoning, personal attack, straw man, false cause, false comparison, or either-or. Explain how the author supports his/her argument. <u>Does he/she use relevant and adequate support, or do fallacies exist?</u> <u>Explain.</u>

Good - transfer

13. The seven most common propaganda techniques are bandwagon, testimonial, transfer, plain folks, name calling, glittering generalities, and card staking. <u>Which techniques are used in this reading selection?</u> <u>Explain.</u>

Plato on Education

From Plato's Republic

translated by Benjamin Jowett

And what shall be their education? Can we find a better than the traditional sort? -- and this has two divisions, gymnastics for the body, and music for the soul.

True.

Shall we begin education with music, and go on to gymnastics afterward?

By all means.

And when you speak of music, do you include literature or not?

I do.

And literature may be either true or false?

Yes.

And the young should be trained in both kinds, and we begin with the false?

I do not understand your meaning, he said.

You know, I said, that we begin by telling children stories which, though not wholly destitute of truth, are in the main fictitious; and these stories are told them when they are not of an age to learn gymnastics.

Very true.

That was my meaning when I said that we must

teach music before gymnastics.

Quite right, he said.

You know also that the beginning is the most important part of any work, especially in the case of a young and tender thing; for that is the time at which the character is being formed and the desired impression is more readily taken.

Quite true.

And shall we just carelessly allow children to hear any casual tales which may be devised by casual persons, and to receive into their minds ideas for the most part the very opposite of those which we should wish them to have when they are grown up?

We cannot.

Then the first thing will be to establish a censorship of the writers of fiction, and let the censors receive any tale of fiction which is good, and reject the bad; and we will desire mothers and nurses to tell their children the authorized ones only. Let them fashion the mind with such tales, even more fondly than they mould the body with their hands; but most of those which are now in use must be discarded.

Of what tales are you speaking? he said.

You may find a model of the lesser in the greater, I said; for they are necessarily of the same type, and there is the same spirit in both of them.

Very likely, he replied; but I do not as yet know what you would term the greater.

Those, I said, which are narrated by Homer and Hesiod, and the rest of the poets, who have ever been the great story-tellers of mankind.

But which stories do you mean, he said; and what fault do you find with them?

A fault which is most serious, I said; the fault of telling a lie, and, what is more, a bad lie.

But when is this fault committed?

Whenever an erroneous representation is made of the nature of gods and heroes -- as when a painter paints a portrait not having the shadow of a likeness to the original.

Yes, he said, that sort of thing is certainly very blamable; but what are the stories which you mean?

First of all, I said, there was that greatest of all lies in high places, which the poet told about Uranus, and which was a bad lie too -- I mean what Hesiod says that Uranus did, and how Cronus retaliated on him. The doings of Cronus, and the sufferings which in turn his son inflicted upon him, even if they were true, ought certainly not to be lightly told to young and thoughtless persons; if possible, they had better be buried in silence. But if there is an absolute necessity for their mention, a chosen few might hear them in a mystery, and they should sacrifice not a common [Eleusinian] pig, but some huge and unprocurable victim; and then the number of the hearers will be very few indeed.

Why, yes, said he, those stories are extremely objectionable.

Yes, Adeimantus, they are stories not to be repeated in our State; the young man should not be told that in committing the worst of crimes he is far from doing anything outrageous; and that even if he chastises his father when he does wrong, in whatever manner, he will only be following the example of the first and greatest among the gods.

I entirely agree with you, he said; in my opinion those stories are quite unfit to be repeated.

Neither, if we mean our future guardians to regard the habit of quarrelling among themselves as of all things the basest, should any word be said to them of the wars in heaven, and of the plots and fightings of the gods against one another, for they are not true. No, we shall never mention the battles of the giants, or let them be embroidered on garments; and we shall be silent about the innumerable other quarrels of gods and heroes with their friends and relatives. If they would only believe us we would tell them that quarrelling is unholy, and that never up to this time has there been any quarrel between citizens; this is what old men and old women should begin by telling children; and when they grow up, the poets also should be told to compose them in a similar spirit. But the narrative of Hephaestus binding Here his mother, or how on another occasion Zeus sent him flying for taking her part when she was being beaten, and all the battles of the gods in Homer -- these tales must not be admitted into our State, whether they are supposed to have an allegorical meaning or not. For a young person cannot judge what is allegorical and what is literal; anything that he receives into his mind at that age is likely to become indelible and unalterable; and therefore it is most important that the tales which the young first hear should be models of virtuous thoughts.

There you are right, he replied; but if anyone asks where are such models to be found and of what tales are you speaking -- how shall we answer him?

I said to him, You and I, Adeimantus, at this moment are not poets, but founders of a State: now the founders of a State ought to know the general forms in which poets should cast their tales, and the limits which must be observed by them, but to make the tales is not their business.

Very true, he said; but what are these forms of theology which you mean?

Something of this kind, I replied: God is always to be represented as he truly is, whatever be the sort of poetry, epic, lyric, or tragic, in which the representation is given.

Right.

And is he not truly good? and must he not be represented as such?

Certainly.

And no good thing is hurtful?

No, indeed.

And that which is not hurtful hurts not?

Certainly not.

And that which hurts not does no evil?

No.

And can that which does no evil be a cause of evil?

Impossible.

And the good is advantageous?

Yes.

And therefore the cause of well-being?

Yes.

It follows, therefore, that the good is not the cause of all things, but of the good only?

Assuredly.

Then God, if he be good, is not the author of all things, as the many assert, but he is the cause of a few things only, and not of most things that occur to men. For few are the goods of human life, and many are the evils, and the good is to be attributed to God alone; of the evils the causes are to be sought elsewhere, and not in him.

That appears to me to be most true, he said.

Then we must not listen to Homer or to any other poet who is guilty of the folly of saying that two casks

"Lie at the threshold of Zeus, full of lots, one of good, the other of evil lots," and that he to whom Zeus gives a mixture of the two

"Sometimes meets with evil fortune, at other times with good;" but that he to whom is given the cup of unmingled ill,

"Him wild hunger drives o'er the beauteous earth." And again --

"Zeus, who is the dispenser of good and evil to us." And if anyone asserts that the violation of oaths and treaties, which was really the work of Pandarus, was brought about by Athene and Zeus, or that the strife and contention of the gods were instigated by Themis and Zeus, he shall not have our approval; neither will we allow our young men to hear the words of AEschylus, that

"God plants guilt among men when he desires utterly to destroy a house." And if a poet writes of the sufferings of Niobe -- the subject of the tragedy in which these iambic verses occur -- or of the house of Pelops, or of the Trojan War or on any similar theme, either we must not permit him to say that these are the works of God, or if they are of God, he must devise some explanation of them such as we are seeking: he must say that God did what was just and right, and they were the better for being punished; but that those who are punished are miserable, and that God is the author of their misery -- the poet is not to be permitted to say; though he may say that the wicked are miserable because they require to be punished, and are benefited by receiving punishment from God; but that God being good is the author of evil to anyone is to be strenuously denied, and not to be said or sung or heard in verse or prose by anyone whether old or young in any well-ordered commonwealth. Such a fiction is suicidal, ruinous, impious.

I agree with you, he replied, and am ready to give my assent to the law.

Let this then be one of our rules and principles concerning the gods, to which our poets and reciters will be expected to conform -- that God is not the author of all things, but of good only.

That will do, he said.

The questions that follow may be used for further discussion of the reading selection or as topics for essay writing.

1. Many Nursery Tales involve fear and violence. What would Plato's viewpoint be on that? What do you think?

2. Plato believed in censorship. We live in a society where very little is censored. Discuss the different viewpoint relating to censorship and what Plato might want to censor if he were alive today.

3. Discuss the successes and failures of our modern educational system. Include Plato's views when relevant.

4. _____
   _____
   _____
   _____
   _____
   _____

5. _____
   _____
   _____
   _____
   _____

6. _____
   _____
   _____
   _____
   _____

7. _____
   _____
   _____
   _____
   _____

Applying Reading Skills
(Neatly **PRINT** all answers using ink **not** pencil)

Title of the Reading Selection: _____

1. **What is the author's overall main idea, (central point, or thesis)?**

   What is a good education? _____

   _____

2. **There are two kinds of supporting details--major and minor. Major details are the primary points that support the main idea and minor details expand major details. List three details and explain how they support the author's primary point?**

Details used	Explanation of how they support the thesis
1. Discussion about God & God	

Details used	Explanation of how they support the thesis
2. Children's stories full of lies	

Details used	Explanation of how they support the thesis
3. Should censor childrens book	

3. **The five major patterns of organization are the list of items pattern, the time order pattern, the example pattern, the comparison and/or contrast pattern, and the cause/effect pattern. What is the <u>main</u> pattern of organization used in this article? <u>Explain</u> why it is the major pattern. What other patterns are used? Give some examples.**

Main pattern: _____ example pattern / Listing _____

Explain how the main pattern was used:

_____

Other pattern(s) used: _____ Cause & Effects _____

Explain how the additional pattern(s) were used:

_____

_____

4. If applicable: Give <u>two</u> examples that were used in the writing. <u>Explain</u> how they affected your understanding of the reading selection.

The example(s) given	How example(s) contributed to your understanding
1. Homer	1.
2. Zeus	2.

5. If applicable: what is being compared and/or contrasted?

Show <u>two</u> comparisons between items A and B:

A	B
Writing of some poets good	Bad pies good

Show <u>two</u> contrasts between items A and B:

A	B
Fairy tales vice Gymnastic	Reality Virtues Music

6. Show <u>two</u> cause/effect relationships:

Cause	Effect
1. Good Bad	No' hurt Hurt
2.	

7. List <u>three</u> facts and <u>three</u> opinions from the article. <u>Explain why</u> it is either a fact or an opinion.

	Explanation:
A.) fact: Various writers and tales	A.)
B.) fact: Aeschylus	B.)
C.) fact: having a connection	C.)

279

	Explanation:
A.) opinion *no convenation*	**A.)**
B.) opinion: *God and morality*	**B.)**
C.) opinion: *Law on censorship*	**C.)**

8. What is the author's purpose in this article? Is it to inform, persuade, or entertain? <u>Tell me how you arrived at that conclusion.</u>

_____

_____

_____

9. What is the author's tone? <u>Explain your answer.</u>

_____

_____

_____

10. Discovering the ideas in writing that are <u>not stated directly</u> is called making inferences, or drawing conclusions. What inferences did you draw from the article you read? <u>Explain</u>.

_____

_____

_____

11. Authors often use connotative language. Return to the reading selection and circle (in red or green) all connotative words. List 10 of those words here and explain how those words might affect the reader.

_____

_____

_____

_____

How the connotative words above might affect the reader:

_____

_____

_____

_____

_____

_____

_____

12. **A good argument makes a point and then provides persuasive and logical evidence to back it up. However, a bad argument uses fallacies to support itself such as changing the subject, hasty generalization, circular reasoning, personal attack, straw man, false cause, false comparison, or either-or. Explain how the author supports his/her argument. <u>Does he/she use relevant and adequate support, or do fallacies exist? Explain.</u>**

_____
_____
_____
_____
_____
_____
_____
_____
_____
_____
_____
_____
_____
_____
_____
_____

13. **The seven most common propaganda techniques are bandwagon, testimonial, transfer, plain folks, name calling, glittering generalities, and card staking. <u>Which techniques are used in this reading selection? Explain.</u>**

_____
_____
_____
_____
_____
_____
_____
_____
_____
_____
_____
_____
_____
_____
_____

Excerpts from
Tao-te Ching

By Lao – Tzu

The Sage

The sage has no mind of his own. He takes as his own the mind of the people.

Those who are good I treat as good. Those who are not good I also treat as good. In so doing I gain in goodness. Those who are of good faith I have faith in. Those who are lacking in good faith I also have faith in. In so doing I gain in good faith.

The Sage in his attempt to distract the mind of the empire seeks urgently to muddle it. The people all have something to occupy their eyes and ears, and the sage treats them all like children.

Governing

Govern the state by being straightforward; wage war by being crafty; but win the empire by not being meddlesome.

How do I know that? By means of this.
The more taboos there are in the empire
The poorer the people;
The more sharpened tools the people have;
The more benighted the state;
The more skills the people have
The further novelties multiply;
The better known the laws and edicts
The more thieves and robbers there are.

Hence the sage says,
I take no action and the people are transferred of themselves;
I prefer stillness and the people are rectified of themselves;
I am not meddlesome and the people prosper of themselves;
I am free from desire and the people of themselves become simple like the uncarved block.

The State

Reduce the size and population of the state. Ensure that even though the people have tools of war for a troop or a battalion they will not use them; and also that they will be reluctant to move to distant places because they look on death as no light matter.

Even when they have ships and carts, they will have no use for them; and even when they have armor and weapons, they will have no occasion to make a show of them.

Bring it about that the people will return to the use of the knotted rope,
Will find relish in their food
And beauty in their clothes,
Will be content in their abode
And happy in the way they live.

Though adjoining states are within sight of one another, and the sound of the dogs barking and cocks crowing in one state can be heard in another, yet the people of one state will grow old and die without having had any dealings with those of another.

283

The questions that follow may be used for further discussion of the reading selection or as topics for essay writing.

1. How does Lao view and treat his subjects? Do you think he is wise? Explain.

2. Discuss the meanings found in the section on governing. Do you agree or disagree with Lao? Explain.

3. What does Lao think brings contentment? Do you agree or disagree? Explain.

4. _____
   _____
   _____
   _____
   _____
   _____
   _____

5. _____
   _____
   _____
   _____
   _____

6. _____
   _____
   _____
   _____
   _____

7. _____
   _____
   _____
   _____
   _____

Applying Reading Skills
(Neatly <u>PRINT</u> all answers using ink <u>not</u> pencil)

Title of the Reading Selection: _____

1. **What is the author's overall main idea, (central point, or thesis)?**

   _____

   _____

2. **There are two kinds of supporting details--major and minor. Major details are the primary points that support the main idea and minor details expand major details. List <u>three</u> details and explain how they support the author's primary point?**

Details used	Explanation of how they support the thesis
1.	

Details used	Explanation of how they support the thesis
2.	

Details used	Explanation of how they support the thesis
3.	

3. **The five major patterns of organization are the list of items pattern, the time order pattern, the example pattern, the comparison and/or contrast pattern, and the cause/effect pattern. What is the <u>main</u> pattern of organization used in this article? <u>Explain</u> why it is the major pattern. What other patterns are used? Give some examples.**

Main pattern: _____

Explain how the main pattern was used:

_____

Other pattern(s) used: _____

Explain how the additional pattern(s) were used:

_____

_____

285

4. If applicable: Give <u>two</u> examples that were used in the writing. <u>Explain</u> how they affected your understanding of the reading selection.

The example(s) given	How example(s) contributed to your understanding
1.	1.
2.	2.

5. If applicable: what is being compared and/or contrasted?

Show <u>two</u> comparisons between items A and B:

A	B

Show <u>two</u> contrasts between items A and B:

A	B

6. Show <u>two</u> cause/effect relationships:

Cause	Effect
1.	
2.	

7. List <u>three</u> facts and <u>three</u> opinions from the article. <u>Explain why</u> it is either a fact or an opinion.

	Explanation:
A.) fact:	A.)
B.) fact:	B.)
C.) fact:	C.)

	Explanation:
A.) opinion	A.)
B.) opinion:	B.)
C.) opinion:	C.)

8. What is the author's purpose in this article? Is it to inform, persuade, or entertain? <u>Tell me how you arrived at that conclusion</u>.

_____

_____

_____

9. What is the author's tone? <u>Explain your answer</u>.

_____

_____

_____

10. Discovering the ideas in writing that are <u>not stated directly</u> is called making inferences, or drawing conclusions. What inferences did you draw from the article you read? <u>Explain</u>.

_____

_____

_____

11. Authors often use connotative language. Return to the reading selection and circle (in red or green) all connotative words. List 10 of those words here and explain how those words might affect the reader.

_____

_____

_____

_____

How the connotative words above might affect the reader:

_____

_____

_____

_____

_____

_____

_____

12. A good argument makes a point and then provides persuasive and logical evidence to back it up. However, a bad argument uses fallacies to support itself such as changing the subject, hasty generalization, circular reasoning, personal attack, straw man, false cause, false comparison, or either-or. Explain how the author supports his/her argument. <u>Does he/she use relevant and adequate support, or do fallacies exist?</u> <u>Explain</u>.

_____
_____
_____
_____
_____
_____
_____
_____
_____
_____
_____
_____
_____
_____
_____
_____

13. The seven most common propaganda techniques are bandwagon, testimonial, transfer, plain folks, name calling, glittering generalities, and card staking. <u>Which techniques are used in this reading selection?</u> <u>Explain</u>.

_____
_____
_____
_____
_____
_____
_____
_____
_____
_____
_____
_____
_____
_____
_____
_____

From **The Koran:**

[**9.1**] (This is a declaration of) immunity by Allah and His Apostle towards those of the idolaters with whom you made an agreement.

[**9.2**] So go about in the land for four months and know that you cannot weaken Allah and that Allah will bring disgrace to the unbelievers.

[**9.3**] And an announcement from Allah and His Apostle to the people on the day of the greater pilgrimage that Allah and His Apostle are free from liability to the idolaters; therefore if you repent, it will be better for you, and if you turn back, then know that you will not weaken Allah; and announce painful punishment to those who disbelieve.

[**9.4**] Except those of the idolaters with whom you made an agreement, then they have not failed you in anything and have not backed up any one against you, so fulfill their agreement to the end of their term; surely Allah loves those who are careful (of their duty).

[**9.5**] So when the sacred months have passed away, then slay the idolaters wherever you find them, and take them captives and besiege them and lie in wait for them in every ambush, then if they repent and keep up prayer and pay the poor-rate, leave their way free to them; surely Allah is Forgiving, Merciful.

Right off the bat Allah, seems like a really strict a set on his rules.

Don't know what it exactly mean to not have the ability to weaken allah

289

[**9.6**] And if one of the idolaters seek protection from you, grant him protection till he hears the word of Allah, then make him attain his place of safety; this is because they are a people who do not know.

[**9.20**] Those who believed and fled (their homes), and strove hard in Allah's way with their property and their souls, are much higher in rank with Allah; and those are they who are the achievers (of their objects).
[**9.21**] Their Lord gives them good news of mercy from Himself and (His) good pleasure and gardens, wherein lasting blessings shall be theirs;
[**9.22**] Abiding therein for ever; surely Allah has a Mighty reward with Him.

Interesting to know what exactly is Allah's word.

According to this passage if you leave your property for Allah, then you are rank high.

[9.29] Fight those who do not believe in Allah, nor in the latter day, nor do they prohibit what Allah and His Apostle have prohibited, nor follow the religion of truth, out of those who have been given the Book, until they pay the tax in acknowledgment of superiority and they are in a state of subjection.

[9.30] And the Jews say: Uzair is the son of Allah; and the Christians say: The Messiah is the son of Allah; these are the words of their mouths; they imitate the saying of those who disbelieved before; may Allah destroy them; how they are turned away!

[9.31] They have taken their doctors of law and their monks for lords besides Allah, and (also) the Messiah son of Marium and they were enjoined that they should serve one God only, there is no god but He; far from His glory be what they set up (with Him).

[9.32] They desire to put out the light of Allah with their mouths, and Allah will not consent save to perfect His light, though the unbelievers are averse.

[9.33] He it is Who sent His Apostle with guidance and the religion of truth, that He might cause it to prevail over all religions, though the polytheists may be averse.

[9.34] O you who believe! most surely many of the doctors of law and the monks eat away the property of men falsely, and turn (them) from Allah's way; and (as for) those who hoard up gold and silver and do not spend it in Allah's way, announce to them a painful chastisement,

This is probably the reason that terrorist exist. This is no made clear and people can take this in a level of violence that will destroy humanity.

Seems like Allah don't care about anything but money.

[**9.35**] On the day when it shall be heated in the fire of hell, then their foreheads and their sides and their backs shall be branded with it; this is what you hoarded up for yourselves, therefore taste what you hoarded.

[**9.36**] Surely the number of months with Allah is twelve months in Allah's ordinance since the day when He created the heavens and the earth, of these four being sacred; that is the right reckoning; therefore be not unjust to yourselves regarding them, and fight the polytheists all together as they fight you all together; and know that Allah is with those who guard (against evil).

[**9.38**] O you who believe! What (excuse) have you that when it is said to you: Go forth in Allah's way, you should incline heavily to earth; are you contented with this world's life instead of the hereafter? But the provision of this world's life compared with the hereafter is but little.

[**9.39**] If you do not go forth, He will chastise you with a painful chastisement and bring in your place a people other than you, and you will do Him no harm; and Allah has power over all things.

So basically if you use your earning towards anything else other than Allah, hell is waiting to torment you? I don't know about this logic.

Very similar to the Bible, but I'm sure both have very different meaning.

292

[**9.72**] Allah has promised to the believing men and the believing women gardens, beneath which rivers flow, to abide in them, and goodly dwellings in gardens of perpetual abode; and best of all is Allah's goodly pleasure; that is the grand achievement.

[**9.73**] O Prophet! strive hard against the unbelievers and the hypocrites and be unyielding to them; and their abode is hell, and evil is the destination.

[**9.74**] They swear by Allah that they did not speak, and certainly they did speak, the word of unbelief, and disbelieved after their Islam, and they had determined upon what they have not been able to effect, and they did not find fault except because Allah and His Apostle enriched them out of His grace; therefore if they repent, it will be good for them; and if they turn back, Allah will chastise them with a painful chastisement in this world and the hereafter, and they shall not have in the land any guardian or a helper.

Don't what pleasure this passage is talking about, but if all your working for is to achieve pleasure then that's probably not the best route.

293

The questions that follow may be used for further discussion of the reading selection or as topics for essay writing.

1. This selection was chosen because it was so often referred to by the News media after the 9/11/2001 attack on America. Discuss your interpretation of the reading selection.

2. In 9.5, Koran speaks of violence to the unbelievers or idolaters. This selection was chosen because many people pointed to that as having possibly incited the terrorists of 9/11/2001 to attack the United States. Discuss the effect this may have had on their thinking.

3. In 9.29 and 9.30, the Koran talks about the latter days. The Bible (as we will see in the next reading) also talks about the Latter Days. The Koran also here talks about the destruction of all Christians and Jews. It seems as though we are watching the Nightly News or reading the morning newspaper. Discuss your thoughts concerning this.

4. The passage seems to be encouraging conversion or death. How might some of the earlier writers respond to this ultimatum and the post 9/11 world that we live in?

5. _____
   _____
   _____
   _____
   _____
   _____

6. _____
   _____
   _____
   _____
   _____
   _____

Applying Reading Skills
(Neatly **PRINT** all answers using ink **not** pencil)

Title of the Reading Selection: _____

1. What is the author's overall main idea, (central point, or thesis)?

    If you don't repent and believe in Allah
    then you will be rebuke with punishment

2. There are two kinds of supporting details--major and minor. Major details are the primary points that support the main idea and minor details expand major details. List <u>three</u> details and explain how they support the author's primary point?

Details used	Explanation of how they support the thesis
1. _Painful punishment_	
Chastise	

Details used	Explanation of how they support the thesis
2.	

Details used	Explanation of how they support the thesis
3.	

3. The five major patterns of organization are the list of items pattern, the time order pattern, the example pattern, the comparison and/or contrast pattern, and the cause/effect pattern. What is the <u>main</u> pattern of organization used in this article? <u>Explain</u> why it is the major pattern. What other patterns are used? Give some examples.

Main pattern: _Listing_

Explain how the main pattern was used:

Other pattern(s) used: _Cause and effect_

Explain how the additional pattern(s) were used:

_____
_____

295

4. If applicable: Give <u>two</u> examples that were used in the writing. <u>Explain</u> how they affected your understanding of the reading selection.

The example(s) given	How example(s) contributed to your understanding
1. Abiding will give you mighty award	1.
2.	2.

5. If applicable: what is being compared and/or contrasted?

Show <u>two</u> comparisons between items A and B:

A	B
Jews	No Christian

Show <u>two</u> contrasts between items A and B:

A	B
believers	Non-believers

6. Show <u>two</u> cause/effect relationships:

Cause	Effect
1. Don't abide	Punish
2. Don't spend on Allah	burn in hell

7. List <u>three</u> facts and <u>three</u> opinions from the article. <u>Explain why</u> it is either a fact or an opinion.

	Explanation:
A.) fact:	A.)
B.) fact:	B.)
C.) fact:	C.)

296

	Explanation:
A.) opinion *Fight the Non -believer*	A.)
B.) opinion: *Go forth in Allahs way*	B.)
C.) opinion:	C.)

8. What is the author's purpose in this article? Is it to inform, persuade, or entertain? **Tell me how you arrived at that conclusion.**

   To persuade that allah is way to go.

9. What is the author's tone? **Explain your answer.**

   Rebuking, mean, enrage

10. Discovering the ideas in writing that are **not stated directly** is called making inferences, or drawing conclusions. What inferences did you draw from the article you read? **Explain.**

    Allah is very strict.

11. Authors often use connotative language. Return to the reading selection and circle (in red or green) all connotative words. List 10 of those words here and explain how those words might affect the reader.

    hell, phastise, captives

How the connotative words above might affect the reader:

12. A good argument makes a point and then provides persuasive and logical evidence to back it up. However, a bad argument uses fallacies to support itself such as changing the subject, hasty generalization, circular reasoning, personal attack, straw man, false cause, false comparison, or either-or. Explain how the author supports his/her argument. <u>Does he/she use relevant and adequate support, or do fallacies exist?</u> <u>Explain</u>.

_____
_____
_____
_____
_____
_____
_____
_____
_____
_____
_____
_____
_____
_____
_____
_____

13. The seven most common propaganda techniques are bandwagon, testimonial, transfer, plain folks, name calling, glittering generalities, and card staking. <u>Which techniques are used in this reading selection?</u> <u>Explain</u>.

_____
_____
_____
_____
_____
_____
_____
_____
_____
_____
_____
_____
_____
_____
_____
_____

FreeStockPhotos.com

Excerpt From The Old Testament Jewish Bible:

The Ten Commandments

1: And God spake all these words, saying,

2: I am the LORD thy God, which have brought thee out of the land of Egypt, out of the house of bondage.

3: Thou shalt have no other gods before me.

4: Thou shalt not make unto thee any graven image, or any likeness of any thing that is in heaven above, or that is in the earth beneath, or that is in the water under the earth:

5: Thou shalt not bow down thyself to them, nor serve them: for I the LORD thy God am a jealous God, visiting the iniquity of the fathers upon the children unto the third and fourth generation of them that hate me;

6: And shewing mercy unto thousands of them that love me, and keep my commandments.

7: Thou shalt not take the name of the LORD thy God in vain; for the LORD will not hold him guiltless that

I see alot of logos and image of heaven and hell these days.

It's sad because even believes fail this commandments

299

taketh his name in vain.

8: Remember the sabbath day, to keep it holy.

9: Six days shalt thou labour, and do all thy work:

10: But the seventh day is the sabbath of the LORD thy God: in it thou shalt not do any work, thou, nor thy son, nor thy daughter, thy manservant, nor thy maidservant, nor thy cattle, nor thy stranger that is within thy gates:

11: For in six days the LORD made heaven and earth, the sea, and all that in them is, and rested the seventh day: wherefore the LORD blessed the sabbath day, and hallowed it.

12: Honour thy father and thy mother: that thy days may be long upon the land which the LORD thy God giveth thee.

13: Thou shalt not kill.

14: Thou shalt not commit adultery.

15: Thou shalt not steal.

16: Thou shalt not bear false witness against thy neighbour.

17: Thou shalt not covet thy neighbour's house, thou shalt not covet thy neighbour's wife, nor his manservant, nor his maidservant, nor his ox, nor his ass, nor any thing that is thy neighbour's.

18: And all the people saw the thunderings, and the lightnings, and the noise of the trumpet, and the mountain smoking: and when the people saw it, they removed, and stood afar off.

19: And they said unto Moses, Speak thou with us, and we will hear: but let not God speak with us, lest we die.

20: And Moses said unto the people, Fear not: for God is come to prove you, and that his fear may be before your faces, that ye sin not.

Glad majority of job's and store are closed during Sunday

Alot of young youth really need help on this one.

Competing with your neighbors is probably coveting them, so this commandment is likely to be broken

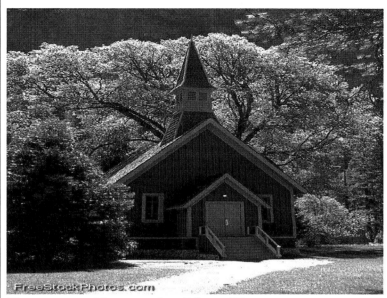

Excerpts From the New Testament Bible:

The Sermon On The Mount

1: And seeing the multitudes, he (Jesus) went up into a mountain: and when he was set, his disciples came unto him:

2: And he opened his mouth, and taught them, saying,

3: Blessed are the poor in spirit: for theirs is the kingdom of heaven.

4: Blessed are they that mourn: for they shall be comforted.

5: Blessed are the meek: for they shall inherit the earth.

6: Blessed are they which do hunger and thirst after righteousness: for they shall be filled.

7: Blessed are the merciful: for they shall obtain mercy.

8: Blessed are the pure in heart: for they shall see God.

9: Blessed are the peacemakers: for they shall be called the children of God.

10: Blessed are they which are persecuted for righteousness' sake: for theirs is the kingdom of heaven.

11: Blessed are ye, when men shall revile you, and persecute you, and shall say all manner of evil against you falsely, for my sake.

12: Rejoice, and be exceeding glad: for great is your reward in heaven: for so persecuted they the prophets which were before you. (Matt. 5:1-12)

Prophecy of the "End Times"

1: And I saw when the Lamb opened one of the seals, and I heard, as it were the noise of thunder, one of the four beasts saying, Come and see.

2: And I saw, and behold a white horse: and he that sat on him had a bow; and a crown was given unto him: and he went forth conquering, and to conquer.

3: And when he had opened the second seal, I heard the second beast say, Come and see.

4: And there went out another horse that was red: and power was given to him that sat thereon to take peace from the earth, and that they should kill one another: and there was given unto him a great sword.

5: And when he had opened the third seal, I heard the third beast say, Come and see. And I beheld, and lo a black horse; and he that sat on him had a pair of balances in his hand.

6: And I heard a voice in the midst of the four beasts say, A measure of wheat for a penny, and three measures of barley for a penny; and see thou hurt not the oil and the wine.

7: And when he had opened the fourth seal, I heard the voice of the fourth beast say, Come and see.

8: And I looked, and behold a pale horse: and his name that sat on him was Death, and Hell followed with him. And power was given unto them over the fourth part of the earth, to kill with sword, and with hunger, and with death, and with the beasts of the earth.

9: And when he had opened the fifth seal, I saw under the altar the souls of them that were slain for the word of God, and for the testimony which they held:

10: And they cried with a loud voice, saying, How long, O Lord, holy and true, dost thou not judge and avenge our blood on them that dwell on the earth?

11: And white robes were given unto every one of them; and it was said unto them, that they should rest yet for a little season, until their fellow servants also and their brethren, that should be killed as they were, should be fulfilled.

12: And I beheld when he had opened the sixth seal, and, lo, there was a great earthquake; and the sun became black as sackcloth of hair, and the moon became as blood;

13: And the stars of heaven fell unto the earth, even as a fig tree casteth her untimely figs, when she is shaken of a mighty wind.

14: And the heaven departed as a scroll when it is rolled together; and every mountain and island were moved out of their places.

15: And the kings of the earth, and the great men, and the rich men, and the chief captains, and the mighty men, and every bondman, and every free man, hid themselves in the dens and in the rocks of the mountains;

16: And said to the mountains and rocks, Fall on us, and hide us from the face of him that sitteth on the throne, and from the wrath of the Lamb:

17: For the great day of his wrath is come; and who shall be able to stand? (Rev 6:1-17)

USDOE

The questions that follow may be used for further discussion of the reading selection or as topics for essay writing.

1. The Ten Commandments have been banned from being displayed in our Nation's public schools and even some courthouses. This has been done under the banner of "Separation of Church and State." This is a very controversial subject with some saying that there must be a clear separation, and others saying that the Founders never meant that but rather that no State religion would be established. It's a controversy that will continue. Discuss the reading selection as it relates to the society that we live in. Are the laws or rules sensible? Are they harmful? Are they necessary for a society to function? Which would you keep and which would you discard?

2. In the Sermon on the Mount, it is said that the righteous, the meek, and those who do good, will inherit the Earth. Compare/contrast this with the reading from the Koran, the Bhagavad-Gita and the sayings of Lao.

3. In reading the New Testament Prophesies, how accurate do you think that they are? Discuss these selections in relationship to recent events. Are they Prophetic or coincidental?

4. You have read selections from many writers. All of them have belief systems concerning this world and their relationship to it. Discuss the many viewpoints. Which ones seem to make the most sense? What was you viewpoint before you read these authors? What is your viewpoint now? Do you feel that these works are influential in our world today?

5. _____
   _____
   _____
   _____
   _____
   _____

Applying Reading Skills
(Neatly PRINT all answers using ink not pencil)

Title of the Reading Selection: _____

1. What is the author's overall main idea, (central point, or thesis)?

_____

_____

2. There are two kinds of supporting details--major and minor. Major details are the primary points that support the main idea and minor details expand major details. List __three__ details and explain how they support the author's primary point?

Details used	Explanation of how they support the thesis
1.	

Details used	Explanation of how they support the thesis
2.	

Details used	Explanation of how they support the thesis
3.	

3. The five major patterns of organization are the list of items pattern, the time order pattern, the example pattern, the comparison and/or contrast pattern, and the cause/effect pattern. What is the __main__ pattern of organization used in this article? __Explain__ why it is the major pattern. What other patterns are used? Give some examples.

Main pattern: _____

Explain how the main pattern was used:

_____

Other pattern(s) used: _____

Explain how the additional pattern(s) were used:

_____

_____

305

4. If applicable: Give <u>two</u> examples that were used in the writing. <u>Explain</u> how they affected your understanding of the reading selection.

The example(s) given	How example(s) contributed to your understanding
1.	1.
2.	2.

5. If applicable: what is being compared and/or contrasted?

Show <u>two</u> comparisons between items A and B:

A	B

Show <u>two</u> contrasts between items A and B:

A	B

6. Show <u>two</u> cause/effect relationships:

Cause	Effect
1.	
2.	

7. List <u>three</u> facts and <u>three</u> opinions from the article. <u>Explain why</u> it is either a fact or an opinion.

	Explanation:
A.) fact:	A.)
B.) fact:	B.)
C.) fact:	C.)

	Explanation:
A.) opinion	A.)
B.) opinion:	B.)
C.) opinion:	C.)

8. What is the author's purpose in this article? Is it to inform, persuade, or entertain? <u>Tell me how you arrived at that conclusion.</u>

_____
_____
_____

9. What is the author's tone? <u>Explain your answer.</u>

_____
_____
_____

10. Discovering the ideas in writing that are <u>not stated directly</u> is called making inferences, or drawing conclusions. What inferences did you draw from the article you read? <u>Explain.</u>

_____
_____
_____

11. Authors often use connotative language. Return to the reading selection and circle (in red or green) all connotative words. List 10 of those words here and explain how those words might affect the reader.

_____
_____
_____
_____
_____

How the connotative words above might affect the reader:

_____
_____
_____
_____
_____
_____
_____

307

12. A good argument makes a point and then provides persuasive and logical evidence to back it up. However, a bad argument uses fallacies to support itself such as changing the subject, hasty generalization, circular reasoning, personal attack, straw man, false cause, false comparison, or either-or. Explain how the author supports his/her argument. <u>Does he/she use relevant and adequate support, or do fallacies exist? Explain.</u>

_____
_____
_____
_____
_____
_____
_____
_____
_____
_____
_____
_____
_____
_____
_____
_____
_____
_____

13. The seven most common propaganda techniques are bandwagon, testimonial, transfer, plain folks, name calling, glittering generalities, and card staking. <u>Which techniques are used in this reading selection? Explain.</u>

_____
_____
_____
_____
_____
_____
_____
_____
_____
_____
_____
_____
_____
_____
_____
_____

Appendix

Some Interesting Topics for Internet Assignments

Topic:	Date Due:	Related Internet Site:
Irradiation of food		
Dangers of Canola Oil		
Gulf War Syndrome		
Microwave ovens dangers		
Rbst or RGBH		
Ebola virus		
Genetic engineering		
Magazine search		
Newspaper search		
HAARP Technology		
Fleas/Ticks/Mites		
European Union/the EURO dollar		
Cell phone hazards		
Famous person		
Aspartame Dangers		www.dorway.com
Human Rights abuses		
Pfiesteria		
Love Canal of Niagara Falls, NY		
The Dangers of Fluoride		
Echelon spy network/NSA		
Accutane acne medicine dangers		
Deformed frogs		
MTBE gasoline additives		
Current Events		
Genealogy		
Stem Cell Research		
Earthquakes		
The Great Chicago Fire		
Anthrax		
Child Soldiers		
Atomic bomb and fluoride waste		
Food additives, colorings, flavorings		
Allergies		
Dangers of Fertilizers		
Defective products/product recalls		www.cpsc.gov
Museum of Tolerance (Los Angeles)		
Anhydrous Dextrose		
Sucralose		
Tea Tree Oil		
The Middle East		
Acesulfame - K		
Atrazine (weed killer)		
Luvox and/or SSRI Drugs		
Benefits of Aloe Vera		
Mercury poisoning		
Citric Acid dangers		

How to Copy and Paste

From the Internet into MS Word

Highlight the text

•Highlight the text that you want to copy by clicking the left mouse button in front of the 1st word of that text.
•While holding down the left button on your mouse, drag the cursor over the text until all of the text (that you want) is highlighted.
• To copy all of the text, press "Ctrl" and "A".

Copy

•Move the cursor to the copy symbol, or select "copy" from the pull down menu under <u>Edit</u>.

Minimize the Internet article

•Minimize the Internet article by clicking on the minimize symbol at the top right corner of the page.

•It looks like this: ▬

Open MS Word

•Open your Microsoft Word program by double clicking on the Microsoft Word symbol.
•A blank document should appear. If a blank document does not appear, choose "blank document" from the choices given.
•You may use the blank document or prefer to use a template (see next slide).

If **I**ing a Template:

•If you use a template, do the following:
    –1. Click on the open folder.
    –2. At "Look in:" select the down arrow and choose the drive that your disk is in (indicated by a string of numbers following the disk drive letter).
    –3. Click on that drive and then find the download template that you want. Click on that template.

Paste

• Next, place your cursor onto the blank document.
•Click on the paste symbol, or click on "Paste" in the <u>Edit</u> pull down menu.

Your Document Should Now Appear

•Your document should now appear.
      –You can edit it.
      –You can increase, or decrease, the font size.
      –You can check the length of your article.
      –You can print it.
      –You can save it to a disk.

Minimize MS Word and Restore the Internet to Your Screen

•Once you have completed your task, you can minimize (**−**), or close (**X**) MS Word.
•You can restore your Internet site by moving your cursor to the bottom of the screen, then click on the site information found there on the hidden toolbar (which will appear when your cursor reaches the bottom of the screen). It will then restore you to your Internet site.

C

How to Use the Enclosed CD Rom

Step 1: <u>**Carefully**</u> remove the CD from the CD pocket holder attached to the back cover.

Step 2: Insert the CD into your computer. Double click on "My Computer."

Step 3: Double click on the drive that contains the CD as indicated by the name ACVRW&SS – Scheg 8.0 following that drive letter. This will open the CD.

Step 4: Double click on each of the following folders to install the readers or other information contained within them:

A. Adobe Reader & Adobe e-book Reader: Double click on "Adobe Reader Installer." This installs the Adobe Reader & Adobe e-book Reader 6.0 which will let you view and print any enclosed Adobe files as indicated by PDF on the disk.

B. PowerPoint Reader: Double click on the "PowerPoint Reader Installer," to install the PowerPoint Reader. Follow the directions as they appear on the screen. This allows you to view the PowerPoint presentations.

Note:
Word 2000 or greater is needed to view and print most of the Word documents. Some Word documents might work with earlier versions of Word. **MS Works is <u>not</u> the same as MS Word and will not open or print these documents.**
Codes:
> PDF = Adobe File
> W - Word file
> PPT = PowerPoint created document

Please, do not scratch, dirty, or allow fingerprints to corrupt your CD. Handle with care and only by the edges or center opening. If CD malfunctions, clean with mild dish detergent and dry with a soft lint free cloth. If it still malfunctions, e-mail ProfessorScheg@Yahoo.Com for instructions on how to receive a replacement disk.